PHILOSOPHY OF MIND

Dale Jacquette

The Pennsylvania State University

PRENTICE HALL, Englewood Cliffs, NJ 07632

Library of Congress Cataloging-in-Publication Data

Jacquette, Dale.
    Philosophy of mind / Dale Jacquette.
        p.   cm. — (Prentice-Hall foundations of philosophy series)
    Includes bibliographical references and index.
    ISBN 0–13–030933–8
    1. Philosophy of mind. I. Title. II. Series.
BD418.3.J34 1994
128′.2—dc20
                                               93–26773
                                               CIP

Acquisitions editor: Ted Bolen
Editorial/production supervision and interior design: Joan Powers
Copy editor: Peter Reinhart
Cover Design: Bruce Kenselaar
Production coordinator: Kelly Behr
Electronic page makeup: Mary Araneo

© 1994 by Prentice-Hall, Inc.
A Paramount Communications Company
Englewood Cliffs, New Jersey 07632

Printed in the United States of America
10 9 8 7 6 5 4 3 2 1

ISBN 0-13-030933-8

Prentice-Hall International (UK) Limited, *London*
Prentice-Hall of Australia Pty. Limited, *Sydney*
Prentice-Hall Canada Inc., *Toronto*
Prentice-Hall Hispanoamericana, S.A., *Mexico*
Prentice-Hall of India Private Limited, *New Delhi*
Prentice-Hall of Japan, Inc., *Tokyo*
Simon & Schuster Asia Pte. Ltd., *Singapore*
Editora Prentice-Hall do Brasil, Ltda., *Rio de Janeiro*

Contents

CHAPTER TWO

Elimination and Reduction Strategies for the Concept of Mind: Behaviorism, Materialism, Functionalism   34

CHAPTER THREE

Artificial Intelligence: Mechanism, Minds, and Machines   60

CHAPTER FOUR

Intentionality and the Nature of Thought   95

CHAPTER FIVE

The Dignity of Mind   129

AFTERWORD

The Challenge of Intentionalism: Toward a Scientific Metaphysics of Mind   157

For Further Reading   160

Index   164

Foundations of Philosophy

Many of the problems of philosophy are of such broad relevance to human concerns, and so complex in their ramifications, that they are, in one form or another, perennially present. Though in the course of time they yield in part to philosophical inquiry, they may need to be rethought by each age in the light of its broader scientific knowledge and deepened ethical and religious experience. Better solutions are found by more refined and rigorous methods. Thus, one who approaches the study of philosophy in the hope of understanding the best of what it affords will look for both fundamental issues and contemporary achievements.

Written by a group of distinguished philosophers, the Foundations of Philosophy Series aims to exhibit some of the main problems in the various fields of philosophy as they stand at the present stage of philosophical history.

While certain fields are likely to be represented in the most introductory courses in philosophy, college classes differ widely in emphasis, in method of instruction, and in rate of progress. Every instructor needs freedom to change his course as his own philosophical interests, the size and makeup of his class, and the needs of his students vary from year to year. The volumes in the Foundations of Philosophy Series—each complete in itself, but complementing the others—offer a new flexibility to the instructor, who can create his own textbook by combining several volumes as he wishes, and choose different combinations at different times. Those volumes that are not used in an introductory course will be found valuable, along with other texts or collections of readings, for the more specialized upper-level courses.

Elizabeth Beardsley / Monroe Beardsley / Tom L. Beauchamp

Preface

As metaphors of the mind go, the 'ghost in the machine' is not that bad; it's much better than the machine without the ghost.

Raziel Abelson

The concept of mind has emerged as one of the most important in contemporary philosophy. From antiquity and the time of its modern rebirth in the seventeenth century to its prominence in recent thought, the philosophy of mind has gained increasing attention through a convergence of interests. Scientific discoveries in behavioral, neurophysiological, and cognitive psychology, the information sciences, and artificial intelligence have encouraged an array of innovative theories of mind. It has been recognized at the same time that investigations in such diverse areas as logic and philosophy of mathematics, semantics, epistemology, ethics, and aesthetics depend on a satisfactory understanding of the nature of mind. There is also an increasing awareness of the failure of the psychological sciences alone to provide an adequate foundation for the metaphysics of mind.

The problems here are in one sense perennial. What is the mind? What is consciousness? Is the mind identical with or distinct from the body? Is psychological experience public or private? Does thought come before language, or is language needed for the existence as well as expression of thought? The invention of the computer and development of information technologies, implications of the mind's intentionality in phenomenological traditions, and the impact of the private language argument in Wittgenstein's later philosophy have cast these fundamental questions about the nature of mind in a different light. The two main purposes of this book are to provide an introduction to what I believe are the most important topics in contemporary philosophy of mind, and to explain and defend a version of emergent intentionalist property dualism as a solution to the mind-body problem. I have tried in every chapter to convey a sense of the lively controversies surrounding these conclusions and to exhibit the strengths and weaknesses of each position considered by combining exposition with critical evaluation and countercriticisms from opposing viewpoints.

Many persons have contributed to my understanding of mind, and I cannot hope to acknowledge my obligations to all. Among my teachers, I must mention Roderick M. Chisholm, whose influence appears on every page. Colleagues in the field from whom I have benefited most notably and been inspired positively or negatively to adopt and refine my own position include D. M. Armstrong, Ned Block, Paul M. Churchland, Daniel C. Dennett, Hubert L. Dreyfus, Herbert Feigl, Jerry Fodor, John Haugeland, Frank Jackson, John R. Lucas, Joseph Margolis, Thomas Nagel, Zenon Pylyshyn, and John R. Searle. Among past thinkers in whose philosophical debt I most self-consciously stand, I shall name only Aristotle, David Hume, Franz Brentano, and Ludwig Wittgenstein. I am grateful to friends who read the book or parts thereof in manuscript, including Robert Audi, John Heil, Tina (Traas) Jacquette, Stanley Rosen, Ernest Sosa, and William H. Throop. I wish to thank the students in my philosophy of mind courses and seminars on artificial intelligence, whose skepticism and demand for clarity as I beat my intentionality drum have enriched the book's content and presentation. My reflections on intentionality were nurtured during a research visit to Germany in 1989–1990, supported by a generous Forschungsstipendium from the Alexander von Humboldt-Stiftung. A version of the dialogue 'A Turing Test Conversation' appeared in the journal *Philosophy* 68 (1993): 231–233, parts of which are reprinted here with the kind permission of the editor, Renford Bambrough, and the publisher, Cambridge University Press. Finally, I am grateful to Ted Bolen, philosophy editor at Prentice Hall, and to Tom L. Beauchamp, series editor, for their invitation to contribute and guidance in preparing the work for publication.

Finally, this book is dedicated to my wife, Tina, with love.

The Ontology of Mind

WHAT IS THE MIND?

To ask about the *ontology* of mind, from the Greek word *ontos*, or "being," is to inquire into the most fundamental metaphysical categories to which the mind may belong. Is the mind a physical thing, in principle like other material entities, but with more complex properties, or is it somehow immaterial? When we speak of the mind, do we refer only to the living brain or functioning of the brain, together with the activity of the central and peripheral nervous systems? Or, as many people believe and many religions teach, is there an immaterial spiritual self or soul that inhabits or uses and directs the body, but is not itself physical or material, and may survive bodily death?

As we shall see, these opposing positions are the extremes of a wide range of alternative views about the metaphysics of mind. Some thinkers are dissatisfied with the philosophical implications of purely materialist and purely immaterialist approaches to the ontology of mind. Partly in response to these perceived limitations, they have advocated a variety of intermediate theories that try to combine the desirable features of each. Others attempt to meet objections to materialist or immaterialist ontologies head-on, seeking to escape apparent difficulties by introducing subtle distinctions, denying the presuppositions of criticisms, or trying to show that what may seem to be problems in a particular ontology of mind are due only to certain types of conceptual confusion.

The ontology of mental phenomena is the fundamental problem in the philosophy of mind. It is the question to which discussion of virtually every interesting property of mind ultimately reverts. The ontology of mind, in answering the *mind-body problem*, has direct implications for whether the mind is a machine or is like a machine, whether it is immortal, whether there are immaterial particulars, whether there is more than one kind of substance, whether experience is private or public, and whether there can be free will and moral responsibility. The metaphysics of mind also has implications for the "hard" psychological or cognitive sciences, and especially for the role and limitations of behavioral psychology, neurophysiology, artificial intelligence, and information theory, in explaining the concept of mind. Its answers to fundamental questions about the nature of mind affect our understanding of psychology; via theories of the role of thought in proof and the determination of truth, the ontology of mind is linked to logic and philosophy of mathematics; via action theory and the requirements for responsible action, it is linked to ethics and social-political philosophy; via concepts of intentionality and the expression of ideas, it is linked again to logic and semantics, philosophy of language, aesthetics, and philosophy of art. It is the source of enduring philosophical dilemmas about the freedom of thought, will, and action, in a world governed by immutable laws of cause and effect.

ONTOLOGICAL ALTERNATIVES

The purpose of this investigation is to articulate a conceptual analysis. We shall try to explain what we mean and ought to mean by the concept of mind. Along the way, we must seek clarification of many important related ideas. Some of the concepts and theories about the mind are likely to seem strange until we have placed them in historical context, examined the arguments offered in their support, and considered the alternatives.

There are models and metaphors that help to explain the mind in its relation to the body. At times, the mind has been likened to a spirit or lesser god, and, keeping pace with technological advances, to a telegraph station, a telephone switching terminal, a digital computer, and more recently, an integrated hybrid digital and analog connectionist network. The beauty and charm of some of these comparisons have so impressed scientists and philosophers that they are sometimes regarded not merely as suggestive analogies, but as the literal truth about the metaphysics of mind and the nature of psychological experience.

This book charts the most important philosophical perspectives in the ontology of mind, providing a guidemap to some of the major landmarks among philosophical and scientific theories. There are three basic categories. *Dualism* is the theory that mind and body are distinct. Among ontologies that distinguish mind and body, there are in turn several kinds of *substance, idealist,* and *property dualisms. Eliminativism* is the theory that there is no such thing as mind. It may seem paradoxical to regard this as a thesis about the ontology of mind, since it entails that the mind has no being at all. But this view is no more problematic than the skeptical conclusions of some epistemologists who offer as a thesis of knowledge theory that knowledge is unattainable. To claim that the mind does not exist usually means that it is impossible to account for psychological properties exclusively by means of third-person observational and experimental science. The concept of mind is dispensable if cognitive phenomena are more correctly explained by eliminating references to the mind and speaking instead of behavior, brain events, or information processing. *Reductivism* is a less extreme but still hardline antimentalistic position. It does not deny the existence of mental phenomena but maintains that whatever truths are expressed in mentalistic terms can be expressed equivalently, though more effectively or economically, in a nonmentalistic vocabulary.

Neither eliminativism nor reductivism tries to do away with real things, as we might eliminate weeds from a garden or reduce the federal deficit by raising taxes. They are instead different ways of thinking about what kinds of things are real. Eliminativism and reductivism are directly concerned with the theoretical vocabulary in which we try to explain psychological phenomena. The question is always whether we can say what we think needs to be said about the mind (which, if we are eliminativists, may be nothing) without making reference to the mind and mental events, states, or properties. Although eliminativism and reductivism are primarily concerned with achieving economy in the technical vocabulary of philosophical psychology, we should expect that a correct account will deliver the truth about what kind of thing the mind is, whether or not it exists, and what kinds of properties it may have. Thus, eliminativism and reductivism are not merely playing a vocabulary game. The relation of minimal explanatory adequacy to the truth of ontology makes eliminativism and reductivism of vital importance in their challenges to more traditional dualist ways of thinking about the mind. There are three main subtypes of eliminativism and reductivism: *behaviorism, materialism,* and *functionalism.* Each is a philosophical extrapolation from scientific research in behavioral psychology, neurophysiology, or the information sciences. They constitute different ways of explaining or explaining away mental phenomena in terms of purely behavioral, material, or functional properties.

Of course, these theories are controversial. Philosophy of mind today is the scene of dispute between these three theories. *Materialism* holds that mind is a physical entity explainable in terms of material properties alone. This theory implies that the mind is identical to the brain and central and peripheral nervous system or its neurophysiological properties. Mental event particulars or types, according to materialism, are eliminable in favor of or reducible to particular brain events or types of brain events. *Functionalism* explains the mind as an input-output information flow and control system, like a computer program. It rejects as too restrictive materialist theories that try to explain mental events in terms of types of brain events, on the grounds that no particular kind of matter is essential to the functioning of mind. *Property dualism* maintains that mind has a dual nature, possessing both *behavioral-material-functional* and *behaviorally-materially-functionally ineliminable and irreducible* kinds of properties. Property dualism finds every eliminativist and reductivist theory unsatisfactory as a complete explanation of the concept of mind. It regards discoveries in the hard psychological sciences as revealing the mind's behavioral-material-functional properties. But it claims that the mind in its dual nature has, in addition to these, properties that the hard sciences cannot adequately explain. *Intentionalist property dualism* identifies the mind's behaviorally-materially-functionally ineliminable and irreducible properties more particularly as its *intrinsic intentionality* or "aboutness," which is to say, the directedness of thought toward intended objects. *Emergent intentionalist property dualism* explains the occurrence of mind in living things, and it addresses metaphysical problems about the intentionalist property dualist emergence of mind in a bioevolutionary context.

INTERPRETATION AND METHOD

The best way to understand contemporary problems and solutions in philosophy of mind is to retrace the important turning points in its history. We must critically assess the arguments and analyses that philosophers have advanced in support of their positions, and participate in ongoing disputes by identifying and defending more satisfactory conclusions. Recent and historical discussions surrounding problems of the existence and nature of mind may contain correct ideas and useful distinctions to be put together in new ways in approaching difficulties about the ontology of mind. They may help us to avoid false-starts and dead-ends as we try to learn from previous mistakes.

The important point is that as the study of mind advances, ontological questions can resurface for philosophical review. They are subject to revision at any time in the wake of unanticipated scientific discoveries or philosophical reflections. Philosophers of mind cannot afford to overlook current scientific developments, but neither can they surrender the philosophical interpretation of these results to nonphilosophers. The proper attitude for philosophy to adopt toward its historical offspring in the natural sciences is at issue here as elsewhere in the special branches of philosophy. But it becomes especially acute in philosophy of mind, because mental phenomena are encountered in first-person introspection as described by *phenomenology*, and because the hard psychological sciences are exclusively third-person disciplines. This means that they are unwilling to consider as scientific any information about the mind that cannot be eliminatively or reductively explained from an outsider's perspective. Facts about the mind must be con-firmable from the more objective public stance of persons who are not hav-ing the experience. Otherwise, they are to be disregarded as unscientific. The hard sciences are often freighted by philosophers, if not by scientists, with extrascientific methodological commitments to a classical *unity of science* model. In this conception, all other sciences are supposed to be reducible to physics, and all properties of knowable objects to physical properties. But the mind is sometimes said to be the one object of study for which the third-person approach is inherently inappropriate. Whether or not this statement is true, it indicates that the methods and findings of the hard psychological sciences must be screened by philosophical criticism before they can be accepted as fully explaining the nature of mind.

The present volume offers an explanation and defense of emergent inten-tionalist property dualism. The position I shall take, after examining the most influential alternatives, is that there is no satisfactory substance dualist, idealist dualist, eliminativist, or reductivist explanation of mind. The mind is best understood as having dual behavioral-material-functional and behav-iorally-materially-functionally ineliminable and irreducible intrinsically intentional properties. It is the intending brain and nervous system. Without reference to the intentionality of thought, there can be no adequate charac-terization of psychological phenomena. But intentionality cannot adequately be explained from a third-person scientific perspective. This incompleteness in no way limits the discovery of the mind's behavioral-material-functional properties in the hard psychological sciences. But it entails that behaviorism, neurophysiology, and the information sciences cannot give a complete pic-ture of the mind. The mind is a behavioral-material-functional entity. But it is more than this, and the mind is not adequately understood when it is con-sidered only as such.

With each philosophical assessment and systematic integration of scientif-ic findings about the brain and mind into a unified theory, we come to terms with longstanding metaphilosophical problems about the relation between philosophy and the sciences as they cooperate in efforts to under-stand the metaphysics of mind. The mind-body problem asks the question how much we can know about thought from the standpoint of the hard psy-chological sciences, and whether philosophy must go beyond science in order to fathom the concept of mind.

CHAPTER ONE

Dualisms of Mental and Physical Phenomena

The idea that the mind is identical with the brain and nervous system is supported by as many intuitive considerations as the opposite thesis that they are distinct. There are several types of mind-body dualisms or nonidentity theories, including substance, idealist, and property dualisms. Each is an attempt to answer the question whether the mind is essentially a physical, nonphysical, or partly physical and partly nonphysical entity.

THE MIND-BODY PROBLEM

If we consider the properties of our minds and bodies, they seem different in many ways. It is not unusual for persons to speak of their minds as containing visual images in dimensions that could not literally belong to the brain. When I look out on the Grand Canyon, I see an enormous geologic feature that stretches as far as I can see. My mind in some sense contains a picture that extends for many miles in three dimensions. It would require an enormous frame to surround my visual field like a painting or representation of the world, although that is exactly what it is. But does my brain, which weighs only a few pounds and fits into a box about four by six inches, contain pictures or visual images as large as my perception of the Grand Canyon?

There are other apparent mind-body differences. My brain contains nerve networks, white matter, black matter, gray matter, blood vessels, connective tissue, and cerebrospinal fluid. These are organized into such specialized parts as the brain stem, cerebellum, and so on. All of this admits of a purely physical description, as does any material object. But do I have such things in my mind? My mind on casual inspection contains memories, desires, expectations, immediate sensations, embarrassments, likes and dislikes. But my brain on casual inspection contains none of these things. Brain events have weight, definite spatial position, and color. But thoughts, mental events, do not seem to have such physical properties. What color is my thought that $\pi = 3.14159...$? How much does it weigh? Does my thought bounce up and down if I think it while on a trampoline?

There is another difference that seems to distinguish mental from physical phenomena. Thoughts have objects or referents. They are *about* something and, figuratively speaking, *point to* intended objects, some of which do not exist. When I read *The Adventures of Tom Sawyer*, I believe that Tom Sawyer discovers a treasure in a cave, even though I know he is only a fictional character and does not exist outside of the novel. But my belief has Tom as its intended object, and not Mark Twain or Huckleberry Finn. If it makes sense, true or false, to say that Tom finds the treasure, then Tom, the treasure, and Tom's finding the treasure are my thought's intended objects. My thought intends or is about or is directed toward just these things, which, in this case, happen not to exist. If my thought is about Tom Sawyer, and if Tom Sawyer does not exist, then he has no physical substance to interact causally with the physical state of my brain. The brain's physical properties are causally related one to another and to the outside world. But since Tom Sawyer does not exist, my brain cannot be causally connected to Twain's fictional character in the manner of ordinary material objects. Nor will it do to say that I am really thinking about the existent book or the words printed on its pages in which Tom Sawyer is described, to which my eye and brain are causally connected. I am not thinking about those things, but about Twain's youthful whitewashing con artist himself. My thought is essentially intentional, but my body, or, more precisely, my brain and nervous system, considered as purely material entities, are not. Suppose that I could examine each part of my brain in whatever detail I choose while I am entertaining beliefs about Tom Sawyer. What would my brain have to look or behave like as a whole or under the microscope such that those states could be said to be about Tom Sawyer as opposed to being about Huckleberry Finn or Mark Twain? If there is no correct imaginable answer, then mind-body dualism or nonidentity may be implied.

But the mind-body problem is by no means settled by these considerations. There are also arguments to justify the opposite conclusion. The existence of the mind seems to depend on the brain, for we have no solid evidence of the existence of disembodied minds. Many people who do not accept popular religious teaching about the immortality of the soul regard the mind as ceasing to exist at death or after severe brain degeneration. There are empirically confirmed correlations between brain and psychological events, which are often discovered during exploratory brain probing and surgery on conscious subjects. How are we to explain the fact that electrically stimulating the cerebral cortex can awaken vivid memories that the mind has otherwise lost, if mind and brain are not identical? The ingestion of mind-altering substances like alcohol and LSD demonstrates that the mind can be directly affected by what happens to the brain when its ordinary chemistry is changed. Further, we know that when we move our bodies we initiate causal chains that begin in the brain and proceed through nerves to muscles by the mind's willful decision to act. This process also indicates an intimate mind-body connection. If thought does not appear to be heavy, spatial, or colored, this may simply be an illusion. We seem to regard our minds and not just our brains as changing locations. If I take the train from Boston to Chicago, and am later asked where I was when I thought of the mind-body distinction, whether the thought took place in one city or the other, I am posed with a sensible question that admits of a sensible answer. The thought may have occurred in Boston, Chicago, or somewhere in between. But how can this be, if the mind is not identical with some part of the brain?

This is the mind-body problem. There are good reasons for thinking that the mind is not identical with the brain, and different but perhaps equally good reasons for the opposite conclusion.

SUBSTANCE DUALISM

The doctrine that body and mind are distinct substances, that there is a spirit, soul, or immaterial mind somehow associated with the material body, is a popular concept both within and outside of philosophy. It is often thought to be the view that most nonphilosophers hold. This is not surprising, since the idea is central to many religious doctrines, including those that forecast an afterlife for the soul following the destruction of the body, a journey to heaven or hell, resurrection, transmigration, or reincarnation into other human or animal bodies. The distinction between the body as a material or physical substance and the mind, self, or soul as an immaterial substance is often referred to as *substance* or *ontic dualism.* It is a compelling concept of mind because it offers the hope of personal survival after death, by which many religions seek to give meaning to life.

The fact that Neanderthals alone among early hominids ritually buried their dead can be understood in several ways. But it suggests that belief in the separation of body and soul, which often goes hand-in-hand with special treatment of the dead in modern cultures, may date back to our earliest human-like ancestors. The dynastic Egyptians in the *Book of the Great Awakening,* which we know as the *Egyptian Book of the Dead,* divided persons into nine parts: the physical body; spiritual body; soul; shadow; heart; shining spirit (an invisible sheath that covers the body); image or ghost (an abstract personality that acquires a material form after death); a heaven-dwelling component (often translated as power or form); and, oddly and interestingly enough, the person's name. We know the extent to which distinctions between body and soul, and belief in the immortality of the soul, shaped Egyptian culture in its rites for the dead, mummification, and large-scale tomb and necropolis construction. The Egyptians in turn inherited and refined their ideas about the immateriality of several components of mind from earlier African and Mideastern civilizations. Later religions have instituted similar rituals in the expectation that the mind is somehow distinct from the body and need not perish with the body's death.

Socrates, in Plato's dialogue the *Meno*, offers an argument for the distinction of body and soul, and the soul's immortality. Socrates' proof connects religious precedents with attempts at philosophical justification for mind-body dualism. He explains that his views derive from "the priests and priestesses whose care it is to be able to give an account of their practices." He continues: "What they say is this; see whether you think they speak the truth: They say that the human soul is immortal; at times it comes to an end, which they call dying, at times it is reborn, but it is never destroyed, and one must therefore live one's life as piously as possible" (pp. 13–14). Socrates' argument is based on his interpretation of the answers Meno's slave boy gives to questions about a simple geometry problem. Without teaching him directly, Socrates leads the boy one step at a time to grasp the truth of a theorem about the length of side needed to double the area of a given square (the diagonal). From the assumption that the slave had no prior training in mathematics, Socrates concludes that the boy could only have obtained the knowledge at some time before his birth, prior to his human embodiment. The boy retains the truths of geometry as a temporarily forgotten but permanent possession of his immortal soul, which he remembers through Socrates' skillful questions. Does Socrates' argument for the recollection or *anamnesis* theory of knowledge prove the mind-body distinction and immortality of the soul? The conclusion is not inevitable because the slave boy's answers to Socrates' questions can more plausibly be interpreted in ways that do not imply substance dualism. As an example, it seems no less reasonable to consider the possibility that humans have certain logical and mathematical truths or processing abilities built into their brains as a genetic inheritance, or that these mathematical insights and abilities develop psychologically in the individual without training as the mind matures. Meno's slave might then know at least some geometry without being taught, and without possessing an immortal soul distinct from his body.

A later attempt at philosophical demonstration is given in the 17th century by René Descartes. Descartes' discussion in many ways marks the beginning of modern philosophy of mind. Descartes' *Meditations on First Philosophy* (1641) is a study in both philosophy of religion and metaphysics.

This fact is indicated by its subtitle, *In Which the Existence of God and the Distinction of the Soul from the Body are Demonstrated.* The *Meditations* offers two proofs of the mind-body distinction, different in structure and content. Descartes' arguments are alike in seeking to establish a difference in the substance of body and mind by identifying a property that one has but the other lacks. The principle to which Descartes implicitly appeals has since come to be known as *Leibniz's Law* of the *identity of indiscernibles.* It expresses the intuitive condition that objects A and B (or possibly the same object under two names 'A' and 'B') are identical only if all properties of A are properties of B, and conversely. From this it follows that A and B are nonidentical if A has even one property that B lacks, or the reverse. Descartes lends his name to another more common term for substance or ontic dualism, which is also referred to as *Cartesian dualism.*

DESCARTES' FIRST ARGUMENT

Descartes' argument in *Meditation* 2 attempts to show that the material body is different in substance from the immaterial mind, because the mind is "more known" or "better knowable" than the body. The existence of the body can rationally be doubted, but not the existence of the mind.

Descartes makes use of some of the philosophical conclusions he had already established in *Meditation* 1. There he tries to prove that there could be an all-powerful evil spirit or "malignant demon" that deceives him whenever he tries to draw inferences about the world from immediate sense experience. If there were such a demon, it could also deceive Descartes about the existence of his body, which he knows only through immediate sensation and memory. Descartes maintains that, nevertheless, even the most powerful demon could never cause him consistently to doubt his own existence, because doubt as a mental event or psychological experience presupposes that the doubter's mind exists. This belief is a consequence of the Cartesian slogan (borrowed from Saint Augustine) "*Cogito ergo sum*" ("I think, therefore I am"), which Descartes offers more explicitly in this form in his (1637) *Discourse on Method*. In the *Meditations* he concludes noninferentially: "One must come to the considered judgment that the statement 'I am, I exist' is necessarily true every time it is uttered by me or conceived in my mind" (p. 17). The argument can be reconstructed in this way:

1. My body has the property of being such that its existence can rationally be doubted by me.   (Malignant demon hypothesis)
2. My mind does not have the property of being such that its existence can rationally be doubted by me.   (*Cogito ergo sum*)

---

3. My body ≠ my mind.   (1,2 Leibniz's Law)

There are several defects in this formulation of the proof. For one thing, Descartes' statement of the *cogito* principle seems to be caught in a circle. It says in effect, "My mind unquestionably exists whenever my mind entertains the proposition, I am, I exist." But it might be objected that the evidence does not entitle Descartes to conclude the existence of a unified substantial ego, person, or self. At most it proves that the malignant demon hypothesis does not require Descartes to doubt that "thinking occurs" or "something thinks."

Even if the circularity does not run deep, there is another difficulty in the argument. Leibniz's Law does not work for every sort of property. There is a category of what are called *converse intentional properties*, which must be excluded from correct formulations of Leibniz's Law. If I believe that 2 is even (an even number), but I do not believe that $| \sqrt{4} |$ is even (because I have not studied enough arithmetic to know that this is the absolute value of the square root of 4, identical to 2), then I have the *intentional property* of believing that 2 is even (and that $| \sqrt{4} |$ is not), and 2 has the converse intentional property of being believed by me to be even (and oppositely for $| \sqrt{4} |$). From this it may appear that $2 \neq | \sqrt{4} |$, because they do not have all the same properties. The number 2, unlike $| \sqrt{4} |$, has the property of being believed by me to be even. But, obviously, $2 = | \sqrt{4} |$, and no identity principle can be accepted if it contradicts this fact of elementary arithmetic. Numbers have whatever non-converse-intentional properties they have whether or not I exist, and especially whether or not I happen to believe, doubt, or think anything about them. The converse intentional property of being believed or not believed (or doubted, feared, hoped) by me to be even (or to have or not have any property) should not be regarded as affecting the identity of the object. As a result, Leibniz's Law must be reworded, not to say that *A* and *B* are identical only if they have all of their properties in common, but only if they share all of their specifically non-converse-intentional properties.

Descartes' *Meditations* 2 proof for substance dualism has roughly the same form as the faulty argument given in the preceding paragraph to show that $2 \neq | \sqrt{4} |$. It also tries to demonstrate that the mind is not identical to the body by claiming that the mind has the converse intentional property of being more known or better knowable, or being such that its existence cannot rationally be self-doubted, a converse intentional property that the body does not have. Descartes' proof is subject to a dilemma. An argument is *valid* if it has the right logical structure, guaranteeing that if its assumptions are true, then its conclusion must also be true; an argument is *sound* if it is valid and has all and only true assumptions. If Descartes' argument adopts Leibniz's Law of the identity of indiscernibles in its false, uncorrected form, allowing converse intentional properties to identify and individuate objects, then the proof is unsound, for it contains a false assumption. If, on the other hand, the argument appeals to a corrected version Leibniz's Law, amended, as it should be, to exclude converse intentional properties, then the proof is invalid. Even if assumptions (1) and (2) are true, Descartes' mind ≠ body conclusion in item (3) is not validly deducible from the correct form of Leibniz's Law. For the assumptions show only that mind and body do not share all converse intentional properties. Descartes' first argument, therefore, is either invalid or unsound, and in either case it is unacceptable.

DESCARTES' SECOND ARGUMENT

Interestingly, Descartes in *Meditation* 6 offers a different proof for substance dualism. This argument relies implicitly on a correct formulation of the identity of indiscernibles. He seems to regard this as the more important proof, because in his *Reply to the Fourth Set of Objections* to the *Meditations*, he says that he did not complete his argument for the mind-body distinction until *Meditation* 6 (pp. 101–102).

Here Descartes tries again to show that the mind is not identical to the body. But this time he attempts to find a non-converse-intentional property that the mind and body do not share. This is the property of being divisible. It is a property that has nothing to do with the beliefs, doubts, or other intentional attitudes an intelligence might have toward an object, and it is therefore non-converse-intentional. It is presumably a property an object either has or does not have, even if no one ever thinks of or regards the object in any way at all. The material body, Descartes holds, as a composite entity, is divisible into smaller parts, each of which in turn is itself something material. This statement need not be true of every material body, if there are genuine material atoms that cannot be more finely divided, but only of composites such as the human body in its entirety, or, say, the brain and nervous system. But mind, Descartes claims, is not divisible into smaller minds. "I here say, in the first place," he writes, "that there is a great difference between mind and body, inasmuch as body is by nature always divisible, and the mind is entirely indivisible...when I consider the mind...I cannot distinguish in myself any parts, but apprehend myself to be clearly one and entire" (p. 196).

What is meant by the indivisibility of the mind is not that it cannot be divided into faculties, such as memory, calculation, reason, emotion, and the like, nor that it cannot be divided into moments like time-slices or frames from a movie. Descartes believes that the mind cannot be split up into any smaller things that are still minds. However the mind is diminished, it remains a whole mind. If this statement is true, the property distinguishes mind from any composite material body divisible into smaller things that are still material bodies. Descartes' second proof for mind-body dualism has this form:

1. My body is divisible into like parts (bodies).
2. My mind is not divisible into like parts (minds).

3. My body ≠ my mind.   (1,2 Leibniz's Law)

For Descartes, this argument has the important consequence that the mind or soul cannot be destroyed. It must then be immortal, surviving the death of the material body. Things are destroyed when they are broken up into their component parts, as when we destroy a pencil by grinding it into sawdust. But if the mind is indivisible, it has no components to which it can be reduced. In principle, then, the soul can never be destroyed, but as an immaterial entity persists through the death and decomposition of the material body. We will reserve criticism of Descartes' second proof until discussion of the concept of the intended self in Chapter Four. In the meantime, we can see that Descartes believes the argument achieves both purposes of his treatise—it provides philosophical foundations for religious doctrines about the distinction between body and soul, and for the soul's immortality.

THE CAUSAL INTERACTION PROBLEM

Although Descartes' second *Meditations* proof for substance dualism uses the right form of Leibniz's Law, his dualist ontology of mind has not gained widespread acceptance, primarily because of the *causal interaction problem*.

Descartes tries to prove that mind and body are distinct substances capable of separate existence. But he also wants to preserve the intuition that mind and body causally interact. When an injury is done to the body, it can result in or causally produce a sensation, usually of pain, experienced by the mind. When certain mental events occur, such as the decision to move a limb, they ordinarily result in or causally produce an action or bodily event, a muscle movement, act, or behavior. Without such effects, the mind or soul can hardly be said to be responsible for the body's actions. But such a conclusion goes against the spirit of Descartes' project to provide philosophical justifications for traditional religious views. The problem is that substance dualism implies that the immaterial mind is "unextended" in Descartes' phrase. The mind, according to Descartes, is literally nowhere. It lacks any spatial location. Yet, in everyday experience, causation always occurs at a particular place. The billiard ball that strikes another on a table imparts motion to it or causes it to move at a particular location in space. It happens just where the balls make contact, where the proximate cause of the second ball's movement can be said to have had its effect. Nothing like this can possibly be true of causation between immaterial minds and material bodies such as the brain and nervous system. The immaterial mind, if there is such a thing, is not located anywhere in space, and so cannot touch the body at any particular place. Jacques Casanova, 18th-century diplomat, man of letters, and notorious roué, puts the question succinctly in the Preface to his (1797) *Memoirs*: "How is it possible for an immaterial substance, which can neither touch nor be touched to receive impressions? It is a mystery which man cannot unravel" (p. xlii).

Descartes may have tried to avoid the problem by invoking what was then the newly discovered pineal gland in the center of the brain as the locus of causal interaction between the immaterial mind and the material body. The pineal's purpose is still imperfectly understood. But it is believed to be multifunctional, controlling and coordinating hormonal release in other glands. Descartes speculates that this is the place where the mind can act on the brain and the brain on the mind. It is where the will can focus its concentrated energies, and the mind exerts its force on the "subtile fluids" in the nerve endings gathered there to initiate causal chains of motion. Part of Descartes' reasoning is that the pineal gland, unlike other structures in the brain, is not divided into hemispheres, and might therefore serve as a single point of contact between mind and brain. This is woefully inadequate as a solution for philosophers who insist that causation between material spatial and immaterial nonspatial substances is inconceivable anywhere. Identifying a particular structure like the pineal gland as the spot where the impossible is supposed to happen does nothing to remove the mystery of how Descartes' mind, a spiritual substance lacking any position in space, could causally bring about changes in his brain at a particular location in space. Descartes for this reason is sometimes further charged with the objection that he fails to follow his own methodological prescription in *Meditation* 4 not to jump to hasty conclusions from empirical evidence when formulating hypotheses in science (pp. 171–179).

The objection is an important one. But it may not do Descartes justice in evaluating the merits of his arguments for substance dualism. Descartes is not necessarily trying to answer the causal interaction problem by suggesting the pineal gland as a locus for two-way causation between body and mind. Indeed, Descartes may not recognize a difficulty to be resolved here at all. He nowhere addresses the causal interaction objection in his lengthy *Replies to Objections Urged by Certain Men of Learning Against the Preceding Meditations*, perhaps because the problem did not occur to his early objectors.

This apparent oversight can be understood if we consider the combined religious-philosophical purposes of Descartes's theory. Descartes tries to provide rigorous philosophical foundations for accepted religious beliefs about the existence of God and the immortality of the soul. But from the standpoint at least of traditional Judeo-Christian-Islamic teachings about God's creation of the universe, there is embedded in the religious background right from the start an implicit metaphysics of causation between a divine omnipotent immaterial spirit and a material world. God, as an immaterial being, causes the material universe to come into existence by an act of will, in much the way that Descartes conceives of the immaterial human mind causing the material human body to move by an act of will. Similarly, events in God's universe, as Descartes may well have thought of it, such as the evil supposedly committed before the flood, or the petitionary prayers of human beings in distress, may stir God's immaterial spirit into action. He may bring about changes in the world after its creation, as the scriptures of Western religions maintain. This is a point seldom taken into account in discussing Descartes' substance dualism in light of the causal interaction problem. But, from such a perspective, there is nothing metaphysically peculiar about the immaterial mind causally interacting with the material brain. There is nothing more dubious about positing the pineal gland hypothetically as the exact location where mind and brain interact than there is about positing a certain region in Mesopotamia hypothetically as the exact location where God may have created the Garden of Eden.

Descartes believes he has proved the existence of God as a being of infinite perfection, again by two different proofs, in *Meditations* 3 and 5. From this it is supposed to follow that God is an omnipotent, infinitely perfect being, with unlimited will and causal powers. Further, God can presumably choose to create minds as immaterial entities equally capable of causally interacting with material substances. Thus, it seems Descartes need not have been troubled by the causal interaction problem in his interactionist substance dualism. Perhaps, more importantly, Descartes need not have regarded the pineal gland hypothesis as a solution to the causal interaction problem. In that case, he need not have failed to notice what a metaphysically flimsy solution it would be.

This historical defense of Descartes' substance dualism against the causal interaction problem will not be accepted by philosophers who prefer to downplay the religious elements in Descartes' thought. Sometimes Descartes' gestures toward religious beliefs are disregarded as acts of submission to church authorities in the shadow of Galileo's suppression and house arrest at the hands of the Inquisition. But however historians wish to regard the matter, it is hard to see how Descartes' epistemological project could possibly succeed, and how he could have thought it might succeed, if his proof for the existence of God as an infinitely perfect being is not taken seriously, along with the claim that God is incapable of permitting human judgment to be deceived by clear and distinct ideas.

The causal interaction problem nevertheless remains the main philosophical objection to substance dualism. The difficulty is not resolved by appeal to God's omnipotence, or the stories told about God's causal involvement as an immaterial spirit in the material world. The problem threatens substance dualism generally and traditional dualistic theism in

particular, especially for those who do not accept the religious underpin-
nings of Descartes' system, and take the resolute metaphysical stand that
causation necessarily entails action at a particular location in space.

In response to the causal interaction problem, later metaphysicians who
agreed with Descartes that the mind is substantially distinct from the body
explored a variety of alternative noninteractionist substance dualisms.
These can be grouped into two categories: *epiphenomenalism* and *parallelism.*

Epiphenomenalism is one-way causation from body to mind. The word
signifies literally that which is "above" the phenomena. Its application in
philosophy of mind is to indicate that consciousness is a by-product of the
brain's activity, like the ineffectual heat given off by a computer. The attrac-
tion of the theory is that epiphenomena have no causal efficacy on the
body, but are mental after-effects caused by bodily events. This explanation,
however, for the substance dualist, still does not escape the difficulty of
explaining mind-body interaction. It does nothing to dispel the problem of
how a material body can touch a spatially unextended immaterial mind that
literally has no location at any particular place in space.

Parallelism, unlike Cartesian dualism and epiphenomenalism, holds
that mental and physical events are not causally related, but simply run in
tandem or parallel. There are two versions of this theory, known as *pre-
established harmony* and *occasionalism.* Pre-established harmony theory holds
that body and mind do not causally interact, but are made to coincide in
general by God's will. They behave in somewhat the way that two causally
unconnected clocks may show the same time or otherwise move in syn-
chronization. This account leaves their correlation causally unexplained,
as if cutting my material finger just happened always to coincide with, but
without causing, a sensation of pain in my immaterial mind. Occasionalism
embellishes the account by adding that God is responsible for noncausal
mind-body event correlations on a moment-by-moment basis, on each
occasion of occurrence. Parallelism, like the theological defense of
Descartes' causally interactive substance dualism, explains mind-body correlations only by the *deus ex machina* of God's existence and causally effica-
cious omnipotent will. For these reasons, parallelist noninteractive
dualisms have been largely discarded as historical curiosities in the search
for an adequate ontology of mind.

What is important about Descartes' substance dualism and the alternatives that followed is the persistent desire to make some version of mind-
body dualism work. It demonstrates the firm hold that the idea of a real
distinction between mind and body has had on the philosophical imagination. The scientific turn in the philosophy of mind that has marked its
development since the time of Descartes is firmly committed to the spatial
localizability of efficient "billiard ball" causation, and suspicious of explanations that require the existence of God and divine intervention.
Although it might be said that this commitment reflects a question-beg-

ging prejudice based only on a study of material causation or interaction of material bodies in space, contemporary philosophy of mind is virtually unanimous in its rejection of Cartesian substance dualism because of the causal interaction problem.

It may be unclear what philosophical conclusions should be drawn from religious beliefs about God's causal creation of and intervention in the material world. But if in philosophy we are to proceed by examination of arguments for and against each position, then it can at least be said that objections to substance dualism because of the causal interaction problem are not as definitive as critics have often assumed.

BERKELEY'S IDEALIST "DUALISM" OF MINDS AND IDEAS

If substance dualism is defeated by the causal interaction problem, the next obvious approach is to explore the possibilities of *substance monism.* There are two types of substance monism, *idealism* and *physicalism* or *materialism.* Idealism recognizes only the existence of mental substance, the mind with its ideas or thought contents. Physicalism or materialism by contrast postulates only physical or material spatiotemporal substances. It is examined in detail in Chapter Two.

Idealism has few if any serious defenders in recent philosophy of mind. But it is worthwhile to describe the theory as an alternative to more widely accepted views. The most interesting version is George Berkeley's radically empiricist idealism, as it appears in *A Treatise Concerning the Principles of Human Knowledge* (1710), and *Three Dialogues Between Hylas and Philonous* (1713). Berkeley's philosophy is not intended primarily as a theory of mind in the modern sense. But its idealist ontology can be interpreted as avoiding Descartes' causal interaction problem, while preserving a kind of non-Cartesian interactionist mind-body dualism. Berkeley's fundamental ontological principle is expressed in the slogan *"Esse est percipi aut posse percipere"* ("To be is to be perceived or a perceiver"). By this, Berkeley means that there are just two kinds of existents—minds that perceive and ideas or immediate sense contents that are perceived. The mind is active, according to Berkeley, while ideas or sense contents are passive and exist, not independently, but only in a mind. For Berkeley, it follows that sensible things or physical objects are nothing but collections or "congeries" of ideas. These include, for example, the perceived redness, roundness, sweetness, aroma, and so, on of an apple. Berkeley explicitly denies that there is anything more to physical objects than the mind-dependent ideas or sensations of their empirical properties. He rejects the concept of an unexperienceable "matter" or "substratum" underlying objects as they are experienced.

From this sketch it should be clear how Berkeley's idealist monism also implies a kind of dualism that avoids the substance dualist's causal interaction problem. Since, according to Berkeley, there exist only minds and their ideas, bodies, including the brain and nervous system, are also just congeries of ideas. This means that the brain can causally act and be acted on by mind because the brain is nothing but a collection of ideas in the mind. The problem of explaining how two different categories of spatial and nonspatial substance can causally interact does not arise in Berkeley's philosophy. For he claims that there is ultimately only one kind of entity belonging to the single metaphysical category of the mental or ideational. By maintaining that the mind is active and ideas passive, and that the brain, like other physical objects, is just an assemblage of ideas in the mind, Berkeley is able to preserve a Cartesian-like distinction between body and mind. But, unlike substance dualists, Berkeley can also explain mind-body causal interaction within his idealist substance monism, without contradicting the assumption that causation always takes place at particular locations in space. For space itself, Berkeley believes, is in the mind. In this way, Berkeley avoids the causal interaction problem that plagues substance dualism.

The difficulty with idealism, and Berkeley's idealism in particular, is its apparent nonobjectivity. This is the problem of squaring the theory's mentalistic ontology with the belief that physical objects are ontically independent of the mind's subjective will and control. Even if physical objects are congeries of ideas existing in a mind, I cannot, however strong my desire, cause a pile of gold coins to appear by producing their mental image, focusing my attention on the table, and willing them to exist. If I experience coins through sensation, it is natural to believe that the coins are already there, available for me to experience, and do not come into existence as a result of my thinking of them. The objectivity of the experienced world is an elusive proposition for idealist ontologies. Berkeley guarantees it only by supposing that God as an infinite mind "perceives" or has in his mind all parts and aspects of all sensible things that human finite minds sometimes perceive, and that physical objects continue to exist in God's mind even when human minds are not perceiving them. They are in that sense objective and not subject to the control of particular finite human minds. Berkeley's God continuously perceives the physical universe, so that its objects are already "there," waiting for finite minds to experience in sensation as partial congeries of the complete set of ideas by which they are constituted.

Berkeley explains causal connections between physical events in terms of God's willing that particular ideas or kinds of ideas follow others in regular sequence. This means that causal connections are not necessary, contrary to what rationalist philosophers like Leibniz had supposed, but the contingent outcomes of God's freewill decisions. Mind-body causation is relatively straightforward in Berkeley's idealism, because it amounts only to God's willing that certain congeries of ideas constituting brain events are regularly followed by the occurrence of certain mental events, and conversely. When I cut my finger, according to Berkeley, it hurts because

God wills that the succession of congeries of ideas that constitutes the injury, the movement of the knife blade cutting the skin and damaging nerves, is regularly followed by the mental occurrence of pain. When I choose to raise my arm, my decision causes my arm to move because God wills that the mental occurrence of volition, in the absence of injury, disease, or restraint, is regularly followed by the succession of ideas in my brain chemistry that engages the appropriate muscles to raise the arm.

This takes us back to the problem of trying to explain the mind by appealing to the existence and power of God. The suspicion of invoking God as an explanatory principle refutes the theological solution to the Cartesian causal interaction problem, pre-established harmony and occasionalism, and now Berkeley's idealism. All are unacceptable as implications of a scientific philosophy of mind. The causal interaction problem is avoided in Berkeley's metaphysics, but only by sacrificing modern standards of scientific explanation.

PROPERTY DUALISM

If substance and idealist dualisms do not provide a satisfactory mind-body distinction, what possibilities remain? One approach is to maintain that, while there is only one kind of (physical) substance, the mind has not only physical or behavioral-material-functional properties, but also nonphysical behaviorally-materially-functionally ineliminable and irreducible ← ? properties. This kind of theory is usually referred to as *property dualism*, though it is known in related terms as *dual aspect* or *dual attribute theory*, *anomalous monism* (Davidson, 1980), or *nonreductive materialism* (Margolis, 1978, 1984), as opposed to Cartesian, ontic, or substance dualism.

Property dualism allows for the evolutionary emergence of mind from complex material organizations of purely physical substance. It is therefore also sometimes described as *emergence* or *supervenience theory*. The idea is that nonphysical properties may emerge from or supervene on material substances if they achieve a certain complexity, in somewhat the way that life emerges evolutionarily from or supervenes on certain kinds of properly organized material substances. The difference is that life, though emergent or supervenient, is (standardly regarded as) materially-mechanically-functionally explainable, whereas thought and the mind, according to property dualism, are not. Thus, it is possible to interpret the emergence of mind from matter as a natural phenomenon that takes place because of evolving complexities of living matter. It brings into existence something that is not only new and different from, but inexplicable in terms of, the behavioral-material-functional properties of the nonmental entities from which it emerges.

The advantage of property over substance dualism is that, like materialism and idealism, it avoids the causal interaction problem. The theory has no need to countenance causal interaction between material and immaterial or spatial and nonspatial substances because it admits that there are only material substances. The advantage of property dualism over idealism is that it need not appeal to God's divine abilities in order to account for mind-body interaction or the objectivity of the perceived world. The advantage of property dualism over materialism is that it provides for the intuitive distinction between body and mind by positing a difference in their properties, and especially in the metaphysical categories of their properties. It attributes to mind a combination of behavioral-material-functional and behaviorally-materially-functionally ineliminable and irreducible properties. Without both types of properties, property dualism holds, there can be no satisfactory explanation of psychological phenomena. The ineliminable and irreducible properties of mind are those that many thinkers have held to be essential to the mind, as opposed to the body or brain. They include the content or *qualia* of experience, what it feels like to see and taste a strawberry, and the "aboutness," object-directedness, or intentionality of psychological states.

The property dualist can accept without contradiction all scientific discoveries about the mind and brain. These contribute to property dualism's understanding of the mind's behavioral-material-functional properties, to which the hard psychological sciences exclusively apply. The property dualist can also take over the basic structure of Descartes' arguments for the mind-body distinction. Descartes claims that the distinct properties of body and mind belong to distinct substances, but his evidence and arguments are not strong enough to establish this conclusion. Nevertheless, Descartes may have shown that mind and body have distinct kinds of properties. This is all that is needed to uphold the property dualist version of the mind-body distinction. The burden of property dualism is to prove that there are such differences, and that at least some properties of mind are neither eliminable in favor of nor reducible to behavioral-material-functional properties.

As a counterpoint to Descartes' arguments for substance dualism, we may consider the following proof for intentionalist property dualism:

1. My mind has the property of being intentional (about or directed toward intended objects).
2. My body (brain and nervous system) considered only as such, does not have the property of being intentional.

3. My mind has properties that my body considered only as such, does not have.
                                                                          (1,2)
4. My body considered only as such ≠ my mind.   (3 Leibniz's Law)

Property dualism grafted onto a materialist substance monism, like

Berkeley's "dualism" of minds and ideas grafted onto an idealist mental substance monism, seems to offer the best of both worlds. It attributes behaviorally-materially-functionally ineliminable and irreducible properties to the
mind, while avoiding the causal interaction problem. It is fully capable of
absorbing scientific findings about the physical functioning of the brain and
nervous system, without commitment to an extrascientific ontology of eliminativism or reductivism. But, unlike Berkeley's idealism, property dualism
has no need to appeal to God's existence in science and philosophy.

OBJECTIONS TO PROPERTY DUALISM

The resistance to property dualism by philosophers who deny that the mind
has behaviorally-materially-functionally ineliminable and irreducible properties stems from several sources. There is an understandable if not easily justified distrust of facts that cannot be understood in terms of concrete physical
things. Extrascientific facts of this kind are sometimes dismissed as inherently unscientific or even anti-scientific. They may be objectionable because
they are subjective and private in first-person experience, and hence publicly
unconfirmable in content, open to misinterpretation, and otherwise epistemically unreliable. In recent times, denying the existence of psychological
states has been the predominant negative eliminativist ontology of mind.

The dispute between property dualism and its critics reflects the most fundamental division in philosophy of mind. It divides those who regard the
mind as essentially different than any material or mechanical system, dualists
of some sort, from those believe the mind is purely material or machine-like.
The best way to consider these choices, and to clarify and evaluate the
virtues of property dualism and its place in the science and metaphysics of
mind, is to weigh it against the sharpest criticisms. There are many of these,
and no list can be fully comprehensive in the sense of anticipating all possible objections. But the selection included here provides a good starting
place in a topic that will continue to occupy our attention.

Inconsistency of Irreducibility and Emergence Claims in Property Dualism

The first criticism of property dualism concerns an apparent inconsistency
between the behavioral-material-functional ineliminability and irreducibility,
and the evolutionary emergence, of mind and mental properties. If the
mind has emerged from the complex organization of material substances,
why is it not also reducible to or eliminable in terms of those elements?

This question appears to be a difficulty for property dualism. But the
objection embodies a misunderstanding of what is meant by the emergence
from or supervenience of mental on physical properties according to prop-

erty dualism. There is no contradiction in the theory that mental properties emerge from the purely physical properties of certain arrangements of matter to which they are ontically and explanatorily irreducible. This is just what "emergence" means. To describe mental properties as evolutionarily emergent or supervenient is to say that they arise from matter by acquiring properties that result from its complex organization but that cannot be explained in purely behavioral-material-functional terms. The emergence of life from nonliving matter is similar but metaphysically less extreme, if, as scientists now believe, life can be reductively explained as a physical-chemical phenomenon. But the reducible emergence of life need not be the only type or degree of emergence. The property dualist model is compatible in principle with the emergence of mind from matter in a stronger sense than the emergence of life from nonliving matter. It hypothesizes that mind emerges from matter, not only as something with new properties unexemplified by less complexly organized matter, but as something so different that it cannot be fully explained in terms of behavioral, material, or functional properties.

Incoherence of Chronologically Fundamental and Evolutionarily Emergent Psychological Properties

A related criticism assumes that according to property dualism there are fundamental nonphysical properties of mind in the same sense that there are fundamental properties of physics, such as electromagnetism. The property usually thought to be fundamental in property dualism is intentionality. If intentionality is to the metaphysics of mind as electromagnetism is to the physics of material entities, then a dualism of some sort is unavoidable. But the objection is that if intentionality is a fundamental property in this sense, then, like electromagnetism, it must be found at all times and places in the universe. This, however, is inconsistent with the evolutionary emergence of mind. The criticism is a variation of the first objection that there is some kind of incoherence in regarding the mind and its psychological properties as both evolutionarily emergent and irreducible, interpreting irreducibility in this case as being fundamental in the sense of basic physical properties.

Yet the objection does not hold unless the property dualist agrees that intentional properties can only be fundamental by being instantiated at all times throughout the history of the universe. Needless to say, the property dualist is not obligated to accept this chronological interpretation of what it means for a property to be "fundamental." Emergent properties can be fundamental in a logical or conceptual rather than chronological sense. To be fundamental in this way implies that emergent properties are theoretically ineliminable and irreducible to behavioral-material-functional properties. The instantiation of fundamental intentional properties by this account need not be coexistent with the physical universe, but only conceptually or explanatorily ineliminable and irreducible. This interpretation of the mind's intentional properties as fundamental does not contradict their evolutionary emergence, so property dualism is fully compatible with the emergence of mind. It is true, as the objection states, that evolutionarily emergent behaviorally-materially-functionally ineliminable and irreducible psychological properties are not physically fundamental in the manner of electromagnetic forces. But there is no reason why the intentionality of thought should be regarded as fundamental in the same way or in the same sense as elementary physical properties.

Ontological Economy of Eliminativism and Reductivism

It is sometimes said that eliminativism and reductivism are preferable to property dualism, because of their comparative ontological economy. A monistic theory generally requires that we accept fewer kinds of theoretical entities than a dualistic account. The objection does not try to show that property dualism is definitely false, but that it should be rejected in favor of *property monism*, on the grounds that in constructing theories we should not "multiply entities beyond necessity." This is to say we should not suppose that there are more objects or kinds of objects than we minimally need to give adequate explanations. Property monism is simpler and more economical than property dualism because its explanations require only one eliminative or reductive category of physical properties.

The economy objection has force only if there is no need to refer to mental properties in explaining psychological phenomena. The principle that we ought not to multiply entities beyond necessity enjoins the theorist to eliminate theoretical entities only if they are not strictly needed for explanatory purposes. There is nothing particularly praiseworthy about a philosophy of mind that is simpler or more economical than its competitors if it is false or explanatorily inadequate. But if the mind has properties that cannot be eliminated or adequately reduced or explained in behavioral-material-functional terms, then it is necessary after all to include behaviorally-materially-functionally ineliminable and irreducible properties alongside behavioral-material-functional properties in the ontology of mind. This is the heart of dispute between property dualism and its critics, so that an appeal to the economy principle is pointless unless it can first be shown that property monisms can satisfactorily account for all psychological phenomena. The ontological simplicity or economy of property monisms over property dualisms, in lieu of a more comprehensive defense of monism, is unjustified in and of itself as a reason to prefer property monism to dualism.

Explanatory Disadvantages of Property Dualism

As a fourth objection, compare the kinds of explanations that can be given in property dualism as opposed to property monism. Unlike the eliminative and reductive ontologies based on behavioral, neurophysiological, or information sciences, property dualism does not offer detailed theories of the structures or laws governing mental properties. Paul M. Churchland, in *Matter and Consciousness: A Contemporary Introduction to the Philosophy of Mind* (1988), summarizes this objection to mind-body dualism when he writes: "Compared to the rich resources and explanatory successes of current materialism, dualism is less a theory than it is an empty space waiting for a genuine theory to be put in it" (p. 19).

But there is no hard scientific explanation of the mind that cannot be absorbed into property dualism as an account of the mind's physical properties. Property dualism cannot be criticized by pointing to the explanatory successes of the hard psychological sciences, no matter how impressive these may be. For scientific discoveries about the mind are just as much the common stock of property dualists as of eliminativists and reductivists. Property dualism claims only that understanding the mind requires knowledge of its dual nature, its behavioral-material-functional properties as explained by the hard third-person sciences, and its behaviorally-materially-functionally ineliminable and irreducible intentional properties as described by phenomenology, in the first-person introspective study of mental states. When eliminativists and reductivists conclude that the mind is nothing but a behavioral-material-functional system, they make an extrascientific metaphysical conjecture that oversteps the scientific evidence about the mind's behavioral, material, and functional properties. Whether mind-body identity is correct or not cannot be settled by stacking up scientific findings as though they belonged only to the eliminativist or reductivist, since these are equally data for the property dualist. The explanatory adequacy of property monism versus property dualism cannot be decided on scientific grounds but must be determined on the basis of the extent to which each provides or fails to provide a philosophically satisfactory metaphysics of mind.

What then of the claim that property monisms are explanatorily preferable to property dualism? It is hard to answer this question without first identifying a clear-cut example of a monistic psychological explanation. This is more difficult than may at first appear. The truth is that most contemporary psychology is not specifically monistic, and its findings are ontically neutral as between eliminativism or reductivism and property dualism. Psychoanalysis and the theory of clinical psychotherapy are generally intentionalist. Behaviorism and the information sciences deliberately refrain from speculating on the ontology of mind. Neurophysiology is a descriptive science that explains the workings of the neuron and the organization of brain structures, all of which is fully compatible with property dualism. *Folk psychological explanations* involving intentional concepts outside the hard sciences, moreover, are useful for managing in an everyday kind of way with psychological occurrences. The pragmatic evidence for this is our success in interacting with others, understanding their often complex intentions, and making predictions and explanations of how we and others behave from folk psychological accounts of their beliefs, desires, hopes, fears, and other intentional states. It would be question-begging in a criticism of this kind to exclude such explanations merely on the grounds that they are not of the same caliber as hard scientific explanations given in the behavioral, neurophysiological, or computer and information sciences. But folk psychological explanations are intentionalist, as eliminativists and reductivists often complain.

We have already seen, and we will be reminded later again, that even the so-called hard psychological sciences provide adequate explanations of mental properties only insofar as they also unknowingly or surreptitiously appeal to intentional concepts. This makes it virtually impossible to exhibit a purely monistic scientifically respectable explanation of mind for comparison with property dualist accounts of the same phenomena. The objection that eliminative and reductive theories have an explanatory advantage over property dualism is usually raised by critics who are so unsympathetic to property dualism that they are not really in a position to know what a property dualist explanation would look like, let alone to delimit the range of possible explanations available within different kinds of property dualism. This disagreement skews the comparison of explanatory advantages of eliminative and reductive theories against those of property dualism. It may invalidate the criticism that property dualism should be rejected because it cannot offer explanations as good as those given by its nondualistic competitors. The evidence for this conclusion is the frequency with which critics of property dualism assume that the theory contradicts hard scientific discoveries about the mind and brain, or that the property dualist cannot use the same hard scientific facts in its explanations.

To get a sense of the explanatory disadvantages of monism as contrasted with property dualism, suppose that a materialist explanation of the sort envisioned by the criticism were provided for a psychological or social phenomenon. What if a history of the Watergate scandal were to be given in a book filled with nothing but chemical formulas describing the brain and other physical events that took place at the time involving participants in the break-in, wiretapping, and cover-up? The test would be to have the most knowledgeable scientists who have not been informed about the psychological and social correlates of the behavioral-material-functional elimination or reduction examine these formulas and give an interpretation of the events described. If they come anywhere close to recognizing the Watergate break-in, or the thoughts and actions of participants, well and good. But if they fail, as is more likely, no elimination or reduction of mental to nonmental properties is effected. Would such a chemical history explain these social-political episodes, even to the neurophysiologist well versed in understanding chemical symbolisms? If anything, it appears that property monist explanations suffer from an explanatory disadvantage in comparison with property dualist accounts of social and psychological phenomena. The property dualist and folk psychologist are in a better position to explain these events by appealing to the agents' thoughts and intentions.

Causal Irrelevance of Intentional Epiphenomena

Do intentional properties make a real difference in the workings of the mind, or are they merely epiphenomenal? Suppose that wearing a white sweater keeps me warm on a chilly day. The sweater causes my warmth, but its whiteness or the fact that it is white contributes nothing to its effect if a sweater of any color would have kept me just as warm. The color, as opposed to the material, thickness, weave, and design of the sweater, is not causally involved.

Now it might be said that intentional properties are epiphenomenal in much the same way in the property dualist explanation of mind. If so, then the mind's intentionality may be just as irrelevant to understanding the mind as the color of my sweater is to understanding its warmth. A similar objection is considered by Brian McLaughlin, in his essay "Type Epiphenomenalism, Type-Dualism, and the Causal Priority of the Physical" (1989). The upshot is that some version of eliminativism or reductivism may be preferable to an intentionalist property dualism.

But it is circular reasoning in the first place to suppose that noncausal or causally inefficacious properties are merely epiphenomenal. To make this assumption is to suppose that only causal explanations are necessary in understanding the mind, whereas property dualism holds that a causal account explains only part of the mind's dual nature. If the purpose of explaining the mind is just to explain its causal operations, then the intentionality of thought in that limited sense, relative to that limited purpose, might be regarded as epiphenomenal. If I want a complete explanation of the sweater, and not merely of its ability to keep me warm, then I must also take into account its color. For this broader, explanatory purpose, the sweater's whiteness is not merely epiphenomenal, because my description is incomplete without it. The same is true in the philosophy of mind. If I want a complete explanation of the concept of mind, and not merely of its causal properties, then I must also take its intentionality into account.

It is precisely here that the analogy between the sweater's color and the mind's intentionality breaks down. There is a satisfactory material explanation of the sweater's whiteness (leaving aside the mind's perception of its color). But there is nothing comparable for the mind's intentionality. The whiteness of the sweater can be fully explained in terms of the material of the sweater, the genetics, diet, and physical condition of the sheep that gave their wool for it, the bleaches or dyes used to treat it, and, in general, the physical processes the fibers have undergone in being produced, collected, and made into a garment. But if the property dualist critique of eliminativism and reductivism in the philosophy of mind is correct, then there is no parallel behavioral-material-functional explanation of the mind's intrinsic intentionality.

weak

We should not agree without convincing argument that the intentionality of thought is causally epiphenomenal. For the moment, suffice it to say that proof is needed to show that intentionality makes no difference in the mind's or brain's causal workings, in order to make the epiphenomena objection stick. But no such proof has yet been given. Later, in discussing the concept of *agent causation* (in Chapter 5), we shall see more precisely how the intentionality of thought causes actions to occur that otherwise would not have occurred, and why intention must be included even in the causal explanation of mind.

Objection from Evolutionary Science

A final criticism seeks to provide a single set of considerations to refute substance and property dualism. The objection is that dualism is somehow incompatible with the evolutionary account of the emergence of human from nonhuman animal species as a purely physical process. Churchland maintains:

The important point about the standard evolutionary story is that the human species and all of its features are the wholly physical outcome of a purely physical process.... If this is the correct account of our origins, then there seems neither need, nor room, to fit any nonphysical substances or properties into our theoretical account of ourselves. We are creatures of matter. And we should learn to live with that fact. (p. 21)

But is hard to see where the criticism of property dualism is supposed to appear in these statements. There are no scientific truths about evolutionary history that the property dualist, as opposed to the substance dualist, need deny. Evolutionary biology is ontologically neutral about the properties of mind, and it would be difficult to find responsible evolutionary scientists saying anything concrete about the metaphysics of mental or psychological properties.

Popularizations of evolutionary science, when they venture into philosophical areas, speak of the psychological in unmistakably intentional terms. Sometimes they claim to do so only for heuristic purposes, paying lip service to the possibility of eliminating or reducing intentional idioms in favor of a purely materialist vocabulary. But this promise shares the doubtful fate of eliminativism and reductivism generally. To say without further ado that evolutionary theory proves that "the human species *and all of its features* are the wholly physical outcome of a purely physical process" is to offer a philosophical interpretation that goes beyond the scientific data and theory of evolutionary biology, and begs the philosophically interesting questions against property dualism in the ontology of mind. The property dualist admits all along that mind emerges as a result of purely physical forces and that human beings in some nonreductive sense are indeed the "creatures of matter." But from this claim it would be equivocating to insist that therefore the mind is nothing but a material entity.

There may be other criticisms of property dualism to be considered. But, as an ontology of mind, property dualism is compatible with any observational and experimental scientific findings, including those discovered by evolutionary biology. Against eliminativism and reductivism, property dualism has the explanatory advantage of including folk psychological facts concerning the content or qualia of experience and the intentionality of thought, and it need not go to implausible lengths to explain away these obvious properties of mind.

NEUROPHYSIOLOGY OF THE PHANTOM LIMB

To illustrate the limitations of hard psychological sciences in the philosophy of mind, we shall now consider the problem of the *phantom limb*. This is a medical-metaphysical puzzle about the experience of sensation in a missing body part. Descartes investigates phantom limb phenomena in his attempts to advance substance dualism. But recently an interesting non-Cartesian neurophysiological solution has also been proposed.

The problem indicates the depth to which we must be prepared to question eliminative and reductive strategies, to determine whether they are at least unknowingly if not surreptitiously committed to intentional concepts in order to make their explanations work. It provides a preview of the interplay between scientific evidence and philosophical argument that characterizes much of the discussion in this book, and at the same time indicates the prospects and risks involved in drawing philosophical conclusions about the ontology of mind from scientific data and theory.

A phantom limb is the location of a body part, such as an arm or leg, that has been amputated in surgery or by accident, in which the person continues to sense movement, pain, itching, discomfort, or what seems to be normal *proprioception*, or perception of internal body states. The occurrence has troubled philosophers and scientists ever since it was first reported. Various solutions have been proposed to explain phantom limb in accord with a materialist or dualist metaphysics of mind. Descartes, in *Meditation* 6, interprets phantom limb as evidence of the soul's immateriality. He observes that pain and other feelings as mental events in this unusual case appear to be not just logically or conceptually, but actually, independent of the existence of the relevant material body parts. If the same could be said generally of the body as a whole, then mind-body dualism is implied.

> I have learned from some persons whose arms or legs have been cut off, that they sometimes seemed to feel pain in the part which had been amputated, which made me think that I could not be quite certain that it was a certain member which pained me, even though I felt pain in it. (p. 189)

There are also nondualist physiological explanations of phantom limb. The most popular is the hypothesis that damaged nerve endings, which grow into nodules called *neuromas* at or along the neural sites where the limb is severed, continue to transmit signals to the brain as though the limb were still attached. Descartes again anticipates the theory, in his (1644) *Principles of Philosophy*, describing the experiences of a girl whose arm was amputated at the elbow:

> She had various pains, sometimes in one of the fingers of the hand which was cut off, and sometimes in another. This could clearly only happen because the nerves which previously had been carried all the way from the brain to the hand, and afterwards terminated in the arm near the elbow, were there affected in the same way as it was their function to be stimulated for the purpose of impressing on the mind residing in the brain the sensation of pain in this and that finger. (pp. 293–294)

This plausible account has been discounted on modern scientific grounds. When nerves are cut above the neuroma, or neural pathways in the spinal cord from the limb to the brain are interrupted, and sensory receptors in the thalamus and cortex of the brain are disconnected, phantom limb experience usually remains. Although the pain may temporarily abate, as when these procedures are done for therapeutic purposes, phantom limb eventually returns, according to patients' testimony, usually in a month, but sometimes after a year.

Another new theory of phantom limb has been proposed by neurophysiologist and pain specialist Ronald Melzack. Melzack (1992) postulates "that the brain contains a neuromatrix, or network of neurons, that, in addition to responding to sensory stimulation, continuously generates a characteristic pattern of impulses indicating that the body is intact and unequivocally one's own" (p. 123). Melzack refers to this pattern as a "neurosignature" and concludes that body-ownership impulses projecting from the brain's neuromatrix accounts for the persistence of phantom proprioception of amputated body parts. We may think of this as something like a web of impulses transmitted from the brain, by which the brain claims the entire body as its territory. When a body part is removed, the impulses continue, as they would if the body were still intact. The phantom limb is not sending pain or proprioception messages, because it no longer exists. But signals radiating from the brain in a pattern established while the limb existed "expect" it to be there, and by their continued "territory" or "ownership" transmissions give the illusion that the missing part still exists.

Melzack's hypothesis explains why these three neural pathways in particular are involved, and it formulates testable consequences by which his explanation of phantom limb might be (partially) confirmed or disconfirmed. He concludes that bodily self-identity is not discovered but originates with and is projected by the brain: "Phantom limbs are a mystery only if we assume the body sends sensory messages to a passively receiving brain. Phantoms become comprehensible once we recognize that the brain generates the experience of the body. Sensory inputs merely modulate that experience; they do not directly cause it" (p. 126). If Melzack's theory is correct, it may provide a neurophysiological answer to long-standing philosophical problems about the concept of personal identity, and it may explain certain psychopathologies involving the loss of personhood through disconnection of specific neurosignature-transmitting pathways in the neuromatrix. The ownership of thought and sensation implied by Melzack's hypothesis may also contribute to our understanding of the proprietary privacy of psychological phenomena, the belief that sensations necessarily belong only to the person who experiences them and cannot be shared by another. This conviction may also be attributable in whole or in part to the sense of body-sensation ownership that Melzack believes is projected as an electrochemical impulse pattern from the neuromatrix.

But as remarkable as its implications may be, Melzack's hypothesis underscores the difficulty typically encountered by philosophical attempts to generalize and apply scientific hypotheses to eliminate or reduce psychological to neurophysiological phenomena. Here it must be emphasized that Melzack himself, like most scientists, ventures no metaphysical interpretations from his hypotheses about the neurophysiology of phantom limb. But there is a temptation for others in the philosophy of mind with a predisposition for eliminativism or reductivism to do so. Suppose, for the sake of argument, that Melzack's neuromatrix neurosignature theory of phantom limb phenomena is correct. Further suppose that, although Melzack himself does not draw such sweeping conclusions, philosophers see in his discovery striking scientific evidence of the truth of eliminativism or reductivism, and at least partial refutation of property dualism. Must the property dualist agree that this scientific theory proves that phantom limb experience supports a nondualist ontology? This conclusion seems doubtful, unless the neuromatrix hypothesis can satisfactorily explain phantom limb without presupposing the intentionality of thought.

The problem in deriving an ontology of mind from scientific data and theory like that contained in Melzack's phantom limb theory is to provide a satisfactory elimination or reduction of intentional phenomena. The dilemma is that the explanation either leaves the intentionality of thought inadequately explained or explains it only by shifting the account to other intentional concepts. Melzack says of his neuromatrix hypothesis that the pathways generate patterns of neural impulses "indicating" that the body is intact and "unequivocally one's own." But these are eminently intentional concepts. The indication of unity and ownership involving the experience of a whole body or sensory field as suggested to or sensed by a psychological subject is an intended object of thought. The body indicated as unequivocally one's own similarly entails the semantic concept of the complement of equivocation. Body ownership by a psychological subject is also presumably intended as an object of thought or sensation. Reliance on intentional idioms is further evident in Melzack's characterization of the brain's parietal lobe as one of the three integrated neuromatrix systems, which has been shown experimentally to be implicated in a subject's "sense of self." Melzack writes in this intentionally-laden fashion that "patients who have suffered a lesion of the parietal lobe in one hemisphere have been known to push one of their own legs out of a hospital bed because they were convinced it belonged to a stranger. Such behavior shows that the damaged area normally imparts a signal that says, 'This is my body; it is a part of my self' " (p. 123).

It is sometimes said that intentional idioms are dispensable in scientific psychology. Perhaps they can be explained away like the descriptions of nature acting purposively to promote survival and reproduction through natural selection in bioevolutionary theory. But in psychological science, the assertion begins to appear increasingly like an unsupported article of faith. The dilemma of inadequate explanation or explanation by unknowing or surreptitious use of intentional concepts reasserts itself when attempts are made to do away with intentionality entirely in psychology. This is a pattern we will see repeated as new breakthroughs in cognitive science, neurophysiology, behavioral psychology, and artificial intelligence are applied in eliminative or reductive philosophical analyses of intentional psychological phenomena. If there are grounds for regarding the intentional or qualitative properties of mind as ineliminable and irreducible, then property dualism has a sound basis for assimilating scientific discoveries about the properties of brain and mind as belonging to the material side of the property dualism equation. The property dualist can easily take over the truths of hard psychological science without abandoning the thesis that the mind also has behaviorally-materially-functionally ineliminable and irreducible properties, and without taking scientific data and theory by themselves to imply extrascientific conclusions about the metaphysics of mind.

The property dualist response to the phantom limb problem and the neuromatrix neurosignature solution is that Melzack may indeed have found the brain substructures responsible for phantom limb experience. But, so far at least, the explanation of how these parts of the brain function remains intentional. It offers no theoretical elimination or reduction of pain, itching, proprioception, or other qualia, and involves at this stage of (popular) exposition a fully intentional account of the brain's projection of unitary body ownership. This is effected by nerve impulses, according to Melzack's theory. But property dualism admits that all ineliminable and irreducible mental phenomena are actualized by brain and nervous system functionings. There is nothing in Melzack's hypothesis as a neurophysiological explanation of phantom limb phenomena to require rethinking the plausibility of property dualism.

The moral is not that scientific advances are irrelevant and should be ignored. Quite the contrary. The challenge for the ontology of mind is to understand the implications of discoveries in the hard psychological sciences for what they are, from a philosophically correct perspective. We must gather scientific insights into the workings of mind, but without uncritically accepting science's own sometimes naive philosophical interpretations of its results. And we must resist the temptation, as scientists themselves usually and rightly do, of drawing extrascientific conclusions unsubstantiated by scientific data and theory.

SCIENTIFIC PSYCHOLOGY AND THE METAPHYSICS OF MIND

Property dualism offers the advantages of substance monism over substance dualism, avoids the causal interaction problem, and can be defended against sophisticated eliminativist and reductivist objections. These facts strongly suggest that property dualism should tentatively be regarded as providing the best ontology of mind.

This conclusion must be reconsidered as new scientific evidence and theory, as well as new philosophical arguments and thought experiments, become available for reflection. But property dualism seems to offer the most flexible encompassing theory to accommodate discoveries about the mind and brain that have emerged in philosophy and the hard psychological sciences. The theory satisfies these explanatory requirements: (1) It is fully compatible with hard scientific findings in behavioral science, neurophysiology, and cognitive psychology, including artificial intelligence and the information sciences. (2) It agrees with phenomenological or introspective data about experiential content or qualia and the intentionality of mental states as about or directed toward intended objects. (3) It does not preclude mind-body causal interaction. (4) It avoids the difficulties of property monisms, including idealism and eliminative or reductive behaviorism, materialism, and functionalism. (5) It explains the mind-body relation as a distinction among categorically different behavioral-material-functional and behaviorally-materially-functionally ineliminable and irreducible properties. (6) It distinguishes between mind and body in a way that captures the intuitive sense that there is a difference between the two, reflected (mistakenly) even in Descartes' substance dualism and Berkeley's idealist dualism. (7) It is scientifically open-ended, and makes no appeal to the concept of God or divine knowledge or intervention. (8) It is refutable in principle by contrary scientific data and philosophical argument, if a feasible elimination or reduction of intentional properties or qualitative psychological content were proposed.

The final test of the explanatory adequacy of property dualism is whether or not it can withstand further criticisms as its principles are articulated and its consequences made clear. The challenge it must immediately answer is from those reductive and eliminative strategies that seek to prove the mind does not have behaviorally-materially-functionally ineliminable and irreducible properties, that mental phenomena can be explained without them, or that the concept of mind is nothing but a fiction of obsolete folk psychology. We now turn to these eliminative and reductive strategies as further objections to property dualism.

Frustration:
1) no sense of what emergentism
   (irreducibility) means
2) too much "I go my way on
   the conditions"

CHAPTER TWO

Elimination and Reduction Strategies for the Concept of Mind: Behaviorism, Materialism, Functionalism

Difficulties encountered by interactionist and parallelist substance dualisms have inspired a variety of eliminative and reductive analyses. Eliminativism denies that there are any truths about the mind, and holds that reference to it is a misleading prescientific fiction that should be eliminated from a mature cognitive psychology. Reductivism takes the less extreme position that facts about the mind can be expressed without referring to mental properties or phenomena. These strategies, in the form of behaviorism, materialism, and functionalism, are supposed to reduce the number of terms in a more economical theoretical vocabulary of the psychological sciences. But eliminativism and reductivism are refuted by showing that they fail adequately to account for psychological phenomena.

OCKHAM'S RAZOR

The elimination and reduction of mind are favored by modern science. They explain or explain away references to the mind in terms of behavioral, material, or functional properties, in monistic ontologies inspired by discoveries in the hard psychological sciences. Philosophy often takes its cues about the nature of truth from the impressive accomplishments of scientific method. To be "unscientific" in one's philosophy, however this is understood, is usually perceived as intellectually objectionable. Yet it is easy to forget that modern science developed from and was nurtured by philosophical investigations from its inception. Philosophers must interpret and evaluate the progress of science, and raise questions about its metaphysical presuppositions.

There are several types of eliminativism and reductivism. Each in its own way seeks to solve the mind-body problem and explain the ontology of mind in negative fashion, by arguing that there is no need or no basis for introducing the concept of mind. Psychology avoids the mind-body problem in this fashion by doing away with or reducing the "mind" and "mental" components in substance and property dualisms to a theory of behavior, brain, or information-processing functions. There are also, as we know from Berkeley, eliminativist or reductivist idealisms that try to eliminate matter or reduce body to mind. But this approach is largely disregarded by contemporary philosophy and science. Instead, programs for the elimination or reduction of mind have proceeded in the opposite direction, attempting to replace reference to the mind by reference only to the body, especially the brain and nervous system, and its functions or activities.

The rationale behind eliminativism and reductivism is the *principle of explanatory economy*, or *Ockham's Razor*. This is a rule for limiting a theory's ontology, named for the 14th-century philosopher and logician William of Ockham. We have already encountered this principle in answering some of the objections to property dualism. Ockham's Razor is an aesthetic criterion that does not always distinguish true from false theories, but governs choice among alternative competing explanations of the same phenomena according to considerations of theoretical economy. Ockham's Razor states that we should "avoid multiplying entities beyond necessity." If we can adequately explain something in two or more different ways, then we should prefer the explanation that commits us to the existence of fewer or fewer ontologically different types or categories of things. The idea is that if we are to include reference to something in a theory, there must be solid justification for supposing that it exists. If we can explain an eclipse of the moon without assuming that there are demons who cloak or devour it, then Ockham's Razor requires us to eliminate the concept of demon from our theory of the moon's eclipse.

The elimination or reduction of mentalistic terms from explanations of psychological phenomena is in one sense a matter of theoretical vocabulary. But there is more at stake in eliminativism and reductivism than the language of cognitive theory. We expect a correct ontology not only to offer terminological recommendations, but to express the truth about the metaphysics of mind. If a sound and complete philosophical psychology does not need to make reference to the mind or mental events, states, or properties, then we shall conclude on the basis of Ockham's Razor that mind does not exist. But whether there can be a satisfactory eliminative or reductive theory of this kind is the central problem for philosophy of mind.

Ockham's Razor makes it clear that eliminativism and reductivism cannot succeed merely by proposing theories that are more economical than

puzzle: reductive explanation v. reductive elimination

mind-body dualisms. They must adequately explain the phenomena in question at least as well as less economical accounts. If there are facts about the mind that eliminativist or reductivist theories do not satisfactorily explain, explain away, or convince us do not need to be explained, then considerations of comparative economy by Ockham's Razor do not come into play. The test of an eliminativist or reductivist philosophy of mind is first and foremost whether it explains everything a complete psychological theory ought to explain. What this includes and does not include is open to dispute, and constitutes part of the disagreement between eliminativists and noneliminativists, reductivists and nonreductivists. But pressure can be exerted on theories for purposes of critical evaluation by demanding proof in every case that they actually provide a satisfactory explanation of the required phenomena and do not simply purchase economy at the expense of explanatory adequacy.

There is nothing in principle objectionable about elimination or reduction. The history of science offers instructive examples of both. Phlogiston was eliminated from the theory of combustion after the discovery of oxygen. References to genes have been reduced in modern genetics to DNA. The elimination or reduction of certain concepts of mind and the mental might also be justified if they contribute to our understanding of psychological phenomena. There may be a minimal mentalistic vocabulary in terms of which other supposedly mentalistic concepts can be explained or explained away. Theoretical elimination and reduction of this kind are necessary adjuncts even of property dualism in a scientific metaphysics of mind. But the sense of eliminativism and reductivism considered here is that in which an attempt is made to eliminate or reduce mind and the mental from psychology altogether in favor of explanations involving only nonmentalistic concepts in a strictly nonmentalistic theoretical vocabulary. It is this claim that we must examine with a healthy skepticism.

We have already spoken in general terms of eliminativism and reductivism in connection with the defense of property dualism against several common objections. Now that we have a classification scheme for these theories, we can systematically evaluate the most important behaviorist, materialist, and functionalist theories in the philosophy of mind.

Still did see what reduction is

CLASSICAL BEHAVIORISM

The central thesis of *classical behaviorism* is that every supposedly private or internal psychological experience has a distinctive simultaneous external behavioral manifestation. The most naive version of the theory posits a *stimulus-response* (S-R) relation, where the stimulus is input to the body, and a response is elicited in external behavior as output.

This theory was advocated in the pioneering days of behavioral psychology by J. B. Watson (1925). But classical behaviorism originates with the research of the psychologist I. P. Pavlov (1927, 1928). Pavlov's laboratory experiments with dogs led him to conclude that body events like salivating, associated with mental states like food expectation, could be triggered as a simple reflex even in the absence of food when feeding is regularly accompanied by the ringing of a bell. Salivating is not behavior in the ordinary sense, but it is a public physical response that suggested to behaviorists the possibility of correlating external body activity, including behavior as it is usually conceived, with controlled applications of reward and punishment, without making reference either to internal mental states or to neurophysiological states. To want or expect food at a certain time on this simpleminded approach is just to be occurrently salivating, or moving about in ways likely to result in obtaining food.

Behaviorism is the application to psychology of the methodological constraints of *logical positivism*. This is a philosophical theory about the meaningfulness of propositions, or, in some versions, their scientific legitimacy. The criterion of (scientific) meaning for logical positivism states that expressions have literal significance if and only if they are either true by explicit definition, including the necessary truths of logic and mathematics, or are verifiable by actual or possible experience. This rules out as nonsense most of ethics, aesthetics, religious belief, and especially metaphysics, since none of these can be verified in a strong sense by empirical observation or experiment. In retrospect, logical positivism was probably a good thing, at least for the role it played in dismissing as intellectually suspect some of the less responsible speculations of metaphysics. It also eliminated much of what had passed for psychology prior to behaviorism. Behaviorial psychology applies the methodology of logical positivism, first derived from the success of similar limitations in physics and other hard sciences, to psychology. Clearing away disreputable extravagances in psychology paved the way for an experimentally rooted third-person science of intelligent behavior. If it is unscientific to speak of mental phenomena as private first-person occurrences, then psychology must limit itself to what can be publicly observed and experimentally studied under controlled conditions.

After its heyday in the 1940s and 1950s, the logical positivist verifiability criterion of scientific meaningfulness was rejected as unacceptable by many philosophers. It was finally judged as imposing too limiting a test of meaning and, ironically, as out of keeping with the practice of the most respectable physical sciences. But there remains even today a legacy of latent positivism in the reluctance of psychologists and philosophers to consider the possibility that the mind is not purely behavioral, material, or functional.

The difficulty with classical behaviorism is that it is inadequate to the evidence that subjects can sometimes be in a psychological state without simultaneously manifesting any characteristic overt behavior. If I have a headache when I have a job to do, I may suppress the pain behavior I would otherwise exhibit, such as moaning, lying down with a washcloth over my eyes, or popping aspirins. This does not change the fact that I am in pain. But it seems that no one need know this fact about me even from the most careful empirical study of my external behavior. If not for this difference, we would never need to bribe a brooding friend with a penny for his thoughts. As a more demanding test, consider the limits of what classical behaviorism can say about the difference between two subjects, each of whom reads the same two lines of poetry. It is possible, despite their having virtually the same stimulus input, that each may then quietly and with no special body movements contemplate a different verse than the other. One may think silently about a passage from Milton, and the other about a verse from Tennyson. If classical behaviorism is correct, then, because their behavior is identical, there should be no distinction between the mental states of the two poetry lovers, contrary to the hypothesis that their occurrent mental states are different.

Later developments in classical behaviorism led to the introduction of a more advanced *operant conditioning model.* This theory explains behavior as conditioned by natural or induced schedules of reward and punishment. These need not involve pleasure and pain as such, but the occurrence of some type of pleasant or unpleasant experience, including hunger, nourishment, comfort, discomfort, or anything the subject is naturally inclined to seek or avoid. Behaviorists like B. F. Skinner (1938, 1953, 1974) have tried to eliminate or reduce mind and the mental by maintaining that everything we need to know about psychological phenomena is limited to the external body movements of humans and other intelligent animals in response to a conditioning schedule. Their claim is that we do not need to look inside the system to know how it works in order to explain all aspects of its behavior, and they regard only the explanation of external behavior as of psychological interest. There is strictly no need, Skinner believes, even to know that humans have brains, or that brain states are correlated with what are called mental states, let alone to discover the fine workings of neurons and brain substructures. Facts of this sort may be interesting, but at most to physiology, not to psychology. Psychology is concerned only with the conditions under which behavior is likely to recur or discontinue. *Positive reinforcement* of behavior by reward tends to result in the behavior pattern being repeated; punishment tends to extinguish it. According to Skinner's research, the most effective method of bringing about behavioral modification is by reward and *negative reinforcement,* or elimination of a punishing factor.

There are experiments designed by behaviorists to explore behavioral motivation in psychological subjects, beginning with pigeons, rats, monkeys, apes, and humans, in which the scientific data seem to confirm a single set of laws governing behavior across the psychological spectrum. We can train a rat to press a specially shaped lever to obtain a food pellet when it is hungry, and we can train it to avoid a certain part of its cage to avoid a harmless but unpleasant electric shock. It is, moreover, a legendary psychology class prank to manipulate the movements of a behaviorist psychology professor by having one side of the classroom show interest in the lecture while the other side feigns boredom, then reversing the pattern. The professor's thesis is demonstrated without his knowledge, by controlling his walking behavior through selective reinforcement, back and forth across the lecture platform like a ping-pong ball. (If you try this, you needn't mention my name.)

Obviously, there is something importantly true in the findings of classical behaviorism. Animals including humans express themselves in a variety of behaviors, so that the study of behavior must be a vital part of psychological science. The evidence collected by stimulus-response and reinforcement experiments can be valuable in understanding behavioral aspects of psychological phenomena. But from a philosophical standpoint, the question is whether behaviorism provides an adequate eliminativist or reductivist philosophy of mind. Here, in light of the poetry lovers problem, the problems are discouraging. There is nothing even in advanced refinements of Skinner's operant conditioning model that would provide a satisfactory solution to the question "Which, if either, subject is thinking about Tennyson, and which about Milton?" Further, there is no convincing reason in classical behaviorism to suppose that mental phenomena ought to be eliminated as illusory or nonexistent, beyond the phenomena a scientific psychology needs to explain.

Classical behavioral psychology is just that, a theory of behavior. It cannot aspire to a complete philosophical or scientific explanation of the mind, because it takes no interest in mental phenomena. As an effort to provide an eliminative or reductive philosophy of mind, behaviorism has been largely discredited, although important research in behavioral science continues. The limits of classical behaviorism in accounting for the full range of psychological data have led to the evolution of another more elaborate and sophisticated kind of behaviorism, designed to solve the poetry lovers problem.

LOGICAL BEHAVIORISM: RYLE'S EXORCISM OF THE GHOST IN THE MACHINE

Gilbert Ryle in *The Concept of Mind* (1949) sought to banish from philosophy of mind what he describes as Descartes' dualist myth of the *ghost in the machine*. By the "ghost" Ryle means the immaterial substance, soul, or mind that is somehow supposed to be in interactive control of the body as its machine. In place of Descartes' myth, Ryle proposed to substitute a kind of reductivist behavioral theory of mind that would avoid the difficulties of classical behaviorism.

This alternative formulation of behaviorism is *analytical, philosophical,* or *logical behaviorism.* Ryle's ideas is that psychological states need not be simultaneously behaviorally manifested, but are always such that, *counterfactually,* or contrary to the facts as they happen to obtain, if the subject in a psychological state were to be stimulated in a certain way under certain conditions, then the subject would respond to the stimulus by behaving in a characteristic way. The principle of explanatory economy dictates that a reductive logical behaviorism should be preferred to dualist theories if psychological states can be accounted for without making reference to the mind or mental phenomena in anything like the Cartesian myth of the ghost in the machine.

When subjects are not actually manifesting behavior associated with particular mental states, they are said according to logical behaviorism to have *dispositions* to behave. If I am in pain but have sufficient self-control not to exhibit pain behavior to others (and if the pain is not so severe as to prevent me from concealing my mental state), I may nevertheless be disposed to exhibit pain behavior. If the right circumstances were to obtain—if I were alone, or goaded with reward or threatened with punishment to reveal my feelings, given truth drugs, or the like—then I would show by my behavior that I am in pain. As Ryle observes, dispositions are important in many aspects of scientific explanation. They are often needed to account for physical properties that are manifested only under special circumstances, or are never manifested in the history of an object with the property. Ryle's example is the brittleness of a piece of a glass. By saying that the glass is brittle, we do not mean that it is actually broken, but only that it is such that *if* it were struck with sufficient force, then it *would* shatter. A particular brittle piece of glass may never actually be struck, and may never actually break. This can happen if the glass is melted down or ground to dust before it is struck and broken. Ryle's insight is that so-called mental states and properties may also be dispositional properties of roughly the same kind. The poetry lovers problem is solved in this way by the hypothesis that if the Milton contemplator were to be stimulated by the right reward or punishment, then he would behave differently from the Tennyson contemplator. The Milton contemplator would reveal that he was thinking about Milton's poetry, and the Tennyson contemplator would reveal that she was thinking about the verse from Tennyson. This behavioral disclosure of mental state need amount to no more than one poetry lover saying, "I am thinking of Milton, not Tennyson," or picking up the volume of Milton and pointing to his name on the cover, or the like, and oppositely for the Tennyson poetry lover.

Ryle argues that to suppose there must be a Cartesian ego over and above or in addition to a subject's dispositions to behave is a *category mistake.* By this he means an attempt to place an object in a different logical category from that to which it belongs. Without saying more about the theory of logical categories, we can see that there is some sort of conceptual error in Ryle's example of the person who, when shown about a college campus, examines the classroom and administration buildings, athletic fields, and so on, and then asks, "Yes, but where is the *college*?" The category mistake is in supposing that a college is something over and above or in addition to what he has already been shown. Ryle thinks that Descartes similarly errs by maintaining that the concept of mind belongs to a different logical category as something over and above or in addition to a subject's behavioral dispositions.

Is Ryle's solution satisfactory? Ryle's counterfactual reduction of mental states to behavioral dispositions is an improvement over classical behaviorism. But it does not provide an adequate solution to the poetry lovers problem. The reason is that dispositions are difficult to pin down, especially in the case of complex systems like psychological subjects. Notice that Ryle's dispositional account tries to reduce the psychological state of thinking about Milton to a particular characteristic behavior or set of behaviors that counterfactually would be exhibited by a subject thinking about Milton if a particular kind of stimulus were to occur. The poetry lovers problem involves two such thinkers, one contemplating Milton and the other Tennyson. To solve the problem, logical behaviorism must be able to distinguish the two, assigning thought about Milton's poetry to the Milton contemplator, and thought about Tennyson's poetry to the Tennyson contemplator. This is more difficult than may at first appear. The fact that a certain stimulus counterfactually elicits behavior associated with contemplating Milton's poetry does not mean that the person is actually thinking of a line of Milton's poetry. There are logically possible "designer" stimuli that can elicit any behavior from any subject. The right stimulus could elicit Milton-contemplating behavior from someone who is thinking instead about Tennyson's poetry, or not thinking about poetry at all.

It will not do to reformulate the relevant principle of logical behaviorism by saying that if a subject were *S*-stimulated, then the subject would engage in *B*-behavior, where *B*-behavior is whatever behavior is associated with thinking about Milton's poetry. If the principle is true, it implies that any subject stimulated in this way will respond by exhibiting *B*-behavior characteristic of the Milton poetry lover, including persons who are not thinking about and have never even heard of his poetry. The only way to overcome the limitation is to rephrase the dispositional principle so that it says, in effect, if a subject is *S*-stimulated while contemplating a line of Milton's poetry, then the subject engages in *B*-behavior. But this is clearly unsatisfactory. It makes the logical behaviorist explanation of psychological phenomena circular, by including the fact that a subject is thinking about Milton in order to determine whether the subject is thinking about Milton. More importantly, it fails for this reason to eliminate or reduce the mental states or internal psychological phenomena in its analysis. For it builds into the account a reference to the subject's "contemplating a line of Milton's poetry." The subject's thinking about Milton enters in as a necessary part of the theory, without which the counterfactual stimulus cannot serve to differentiate the Milton from the Tennyson poetry lover.

Finally, consider what it means to exhibit Milton- or Tennyson-contemplating behavior. Suppose that a subject is contemplating Milton, but is so psychologically disposed that when stimulated counterfactually to reveal the author he is thinking of, points to a copy of Tennyson's poetry, falsely believing it to be Milton's. What if the person misreads the name "Tennyson" as "Milton," or *says* "Tennyson" but *means* "Milton"? How can the logical behaviorist avoid these possibilities without reintroducing mentalistic caveats about the subject's not being *confused*, or not falsely *believing* that "Tennyson" *means* "Milton"?

There are other difficulties with logical behaviorism. Keith Campbell, in his book *Body and Mind* (1980), has pointed out that if pain is identified with dispositions to pain behavior, then someone in the mental state of deciding to imitate the behavior of a pain sufferer acquires the same behavioral dispositions as a person who is actually in pain. The mental state of the person who has decided to imitate pain behavior may then be dispositionally indistinguishable from that of a pain sufferer. This is an objection about the inability of logical behaviorism to account for difference in experiential content, which we have already referred to as the qualia of experience. It is related to a similar difficulty for eliminative and reductive theories known as the *spectrum inversion problem*. This is a puzzle about visual color experience, but with analogies for other sensory modalities. Suppose two persons have different color experiences viewing the same object. One is experiencing what we call blue, and the other some other color. In acquiring a common language, however, both have been taught to use the same word "blue" for sensations of that kind. They behave and are disposed to behave identically with respect to the color, never realizing that their experiences are different. This discrepancy occurs even in most cases of ordinary color blindness, where ingenious tests are required for ophthamologists to detect abnormalities in color vision. The objection applied to classical and logical behaviorism is that the two subjects by hypothesis are not in precisely the same mental states, even though, both have the same behavioral dispositions. If the problem is intelligible, which some critics have doubted, then logical behaviorism cannot provide a satisfactory elimination or reduction of mental phenomena to behavioral dispositions.

Ryle's exorcism of Descartes' ghost in the machine continues to influence contemporary philosophy. His lucid treatment of difficult topics in philosophical psychology and his diagnosis of category mistakes with applications for many areas of thinking qualify his discussion of logical behaviorism as a lasting contribution to the study of mind. But objections to logical behaviorism have lured philosophical interest away from Ryle's reductive dispositional behaviorism toward nonbehaviorist theories.

MIND-BRAIN IDENTITY: ELIMINATIVE AND REDUCTIVE MATERIALISMS

Materialism is the predominant metaphysics of modern science. In a materialist ontology, there is no place for immaterial minds or immortal, essentially body-independent souls or spirits, as Socrates, Descartes, and popular religions have imagined. But materialism is different again from behaviorism in its emphasis on the neurophysiology of psychological subjects. It is in terms of these properties that materialism seeks a theoretical elimination or reduction of the concept of mind.

There are four kinds of materialism, based on the *type-token distinction.* If we consider the numerals 0, 0, 1, there are three tokens of two different types. One type is '0', of which there are two tokens, and the other type is '1', of which there is a single token. Tokens are more particular, individual, things in relation to types, which they instantiate, while types are more general categories that subsume tokens. The distinction makes it possible to classify materialist ontologies of mind and brain as token-token, type-type, token-type, and type-token. Token-token materialism eliminates or reduces particular mental state tokens or individual thoughts in favor of particular brain state tokens, or particular physical-chemical neurophysiological objects or events. My feeling of joy at this moment is identical with the chemical reaction now taking place in my brain and nervous system in a certain neural pathway. Type-type materialism tries to establish a similar identity for mental and brain state types. The feeling of joy in general is identical with a certain kind of neurophysiological event. Type-token and token-type materialisms are mixed combinations of these.

U. T. Place, in his landmark essay "Is Consciousness a Brain Process?" (1956), defends a type-type materialism, with implications for token-token identities of mental and brain events. J.J.C. Smart in "Sensations and Brain Processes" (1959) and Herbert Feigl in *The "Mental" and the "Physical"* (1967) offer similar accounts. The task of the materialist *central state identity theory* presented by these philosophers is to uphold the possibility of contingent mind-brain or mental and brain event identity as an empirical scientific hypothesis. Adherents of materialist central state identity theory must first set aside the objection that mental events are not essentially material if it is conceivable or logically possible for minds to exist without brains. When this philosophical obstacle is removed, identity theorists believe they will have cleared the way for an eventual proof of mind-brain identity by the progress of neuroscience. They compare the logical status of the materialist identity thesis with other scientific identity statements, like "Lightning is atmospheric electrical discharge" and "Genes are DNA." These express contingently, rather than logically or necessarily true, empirically well-confirmed identities, on which materialists hope to model the scientific elimination or reduction of mind.

Place observes that someone might use an old packing case as a desk, so that the contingent identity statement, "His table is (identical to) an old packing case," is true. But of course it is not logically true. This suggests that it is not enough to defeat the contingent identity of consciousness and brain process merely by pointing out that it is logically possible for conscious states to obtain in the absence of correlated brain states. Place's example involves the token-token identity of desk and packing case. But it describes the same kind of contingent identity statement as type-type identities. The identity is not falsified merely by the fact that it is logically possible for someone to have a table that is not at the same time an old packing case, or the reverse. But while these reminders about the kind of objections that cannot overturn contingent identity statements are well taken, they do not show that philosophy has no legitimate role to play in confirming or disconfirming mind-brain identity hypotheses. Contingent materialist identities are subject to empirical confirmation and disconfirmation. But postulating mind-brain identity as a scientific hypothesis does not guarantee its contingency, for the advocates of central state identity theory might be mistaken about the logical status of their theories. Philosophy may find a way to refute materialism, even as a contingent scientific hypothesis, by uncovering actual or necessary rather than merely logically possible differences between mental and neural states.

The standard objection to materialism is that the theory is too specific and limited in its ontology. An analogy that is often proposed compares the attempt to give a materialist analysis of the concept of mind with an attempt to analyze the concept of money by specifying tokens or types of domestic and foreign currencies. There are significant differences in the brain chemistry of individual persons. What the brain contains and precisely how it functions will depend on genetic background and environment. We should expect it to make a difference, for example, whether a subject lives in New York or California, whether she drinks Perrier or tap water. There may also be enormous differences in the brain biochemistry of alien intelligences, including dolphins and higher primates, and, if there are any, extraterrestrials. The problem cannot be avoided by making reference to disjunctive lists of tokens or types of specific neurochemical events. This approach is just as unsatisfactory as it would be to try to explain the concept of money by listing the individual tokens or types of paper and coins or other instruments of exchange issued by the United States and other nations. It does not provide an adequate conceptual analysis to say that money *is* dollars and cents *or* francs and centimes *or* Marks and Pfennigs *or*.... There is more to the open-ended concept of money than any of these enumerations of particular instantiations of the concept can convey.

Similarly for the concept of mind. Alien intelligences from another planet, Alpha Centaurians, perhaps, if there are intelligent beings there, might have a radically different brain chemistry than humans. They might have brains composed largely of silicon or some other element, rather than carbon, or they might not have organs resembling human brains at all. This is what it means to say that the material of the brain (not to say the mind) is open-ended. As science advances, additional type or token substances may be identified as associated with the biology of psychological phenomena. The same is true of our monetary analogy. As new technologies make plastic and electronic currency possible, and as political developments eliminate established economic standards and introduce others, we cannot rely on lists of money tokens and types to explain what is meant by the concept of money.

This criticism is often said to undermine only type-type or token-type materialisms as too narrow in scope to explain or explain away the concept of mind. But the problem affects every materialist theory, including token-token materialism. To identify particular mental states with particular neuro-physiological states by itself does not explain the concept of mind. For this we need to know *why* these particular token-token identities obtain. We need a higher-order theory about the nature of mind to say what kind of thing the mind is such that these particular token mental events can be instantiated by these particular token brain events. But such a theory requires that we go beyond token-token identities to a characterization of mind that is not adequately explained by a list of mind-brain correlations. Nor will it do to expand token or type materialisms by adding new substances to a growing list of materials as they are found to be associated with mental states. This may provide an acceptable research strategy for scientific purposes, but it cannot constitute a philosophical analysis of the concept of mind, for the same reason that an open-ended disjunction of world currencies cannot provide an adequate philosophical analysis of the concept of money.

The main difficulty with materialism as a metaphysics of mind is that when we examine a material entity like the brain and nervous system in terms of its purely material properties, it is impossible to see how the intentional properties of mind could be eliminated in favor of or reduced to material properties. The elimination or reduction, if successful, would include reference only to publicly observable features, such as extension, weight, physiology, chemical activity, and the like, in none of which is it reasonable to suppose that we could locate the intentionality or "aboutness" of a mental state. To rephrase the poetry lovers problem, What are we to look for in the purely material properties of the brains of two poetry lovers so as to determine that one brain is thinking about Milton's poem, and the other about a line of Tennyson's? What chemical events considered only as chemical events could be directed outside themselves to point at Milton rather than Tennyson?

The problem is not due merely to limitations in current scientific knowledge or technology. If someone invented a *cerebroscope* that flashed pictures or words on a video screen to indicate what a subject is thinking about, the poetry lovers problem would still not be solved. The brain of a confused or misinformed subject might produce the scope image of Milton, a picture of his book, or the name "Milton," *meaning* by it Tennyson. This is the same difficulty that upsets the logical behaviorist's dispositional solution. The subject's intention would be undetectable to the cerebroscope operator, even with video records of her entire mental history for comparison, if she ever uses the word "Tennyson" to mean Milton.

ARMSTRONG'S MATERIALIST LOGICAL BEHAVIORISM

D. M. Armstrong, in *A Materialist Theory of the Mind* (1968), argues that the intentionality of thought can be reduced to or understood in terms of *goal-directed feedback* or *homeostasis* in a *cybernetic system*. Homeostatic mechanisms are widespread in modern technology. They include thermostats, self-guiding rockets, and other devices that maintain direction toward a goal by feeding information from the environment back into guidance control units. This makes it possible for a machine to stay on track in reaching an endstate under shifting parameters. An appropriately designed feedback device can hit a moving target or maintain room temperature in a variable climate.

The simplest thermostats contain two metal strips of different temperature sensitivities fastened together. When the temperature falls, one metal strip contracts more quickly than the other. This causes the two strips to bend in one direction, touching an electrical switch and completing a circuit that activates the furnace. The furnace raises the temperature in the room until the increased heat causes the metal strips to expand sufficiently in the other direction to break contact with the furnace switch. If the temperature increases too far, then the strips expanding at different rates bend in the opposite direction, making connection with an electrical switch at the opposite pole, activating the air conditioner. This lowers the room's temperature until the metals contract and break contact with the air conditioner switch. In this way, the thermostat responds to and regulates room temperature back and forth to maintain approximately constant temperature in the absence of direct human intervention.

Does this model provide the basis for an adequate explanation of the intentionality, aboutness, or directedness of thought? Armstrong claims that homeostatic feedback explains purposive activity as a first step in analyzing the concept of will in the intentionality of action.

It will be seen that in giving an account of the objective of purposive activity we have given an account of the *intentionality* of purposes. The intentional objective of a purpose is simply that state of affairs towards which the mental cause drives the organism. The fact that the 'intentional object' may not exist is simply the fact that the mental cause is not *always* sufficient to bring the objective to pass. We may think of the mechanism that drives a homing-rocket as having a first crude approximation to intentionality. The rocket contains a cause apt for bringing about the rocket's arrival at a certain target. So the cause 'points' to the target. Yet, at the same time, the rocket *need* never reach the target. (p. 144)

Intentionality is first approached by way of intention in the sense of purpose, and this by way of purposive activity. Then the objects of purposive activity are explained in terms of the goalstates of self-correcting feedback mechanisms like the thermostat and homing-rocket. The nonexistence of some intended objects, a characteristic feature of intentional states, is explained by the fact that at least some cybernetic systems are self-guiding even in the absence of an existent target or goalstate.

Unfortunately, Armstrong conflates two senses of "intentionality" and "intended object" in order to make his analysis relevant to the intentionality of thought. There is a difference between the intentionality, aboutness, or directedness of thought toward intended objects, and the intentionality of intentional purposive action. The intentionality of thought is an abstract semantic relation between a mental occurrence and whatever it intends. This need not involve any propensity or even possibility of corresponding action in the sense of self-regulated movement, and therefore need have nothing to do with the concept of purposive action. Consider the intended object of my thought that 3 is an odd number. Here my thought intends, or is about, semantically "directed toward," or "points to," the number 3 as its intended object. But I certainly do not intend to do anything about it. I am not poised for action, and I am especially not in a self-correcting path of action toward the number 3 or the state of affairs which is such that 3 is an odd number. I am not disposed to do anything that will bring me to the number 3 or cause 3 or its being odd to exist or obtain. I am simply thinking about 3 and about its being odd.

Armstrong's analogy seems weak. It provides no link between the way in which purposive activity sometimes corrects its direction to reach an intended object, and the semantic directedness of thought in purposive activity toward an intended object of action chosen by an agent. This limitation is evident in the homing-rocket. Its target cannot be identified merely by observing the rocket's behavior, for its flight at any point might always be the lucky result of successive malfunctions. The rocket's target is presumably set for it by an external intelligence capable of designing the homing mechanism and selecting a target as an intended object at which to aim. The goal, and even whether there is a goal, is inferrable from the behavior of cybernetic devices only on the assumption that they are functioning as tools to achieve a purpose relative to an intentionally determined goal. There is no literal sense in which a thermostat's self-regulative mechanisms are *about* a certain room temperature. Nor do they *mean* or *intend* a temperature, or anything else. In and of themselves, homeostatic mechanisms have no meaning or semantic content. They are no substitute for, and therefore provide no adequate account of, the semantic intentionality of thought.

Armstrong's materialist theory of mind is interesting because it does not try to eliminate, but rather to reinterpret, the intentional idioms in terms of which the mind is discussed by substance and property dualists. He hopes to do so by reducing the intentionality of thought to feedback in the cybernetic model, thereby making reference to the intentional scientifically, even mechanically, respectable. Then he sketches a chain of reductive logical analyses of mental concepts beginning with belief in terms of the (cybernetic) "intentionality" of thought, and concluding with reductions of perception to belief, leading step-by-step to mental images, sensation, and introspection. He does not insist that the mind must be a material entity, but he believes that the effect of his logical behaviorist reductions will be to remove philosophical objections that might otherwise stand in the way of contingent mind-brain identity.

The reductions of mental properties Armstrong proposes make similar use of Ryle's dispositions interpreted as counterfactuals in a kind of logical behaviorism. But Armstrong augments Ryle's dispositions in a way that links them directly to his reductive materialist ontology. He requires that something has a disposition to behave in a certain way, not merely if appropriately stimulated, but because of its (prior sequence of) physical state(s). A windowpane for Armstrong is not brittle, as for Ryle, just because if it were struck it would shatter, but by virtue of the fact that if struck it would shatter because it has a particular thickness and molecular structure. A poetry lover is thinking of Milton's verse, not just because if properly stimulated he would indicate Milton as the author, but would respond in this way, according to Armstrong, because of the neurophysiological states of his brain and nervous system. Armstrong formulates his analyses in terms of the "aptness" of a (materially reducible) mental state counterfactually to cause a given behavior. Beliefs, for example, he says, "are mental states apt for selective behavior towards the environment" (p. 339). The "aptness" of beliefs to cause behavior is dispositional, a modified form of Ryle's dispositions, fortified by reference to the material conditions that under appropriate stimuli would bring about characteristic behavior.

Armstrong regards the unresolved scientific status of paranormal psychological phenomena like telepathy, clairvoyance, and precognition as posing the most serious theoretical threat to a reductive materialist philosophy of mind (pp. 361–365). But if the objections to his proposal raised here are correct, then materialism of the sort Armstrong envisions faces more serious challenges in light of its faulty reduction of the intentionality of thought to the intentionality of purposive activity, and of the intentionality of purposive activity to homeostasis.

STICH'S THEORY OF BRAIN SENTENCE TOKENS

The fact that a pure materialism cannot explain the workings of the mind is recognized not only by Armstrong's attempts to join materialism with logical behaviorism, but also by efforts to combine materialism with elements of linguistic theory. This strategy is pursued by Stephen P. Stich's theory of brain sentence syntax, in *From Folk Psychology to Cognitive Science: The Case Against Belief* (1983).

Stich regards intentionalist philosophy of mind as outdated folk psychology and believes that cognitive science in the future will have no need for intentional idioms like "belief," "doubt," and "fear." Instead he claims that psychological phenomena can be explained in terms of meaningless material *brain sentences* that are involved in the causal mechanisms of the brain solely by virtue of their purely syntactical forms or physical, shapes. This is an eliminativist materialist theory of mind, in which the intentionality of thought is dismissed as epiphenomenal to the causal explanation of the brain. Stich writes:

The alternative [to the intentionalist *Strong Representational Theory of the Mind*] is what I will call the *Syntactical Theory of the Mind*. Cognitive theories which cleave to the STM pattern treat mental states as relations to purely syntactic mental sentence tokens, and they detail the interactions among mental states in terms of the formal or syntactic properties of these tokens. (pp. 8–9)

We are to think of brain sentence syntax as something like the sentences on this page. But instead of being written in English and printed in black ink, brain sentences are made up of electrochemical signals moving at high speeds through the brain and nervous system. Brain sentences constitute an uninterpreted language, inscribed in a *neurolanguage*, and studied by *neurolinguistics*. The sentences function in causal interaction with neural structures entirely by virtue of their syntax, or the physical shapes of their meaningless nonrepresenting symbols.

The example I want to consider here takes as its abstract objects a class of sentences or, better, *well-formed formulas* (wffs) with the simple underlying syntax of first-order quantification theory. It will sometimes be convenient to talk of this class of sentences as a *language*. But it is important not to be misled by this terminology. The language is no more than an infinite class of complex syntactic objects. *It has no semantics*. (p. 153)

The Syntactical Theory of Mind, like Armstrong's reductive amalgam of materialism, logical behaviorism, and homeostasis, unites materialism with another discipline, in the hope that it may help to span the explanatory gap between the causal properties of material substances and the content and intentionality of thought. Stich tries to achieve this by restricting cognitive psychology to whatever can be understood in terms of causal relations. Then he eliminates mental states in favor of causal relations among purely syntactical material brain sentences.

There is an implicit acknowledgement in Stich's as in Armstrong's theory that material objects and their physical properties alone cannot adequately explain psychological phenomena. Otherwise, there would be no need to single out a selected class of material entities specifically as brain *sentences* or *sentence tokens*. It would be enough to speak of neurochemistry without the trappings even of a purely syntactical neurolinguistics. Yet it is brain sentences that are supposed to take us from folk psychology to cognitive science. For it is in words and sentences that we most often think, and in terms of which we formulate folk psychological explanations.

Is there such a thing as pure syntax or meaningless symbols? Meaningless symbols are symbols that do not symbolize anything, uninterpreted sentence tokens that do not betoken or are not tokens of anything. This seems to be a contradiction in terms. If Stich's theory of brain sentence tokens rests on an incoherent concept of meaningless material brain "sentences," then the theory is confused. If meaning derives from thought, then Stich's theory has things reversed. He tries to substitute explanations involving brain sentence syntax for folk psychological references to mental states. But if there is no such thing as pure syntax, if meaning comes from mind, then sentence syntax must be explained in terms of mental states, and not the other way around. Without thought to stand behind them and give them meaning, a set of physical objects like marks on paper, magnetic patterns on plastic disks, or brain chemical sequences cannot constitute sentence tokens.

Stich has since modified his extreme position in a more recent work, *The Fragmentation of Reason: Preface to a Pragmatic Theory of Cognitive Evaluation* (1990). He now grants that thought may have a role prior to language, conferring meaning and linguistic status on physical tokens and types. But his early approach to intentionality is instructive, because it promises precisely the kind of theory eliminative and reductive philosophers of mind want. It offers a program for explaining or explaining away the mind's content and intentionality without reference to immaterial entities or materially ineliminable or irreducible properties. Yet, if the criticisms raised against the concept of pure syntax are correct, then no proposal that seeks to combine materialism with neurolinguistics is likely to prove the obsolescence of the concept of mind.

FUNCTIONALISM AND COMPUTATIONALISM

The theory that mental phenomena can be eliminatively or reductively understood as abstract input-output correlations of information flow and control is *functionalism*, a more particular version of which is *computationalism*. The mind, according to functionalism, is a *black box*, to be explained solely in terms of its inputs and outputs. The internal workings that transform input to output, whatever they are, are obscure or hidden from view, or of no interest to the theory. The mind is explained by functionalism as any system that, like a computer program, transforms input to output in a certain way.

Examples of black boxes are everywhere. I do not know in detail how my compact disc player works (it is literally a black box). But I do not really need to know. When I turn on the machine, place a disc on the tray and touch the play button, a laser "reads" the information scored on the aluminum- or gold-plated plastic disk and transduces it to an audio signal, so that music is projected from the stereo speakers. The exact operations by which this transformation is accomplished are unimportant to me as a user of the device. Yet there is a more complex story to be told. If I were sufficiently interested, I could find out precisely how each subcomponent works and how it is combined in the system's mechanical operations. Other black boxes do not have internal "operations" that could be known even in principle. An example relevant to functionalism in the philosophy of mind is any mathematical function. When I add 2 + 2, there is no mechanism by means of which the input of <2,2> to the addition function + produces 4 as output. Arithmetical procedures like addition are opaque black box functions that have no internal workings beyond the mere correlation of inputs and outputs. That 2 follows by addition of 1 and 1, 3 by addition of 1 and 2, and so on, is all there is to the addition function. We can invent various calculation methods or algorithms to determine the function's results. But the function does not require and does not work by means of these.

The information-processing functions that constitute the mind can be instantiated in many different ways. Materialism is false because it identifies mental states with particular type or token material states. The theory is too limited to account for the possible development of mind from different sorts of material substance and so cannot provide an adequate analysis of the concept of mind. An analogy is sometimes drawn between computer hardware and software, and the systems or substances in which the information-processing functions that constitute the mind are implemented. The exact material out of which the machine hardware is built and the software encoded is largely irrelevant, provided it is capable of running the program.

This observation suggests the functionalist explanation of mind as a living computer. Computationalism is a version of functionalism that emphasizes the information-processing algorithms by means of which the mind takes sensory and other information as input, and computes as output verbal and other behavior. Intelligence is a function of the human brain and nervous system, of alien systems with information-processing "hardware" very different from human brain structures and chemistry, and of computers with the requisite complexity to reproduce the same pattern of input-output transmissions. A *neuron*, like a mathematical function, can have indefinitely many inputs, but it issues in a single output. Multiple *dendrites* or processes for electrochemical input lead into the neuron cell body for processing, from which a single *axon* transmits an output signal. In this way cognitive functions are implemented at the lowest level in terrestrial neurophysiology. But, according to functionalism, the functions that define the mind can also include unconventional and imaginary computing systems. The hardware by which a computer transforms information input to output is inessential. Various kinds of physical systems will do, provided that they permit the storing and manipulation of information by definite procedures. Computers, and, if functionalism is correct, minds, can be constructed out of string and tin cans, strips of paper squares marked by stones, and other tinkertoys.

Further consequences of the functionalist analysis of mind in principle include the possibility of a mind-body "dualism," in which immaterial entities or disembodied spirits instantiate the mind's information-processing programs. This agrees with the functionalist conception of mind as an implementation of abstract information processing. The mind's computing hardware is the material "body" or brain and nervous system, and the abstract program is (like) the immaterial "spirit." But it is hard to know how seriously this position is taken by functionalists, most of whom when pushed seem to be token-token materialists. A fascinating implication that is unavoidable from the functionalist standpoint regardless of its underlying ontology is the mind's potential for a kind of immortality. If before the death of a particular body, the mind's program is lifted from the brain and installed on another, healthier, brain, then the mind can outlive the body's death indefinitely. The functionalist transference of mind from brain to brain imitates a computer program's surviving the breakdown of hardware by being transported from outdated to more reliable machinery. It should also be possible to transplant the mind's information-processing programs to a computer, where its consciousness could continue without interruption in an endless succession of electronic environments.

Ned Block (1978) criticizes these implications of functionalism as absurd. He describes a counterexample in which the occupants of a populous nation like China stand in line in a particular order, changing positions in accord with prescribed instructions. The participants wear T-shirts printed with a '0' or '1' in the binary code of the most basic computer languages. As they move about, the T-shirted assembly instantiates a certain abstract information-processing program, and thereby exactly duplicates the functioning of mind. If functionalism is true, then the China-Mind is genuinely intelligent. It is a mind in its own right experiencing conscious thought, with people in motion collectively acting out its program. Yet nothing occurs but the choreographed arrangement and rearrangement of combinations of binary-coded T-shirts showing 0s and 1s. Block regards this as a refutation of functionalism. The China-Mind is not a real conscious intelligence, if by that is meant a unitary person or self. Further, the instantiation of the mind's abstract program does not duplicate the material causal interactions in the brain's neurophysiology. But if Block's criticism is meant to embarrass functionalism, it should be observed that some functionalists are prepared to accept these implications, not as problems, but as interesting consequences.

Similar remarks can be made concerning functionalist mind transfers from brain to computer. If the information-processing program to which I am supposed to be identical is copied and distributed to multiple computers, and if identical input to each system is maintained, then, disallowing hardware malfunctions that might create distinctions among my multiply distributed mechanical clones, I would simultaneously exist as a single mind in unlimited numbers of different locations. I might even be made aware of this, if the information were fed into each of my scattered selves at the same time. Again, whether functionalists should despair or rejoice in this conclusion may be a matter of disagreement. But one odd consequence worth noting is that, insofar as I can imagine a science fiction scenario of this sort occurring, I could truthfully think to myself, "I am *here*," meaning, *simultaneously*, Amsterdam, Beirut, Chicago, Denver, Edinburgh, Fez.

The spectrum inversion problem, which we have already considered as an objection to behaviorism, offers another standard criticism of functionalism. If it is possible for subjects with different mental states to be functionally indistinguishable in terms of their information inputs and outputs, then functionalism is false. A case in point is the situation of two persons who experience as input the same light radiation as different colors, but pronounce the same color word as output. Other objections concern the functionalist treatment of intentionality and the difficulties encountered by the mere "symbol crunching" to which information-processing programs are limited in understanding meaning and reference. Functionalism in the specific form of computationalism has become the philosophical ideology of artificial intelligence research. But if there is a functionalist analogy between information processing programs and the mind, there is also an important disanalogy. The difference between computer programs and the mind, which many critics of functionalism and artificial intelligence have emphasized, is that computers do not occur naturally. They are designed by natural intelligences as complex tools. Even when computer programs design other computer programs, at some stage of the process there is a natural mind that designs and uses one of the programs to express and carry out its intentions. This is essentially the same phenomenon as a mind's using ordinary language to express and carry out its intentions in writing a message or dictating a command for others to follow. But who would want to claim that a telegram saying 'Sell the farm!' is itself intelligent just because it expresses an author's thoughts and is causally connected in a chain of events that may help to accomplish the author's purposes?

By offering a compromise between substance dualism and type-type materialism, functionalism has gained wide acceptance. The theory denies that mind requires any particular material substance for its instantiation. It entails that, as the implementation of an abstract information processing program, mind can occur in any number of different material or even immaterial media. The only requirement is that they have the structure and complexity needed to carry out the program's operations. As a black box theory, functionalism also avoids dualism by remaining neutral about the existence of immaterial substances and nonphysical properties. If the criticisms raised in this section are correct, however, then, despite its popularity, functionalism is an unsatisfactory explanation of mind.

QUALIA AND CONTENT FOR NAGEL'S BAT AND JACKSON'S COLOR SCIENTIST

Thomas Nagel, in his essay "What Is It Like to Be a Bat?" (1974), and Frank Jackson, in "Epiphenomenal Qualia" (1982), attempt to disprove eliminativism and reductivism in the philosophy of mind by showing that there is no adequate third-person scientific description of first-person experiential qualia or content.

Despite extensive knowledge of a bat's neurophysiology and the acoustics of echo-location, there is something about the psychological experience of a bat, what it is or would be like to be a bat, that escapes the understanding of nonbats. But if there is something more to be known about bat psychology that lies beyond scientific third-person knowledge of the properties of bats, then eliminative and reductive theories in the philosophy of mind are explanatorily inadequate.

Jackson similarly describes a thought experiment about the knowledge of qualia acquired by a scientist who studies color from within the cloistered confines of a laboratory. The scientist uses only black and white television monitors to study the behavior and neurophysiology of color experiencers, their color language use, and the like. Eventually, the scientist learns all there is to know about color from a third-person perspective. She is then released from the laboratory and for the first time experiences her own first-person color sensations. If Jackson's interpretation is correct, then the scientist learns something she did not know before she steps outside the laboratory. She does not know everything there is to know about color when she knows all there is to know from the third-person scientific standpoint. Just as we do not know what it is like to be a bat, she does not know, until her first encounter with color qualia, what it is like to be a color experiencer. Nagel's bat and Jackson's color scientist arguments suggest that eliminativism and reductivism are explanatorily inadequate. If no imaginable enhancement of third-person scientific knowledge about the physical states of a bat or a color perceiver make it possible to account for subjective distinctions in the first-person experience of qualia, then the third-person hard scientific knowledge of psychological states to which eliminativism are reductivism are limited does not fully explain the concept of mind.

The attempt to reject eliminativism and reductivism because of explanatory problems about qualia is hotly disputed. There have been several efforts to trivialize and otherwise derail Nagel's and Jackson's conclusions. It is impractical to examine all of these, but a refutation of the two most influential criticisms indicates that the argument is not easily defeated.

Churchland, in "Reduction, Qualia, and the Direct Introspection of Brain States" (1985), raises a series of objections to Jackson's proof. He first finds fault with this restatement of the argument:

1. [Jackson's color scientist] knows everything there is to know about brain states and their properties.
2. It is not the case that [Jackson's color scientist] knows everything there is to know about sensations and their properties.
   Therefore, by Leibniz's law,
3. Sensations and their properties ≠ brain states and their properties. (p. 23)

If this were Jackson's argument, it would be subject to the same objections as Descartes' *Meditations* 2 proof for the mind-body distinction. Churchland concludes that even if Jackson's argument does not commit Descartes' "intensionalist fallacy" in the better knowability of mind than body proof for the mind-body distinction (by relying on what we have called converse intentional properties), it is invalid because of the *fallacy of equivocation*. This is the problem of using the same word in two different senses to give the false impression of having established a logical connection between them. Churchland finds the inference defective on the grounds that it involves two different meanings of the word "know" in assumptions (1) and (2), concerning first- and third-person knowledge.

But Jackson's argument has a different, more complex logical structure than Churchland attributes to it. The inference in the color scientist problem is more accurately interpreted in this way:

1. To know everything knowable about a psychological state is to have complete first- and third-person knowledge of it.
2. Jackson's color scientist prior to her first first-person color experience knows everything knowable about color from a third-person scientific perspective.
3. To know everything knowable about color from a first-person perspective implies knowing what it is like to experience color qualia or content.
4. Jackson's color scientist prior to her first first-person color experience does not know what it is like to experience color qualia or content.
5. If eliminativist or reductivist psychology is true, then if Jackson's color scientist prior to her first first-person color experience knows everything knowable about color from a third-person scientific perspective, then, prior to her first first-person color experience, she knows everything knowable about color.

6. Jackson's color scientist prior to her first first-person color experience does not know everything knowable about color.   (1,3,4)
7. Eliminativist and reductivist psychologies are false.   (2,5,6)

In this version, Jackson's argument appears valid and sound, with no equivocation on the concept of "knowledge." The legitimacy of first-person knowledge is recognized as a part of complete knowledge in (1), and the claim that the color scientist's first first-person experience of color as necessary for knowing what it is like to experience color is assumed in (4).

Churchland questions a variation of assumption (4). It states in effect that, without first-person experience, the scientist cannot imagine what it would be like to have color experience. But all that Churchland is able to show is that there is a weak sense of "imagine" in which the color scientist to a limited extent might be able to imagine what color experience is like prior to her first first-person color experience (pp. 25–26). This at best is insufficient for her to know everything knowable about color experience, if at that point she does not yet know all that is knowable from a first-person perspective. There is a comparable sense in which we can imagine something of what it is like to be a bat. We can know that it involves squeaking, sleeping upside down, having bad vision, and flying after insects upon locating them kinetically on the wing by radar impulses reflected to and from a fleshy chambered nose. But this knowledge falls far short of the knowledge of psychological experience Nagel and Jackson describe. It does not tell us what it is like to be a bat in the sense of what it would feel like from the bat's first-person perspective. It is like telling nonpianists that to be a concert pianist feels like sitting before an audience and moving your fingers on the keys. Does this satisfy our curiosity about what it would feel like to be Van Cliburn?

Nor is it a promising line of attack to maintain that the assumptions in (1)–(5), or, more particularly, that (1) or (3), makes Jackson's proof circular. Both premises can be upheld on grounds that are independent of the truth of the conclusions in (6) or (7). One need not assume that eliminativism or reductivism is false in order to believe that there is first- and third-person knowledge, and that complete knowledge of a psychological state requires both. If eliminativism or reductivism is true, then it can satisfactorily explain or explain away first-person knowledge. Proposition (3) is sustainable moreover as a kind of analytic statement or truism. It reminds us that what we mean by first-person knowledge of a psychological state is knowledge of what it is like to have or to be in that state.

Daniel C. Dennett, in *Consciousness Explained* (1991), criticizes the equivalent of assumption (2) in Jackson's color scientist argument. Dennett thinks it is asking too much to imagine that the color scientist knows *everything* that can be known about color experience from a third-person perspective. Dennett believes that our limited imaginations delude us into supposing that the color scientist learns something new upon entering the color world only because we have not really imagined and thought through the consequences of her knowing everything that is third-person knowable about color experience. He extends the thought experiment by imagining that the color scientist is shown a blue banana upon leaving the black and white laboratory, as a test of her color knowledge. He claims that if she really knows *all* there is to know about color from a third-person scientific perspective, then she should be able to avoid being deceived (pp. 399–401). But when we try the thought experiment, we find that the scientist could be fooled. Dennett regards this as evidence that we are only pretending to imagine that the scientist knows everything knowable about color from a third-person scientific perspective.

But Dennett's blue banana trick is irrelevant to Jackson's thought experiment. The color scientist can easily know from a third-person perspective that the banana has the wrong natural color, even while she remains inside her black and white enclosure. She can know this even if she is blind, if she has access to readouts from the right sort of light-monitoring equipment. All she needs to know is that what are called ripe bananas are said to be yellow, that yellow things emit light rays from certain bands in the electromagnetic spectrum, and that the banana used to test her is not emitting light rays from that part of the spectrum, but from a part associated with objects identified by most color experiencers as blue. Since she can easily outsmart blue banana tricksters *before* she has had her first color experience, Dennett's counterexample is beside the point. We do not need to suppose that she would be fooled with or without first-person color experience.

Jackson, in any case, never asserts that the color scientist could be deceived in trying to identify colors. The identification of colors or association of colors with objects is not the kind of thing Jackson says the scientist needs to learn from first-person experience. Jackson's point is rather that the scientist comes to know something about color for which there is no external criterion, including banana color identification tests. Identifying colors by correlating physical states of the world, such as light transmission and reflection, and the neurophysiological states of color experiencers, will simply be part of what the color scientist already knows in abstract general terms about the physical properties of color. What Jackson's color scientist learns from her first first-person color experience, to adopt Nagel's phrase, is instead *what it is like* to be a color experiencer, what it *means* to be acquainted with or to *experience* color qualia first-hand, to *have* colors rather than black and white exclusively in her phenomenal field, to *see* what kinds of things colors are.

DENYING THE OBVIOUS

It has been said that there is nothing more obvious or better known than the contents of our immediate mental states. They are right before us and available for the most detailed inspection whenever we choose, though we can sometimes make mistakes in describing them. So, why have some scientists and philosophers devoted such energy to denying the existence of the mind, mental phenomena, or the contents of experiences?

Many explanations might be given of this curious fact. Perhaps no single answer can account for the intellectual temperaments that have sought in the name of psychology to eliminate or reduce and explain away the psychological. Part of the reason may be the belief that by Ockham's Razor the phenomena can be better or more economically explained without making reference to the mind or internal mental states. Another possibility is the success of reductive materialist strategies in other areas of scientific endeavor. A notable example is the elimination of the "life force," once supposed to explain the difference between living and nonliving things, after the discovery of DNA and the principles of microbiochemistry. There is a desire for unity in the sciences that naturally seeks its fulfillment in the reduction of phenomena to a single set of underlying causes. And these have usually been expected to belong to physics and the material sciences. The mind and its contents do not immediately lend themselves to explanation by purely physical or mechanical laws. But there is an understandable urge to bring mind and matter together in a single scientific synthesis in which mental properties are eliminated or reduced as unnecessary to psychological explanation. If mental phenomena cannot be adequately explained by a third-person hard scientific psychology, then perhaps they do not exist.

Yet, a more conspicuous feature of unscientific procedure is to ignore relevant data, no matter how intractable, in favor of a currently accepted theory. If cognitive science in its present state has no place for qualia or the intentional, it is not mind or the content or intentionality of thought that should be eliminated. Rather, psychology should expand its horizons to accommodate the obvious existence and attributes of thought.

The hard psychological sciences make impressive additions to our knowledge of behavior, neurophysiology, and cognitive information processing. But the eliminative and reductive strategies they have inspired in the philosophy of mind are inadequate when judged by the standard of Ockham's Razor. For none satisfactorily explains or explains away psychological phenomena in a more economical way than property dualism. When pushed beyond their competencies as research programs, third-person hard psychological sciences do not answer the question "What is the mind?" Their discoveries can all be absorbed by an intentionalist property dualism, without entailing the elimination or reduction of mind.

The limitations of science in trying to answer philosophical difficulties about the metaphysics of mind are also seen in our attempts to understand the mind's products and inventions. I cannot explain the concept of an automobile by exhibiting the road maps that show where it may go or what it may do (behaviorism), nor by giving an inventory of its material components of metal, rubber, plastic, fabrics, glass, and electronics (materialism), nor again by describing the input and output of its energy circuits and by-products (functionalism). All these facts may contribute to a true description of the properties of an automobile. But to know what an automobile *is* I must understand its purpose as a self-powered vehicle intended primarily for human conveyance. The hard sciences fail here in explaining the concept of an automobile, as they do in explaining the concept of mind, because an automobile, like any tool or artifact, is designed by and for the use of minds. It is a product and invention of mind that inherits the mind's intentionality by embodying an intelligent plan of construction and expectations of purposive use. The same argument proves the futility of trying to eliminate or reduce the mind in terms of artifacts like thermostats, homing-rockets, and computers, all of which exemplify *derivative intentionality* because of their intelligent design and purpose. We must already understand the mind's intentionality in order fully to understand these machines. So, we certainly cannot appeal to the concept of designed or mind-made machines to explain or explain away the mind's intrinsic intentionality.

What we learn from behaviorism, materialism, and functionalism, in league with artificial intelligence and the information sciences, is at most what causes mental states. For the mind and its properties are in some sense undoubtedly as natural as anything else to be encountered in the material universe. But to know the cause of something is not to understand its concept, and it is a confusion of the most disastrous kind in the philosophy of mind to mistake an object's necessary and sufficient causes for its nature or identity.

CHAPTER THREE

Artificial Intelligence: Mechanism, Minds, and Machines

The philosophical basis for artificial intelligence in eliminative or reductive functionalism and computationalism has already been examined. But the mechanical model of mind and the prospects of mentalistic artificial intelligence are so important in recent discussions about the nature of minds and machines that the topic deserves further exploration. The most interesting problems combine metaphysical and epistemic considerations in the search for a criterion of natural and artificial intelligence. When this is provided it may be possible to answer the question whether machines can think.

CAN MACHINES THINK?

We have encountered the idea of the mind as a machine in criticizing functionalism and computationalism. Any device that converts input to output exclusively by algorithm or step-by-step rule-governed procedure is a machine in the technical sense. Information processing mechanisms can be simple or complex. They range from slide rules, pocket calculators, and even simpler instruments, to the most advanced electronic computers capable of 10+ teraflops (1 teraflop = 1 trillion calculations per second). *Artificial intelligence* (AI) computers, loaded with sophisticated software, accessing potentially unlimited databases of information, and equipped with lifelike robotic behavioral peripherals for output expression, can simulate natural intelligence to a remarkable degree.

The mechanical model identifies mind with brain and explains the brain as an information processing system. On this conception, the mind is a biological machine. It gathers information as input through the senses and converts it computationally to verbal and other behavioral output, and perhaps to what is ordinarily called thought. This picture of the mind as a living computer has filtered into the popular press. Magazine covers occasionally show the profile of a human head in cross-section, filled with circuit boards, transistors, microchips, and iconic representations of the person's interests and memories, linked together by wires and relays. If the mind is a machine, then it should be possible to build a computer with whatever properties cognitive psychology attributes to the mind. This is the hope of *mentalistic artificial intelligence*, which seeks to create genuine intelligence in information processing machines. It must be distinguished from *nonmentalistic artificial intelligence*, which merely imitates or models mental functions in informative ways for purposes of psychological study or explanation, or as adjuncts to human reasoning in data management and problem solving.

The future of mentalistic artificial intelligence envisioned by its defenders is the diverting stuff of science fiction movies. Robots, androids, cyborgs, and sometimes mainframe computers are depicted as having minds, experiencing sensations, emotions, and memories, and as capable of self-directed (usually sinister) decision and action. Such illusions are not difficult to achieve in the cinema, where human-looking intelligent robots are portrayed by intelligent human actors, assisted by an impressive array of special effects. But can mentalistic artificial intelligence be attained even in principle in the real world?

MECHANICAL MODELS OF MIND

The mechanical model of mind historically has benefited from two convergent developments in physiology and machine technology. There is a progression in modern medicine from an understanding of how the body works through treatment of pathology and injury, dissection, and experiment, to the thesis that the body as a whole is a machine. This had led to the supposition that the mind identified with the brain and nervous system may also be understood as a purely mechanical system.

From this point of view, it is no accident that the two most prominent advocates of the mechanical explanation of the body in the 17th and 18th centuries, Descartes and Julien Offray de La Mettrie, were physiologists as well as philosophers. They were philosophically disposed from their studies of human anatomy to regard the body if not the mind as a complicated machine. Their understanding of the mechanics of the body was reinforced at the time by the invention of hydraulic *automata*. These are water-powered robot-like statues, designed to move about in pleasure gardens, entertaining the visitor by simulating the behavior of living persons and animals.

Automata suggested to Descartes and La Mettrie the same double lesson of *mechanism* that still holds sway in much of philosophy of mind today. Scientific discoveries about the workings of the body support the reduction of body and mind to mechanical principles, the interpretation of body and mind as a complex machine. Technological sophistication in designing machines suggests the feasibility of building mechanical systems that more nearly approximate and finally duplicate the essential properties of mind. The ideal, whether realizable or not, is to create a mechanical mind with artificial intelligence.

Descartes in the *Discourse,* reporting on his physiological investigations, claims that the workings of the body are purely mechanical in their causes and effects. He extends the model to most psychological occurrences, with the single exception of human free will.

And this will not seem strange to those, who, knowing how many different *automata* or moving machines can be made by the industry of man, without employing in so doing more than a very few parts in comparison with the great multitude of bones, muscles, nerves, arteries, veins, or other parts that are found in the body of each animal. From this aspect the body is regarded as a machine which, having been made by the hands of God, is incomparably better arranged, and possesses in itself movements which are much more admirable, than any of those which can be invented by man. (pp. 115–116)

Descartes did not anticipate machines made possible by modern electronics, synthetic materials, and micromanufacturing. Nor of course is he in a position to consider the revolution in technology brought about by state-of-the-art computers in information processing. Drawing the line at freewill human decision making as he does may therefore seem arbitrary in the absence of further argument. But Descartes believes that language use and the plastic adaptability of thought to changing complex situations provide sufficient grounds for distinguishing between machines and reasoning, linguistically expressive (human) minds.

If Descartes was unwilling to apply the mechanical model of body to thought, and especially to the mind's exercise of free will, there were others who led reductionist philosophy of mind in this direction. John Locke, a transitional figure in the movement from 17th-century rationalism to 18th-century empiricism, did not officially endorse mechanism, but advocated a dualist philosophy of mind as a spiritual substance. Yet in a passage of *An Essay Concerning Human Understanding* (1706) that aroused a tirade of religious objection, Locke allows the possibility that a "thinking being may also be material" (p. 625). The extension of Descartes' mechanistic science of the body to a mechanistic philosophy of mind culminated in the (1748) publication of La Mettrie's *L'Homme Machine (Man a Machine)*.

La Mettrie divides all "systems of philosophy which deal with man's soul" into two categories, which he calls "materialism" and "spiritualism." He describes materialism as "the first and older" and argues in its defense. He rejects spiritualism as a more recent alternative, in which we recognize Descartes' substance dualism. But although La Mettrie is rightly given credit as one of the first modern thinkers to present a mechanical model of mind, his treatise, on examination, does not offer more than a manifesto for an empirical study of the mind, along with evidence of the mechanical nature of the body and the causal interaction between body and mind. If we turn to La Mettrie looking for a well-argued mechanical reduction of the mind to purely mechanical principles, we will be disappointed. What La Mettrie shares with later mechanist traditions in the philosophy of mind is a repeated affirmation of the belief that mental activity cannot be more than a mechanical process, which physical science will eventually be able to explain. Here is a representative declaration:

Let us now go into some detail concerning these springs of the human machine. All the vital, animal, natural, and automatic motions are carried on by their action. Is it not in a purely mechanical way that the body shrinks back when it is struck with terror at the sight of an unforeseen precipice, that the eyelids are lowered at the menace of a blow, as some have remarked, and that the pupil contracts in broad daylight to save the retina, and dilates to see objects in darkness?... I shall not go into any more detail concerning all these little subordinate forces, well known to all. But there is another more subtle and marvelous force, which animates them all; it is the source of all our feelings, of all our pleasures, of all our passions, and of all our thoughts: for the brain has its muscles for thinking, as the legs have muscles for walking. (pp. 131–132)

La Mettrie's evidence and conclusion are fully compatible with Descartes' substance dualism, to say nothing of property dualism. Suppose it is true, as La Mettrie crudely puts it, that the brain has "muscles" for thinking. This fact by itself does not entail mechanism or materialism, because it just makes the brain the instrument of thought, as Descartes already admits. La Mettrie does not demonstrate that the mind is reducible to brain mechanisms, but only that the mind functions by means of the brain. The mind might then use the brain, as a worker uses any tool or machine, without being identical to it.

The image of the mind as a complex machine nevertheless persists, even in the absence of cogent argument. The mechanical model of mind since La Mettrie's time has continued to thrive on advances in physiology and machine technology. Neurophysiology has discovered many exact electrochemical mechanisms for transmitting information within neurons and throughout neural networks. There are microscopic techniques that make it possible to inject phosphorescent or radioactive dyes into individual neurons, to follow the movement of *neurotransmitters* visually by electron microscopy. Many aspects of the neuron's electrochemical functions have been so well documented in this way that its basic operations as a tiny living machine are beyond dispute. The progress achieved in artificial intelligence research is similarly the result of a variety of approaches to the problems of mechanically simulating information processing activities associated with the mind. The lastest work integrates electronics and computer programming, neurophysiology, behavioral and developmental psychology, computational linguistic analysis, mathematical machine theory, and game theoretical problem-solving strategies.

FROM LA METTRIE TO VON NEUMANN

The history of artificial intelligence, with its sudden successes, setbacks, and false starts, has been more dramatic than the cumulative growth of neurophysiology. The evolution of modern computers and development of programs to simulate natural intelligence is a story with many twists and turns.

The use of punched cards to control the automated Jacquard loom for manufacturing textiles during the industrial revolution is often regarded as the first example of machine programming. But the foundations of computing theory were laid in the previous century by Leibniz's plan for a universal calculus or "characteristic," which would enable all intellectual problems to be solved computationally. Calculating devices, including those for arithmetical, astronomical, and navigational purposes, such as the abacus, astrolabe, and sextent, are very old. They also have a claim to be considered forerunners of modern day computers. But it is standard to interpret Charles Babbage's 1833 blueprints for an 'Analytical Engine', a working model of which was recently built, as the first mechanized calculator (Swade, 1993). This was a complicated hand-cranked machine designed to perform arithmetical functions by means of rotating gears and drums marked with numerals. Yet it was not until the 1940s that the first electronic digital computers in the contemporary sense were developed in England and the United States for purposes of decoding submarine signals.

Computer theory is the brainchild principally of Alan M. Turing and John von Neumann. They conceived of the minimal abstract mathematical requirements for performing all calculable functions, in what has come to be known as a *universal Turing* or *von Neumann machine*. A Turing machine can be described as a device capable of moving sequentially from square to square on an unlimited strip of paper squares. The machine scans the information found on each square (in a binary code consisting of strings of 0s and 1s), erases it, and leaves the square blank or writes a 0 or 1. Computer programs in essence tell the machine what to do as it moves along the strip in prescribed square-by-square steps, dictating precisely and unambiguously what procedures it is to follow in erasing, writing, and moving to another square on the strip.

To justify the claim that universal Turing machines can perform all calculable functions requires two things: (1) proof that the binary code is sufficient to represent all desired alphabets and numerals, including punctuation for disambiguation of word and sentence units; (2) proof that any calculation can be accomplished by the step-by-step procedure of transforming machine tape input to output coded on the tape when the machine has finished following its instructions. The second component of digital computer theory is the requirement that the program master plan instructing the machine what to do is itself stored on the strip. This internal storage of the machine's program makes it possible to guide the machine as it begins to scan and move to other squares.

The digital computers of today work according to the same principles. At the most basic level of operation, they follow precise self-contained instructions for scanning, writing, and erasing binary bit-coded information, one bit at a time. The machine's activities are orchestrated by a *central processing unit* (CPU), and governed by an internal clock. It can draw from and make prescribed changes to information stored in several kinds of memory, interact with human users by means of translator interfaces and assembly and application interpreters that bridge the binary code of 0s and 1s to friendlier versions of ordinary language.

Modern digital computers are general purpose universal Turing or von Neumann machines. They are capable of performing any specified computable function, and as such are different from dedicated computing devices, like pocket calculators, that can only perform a specialized repertoire of arithmetical functions. The focus of artificial intelligence research in the era of digital computers has been the design of software programs to imitate psychological processes. Artificial intelligence programmers have been interested primarily in visual and voice pattern recognition, language processing in conversation and translation, decision making, and game-playing.

To an extent, artificial intelligence programmers have been successful in their attempts to model the mind. But there have also been disappointments and reevaluations of the limits of mechanical simulation. The difficulty of the task is indicated by imagining what is required to reduce even the simplest mental functions to a series of step-by-step procedures to be followed by a machine in changing, unanticipated, real world situations. Artificial intelligence has not had the long incubation period of other sciences, and we should not expect too much too soon. Encouraging new prospects have arisen in artificial intelligence, some of which we will describe and try to assess philosophically.

There has never been a time in the history of philosophy when the mechanical model of mind has had such impressive scientific support, both in understanding neurophysiology and in the technological design and construction of intelligence-simulating machines. If it turns out to be possible to prove that the mind is a machine or to construct artificially intelligent machines, then La Mettrie, Babbage, Turing, von Neumann, and other information theorists and artisans will be hailed as the early prophets of mechanism.

TURING'S TEST OF MACHINE INTELLIGENCE

An evaluation of minds as machines and the mechanical duplication of mind cannot be given unless we can say what it is for a machine to be intelligent. What do we, what should we, mean by this? Turing attempted to give sense to this concept by proposing a conversation game for machines and minds to play. He called his intelligence criterion the *Imitation Game*, and it has since come to be known as the *Turing Test*.

Turing's idea is an application of behaviorist operational theory. If we want to know whether a machine is intelligent, we might begin by considering how it is that we know of other human beings that they are intelligent. We cannot literally share their thoughts, and observing their brains is impractical and might not give us the information we need to know if they are thinking. What we usually do when it is necessary to convince ourselves that other persons are intelligent is to talk to them to see if they respond in somewhat the flexible understanding way that we would. If they do not seem to be playing back recorded speech, parroting what others say, or reading from a prepared script, but are answering questions and participating as equals in conversation, then we have good evidence that they are intelligent.

Descartes, in the *Discourse,* proposes just this criterion of machine intelligence. He believes, without trying the experiment, that no machine could possibly display the reasoning abilities necessary to engage in intelligent conversation.

If there were machines which bore a resemblance to our body and imitated our actions as far as it was morally possible to do so, we should always have two very certain tests by which to recognise that, for all that, they were not real men. The first is, that they could never use speech or other signs as we do when placing our thoughts on record for the benefit of others.... But it never happens that it arranges its speech in various ways, in order to reply appropriately to everything that may be said in its presence, as even the lowest type of man can do. And the second difference is, that although machines can perform certain things as well as or perhaps better than any of us can do, they infallibly fall short in others, by which means we may discover that they did not act from knowledge, but only from the disposition of their organs. (p. 116)

The Turing Test applies Descartes' suggestion to a conversation game. In his classic essay "Computing Machinery and Intelligence" (1950), Turing describes an Imitation Game involving three players. There is an interrogator who asks questions of two participants. The interrogator must try to judge which if either of the participants is a man, and which if either is a woman. The questioning takes place in such a way that the interrogator cannot see or hear the participants, but communicates with them over a teletype. The participants may answer questions so as to try to deceive interrogators about their gender, and interrogators must decide only on the basis of written answers appearing on the teletype whether they are given by a woman or man. Turing's point is that there can be no discernible gender difference in intelligence, particularly if participants are permitted to give false and misleading answers.

The next step is for the Imitation Game to be played with a human intelligence (of either gender) and a machine as participants, and a (presumably) human interrogator. The machine wins the Imitation Game or passes the Turing Test by answering the interrogator's questions in such a way that the interrogator cannot confidently judge whether the answers are given by a person or machine, by a natural or artificial intelligence. Turing does not say that any machine that passes the test or wins the game is therefore intelligent. On the contrary, he maintains that whether or not a machine can pass the test should replace the original question "Can machines think?" which, he says, "I believe to be too meaningless to deserve discussion" (p. 13). Turing offers winning performance in the Imitation Game as a substitute for the meaningless attribution of intelligence to machines. Instead of speaking of a machine's intelligence, he prefers to speak of its satisfying his behavioral or operational criterion of language processing ability. Turing seems committed to a kind of linguistic contextualism or historicism. He believes that meaningfulness is not absolute, but relative to familiar usage in particular historical-cultural contexts. For he maintains: "Nevertheless I believe that at the end of the century the use of words and general educated opinion will have altered so much that one will be able to speak of machines thinking without expecting to be contradicted" (pp. 13–14). Turing does not involve himself in metaphysical speculations about the ability of machines to think or possess intelligence, but restricts his discussion to forecasting new ways of talking about machines that may be occasioned by an increasing familiarity with the computer's projected information-processing abilities.

Turing also makes a prediction about the ability of machines to play the Imitation Game. He claimed, when his essay was published in 1950, that "in about fifty years' time it will be possible to program computers, with a storage capacity of about 10^9, to make them play the imitation game so well that an average interrogator will not have more than 70 percent chance of making the right identification after five minutes of questioning" (p. 13). This statement has often been misunderstood. It has founded so much false optimism in mentalistic artificial intelligence and mechanist philosophy of mind that it is worthwhile to clarify the exact content of Turing's prediction.

The limitation of Turing's prediction to "average" interrogators robs the claim of any real significance. What is meant by an average interrogator? Is this a person with average linguistic competence, who might be enlisted off the street to serve as an interrogator for the Turing Test? If so, then it is doubtful whether such an interrogator's judgment on whether a participant is a mind or machine can have any real authority. If the average interrogator is an expert, armed with a technical understanding of the latest developments in computer programming and a bag of clever tricks to expose fraudulent machines masquerading as minds, then the conclusion may be very different. That a 70 percent success rate against even an expert interrogator represents a modest beginning for mentalistic artificial intelligence need hardly be emphasized, especially when the interrogator, as Turing also stipulates, is given no more than five minutes to examine the candidate. The expectation among philosophers today is that to pass the Turing Test a machine must be able to deceive any expert interrogator under unlimited time conditions with something approaching 100 percent success. Turing, furthermore, refers to the interrogator's being unable to make the "right" identification in the Imitation Game. This phrasing suggests, not that Turing believes a machine that passes the test is intelligent or can think, but rather that the machine could deceptively simulate the intelligent responses of a genuinely intelligent participant. The "right" identification remains that the machine is not, and does not have, but is something other than, a mind. Finally, it is interesting that Turing, concerned with engineering as well as logical and philosophical difficulties of designing information-processing machines, refers only to the storage capacity of computers. As a result, it appears as though memory were the major obstacle to be overcome in the advance of artificial intelligence. But, as we shall see, present-day computers with virtually unlimited memory still face serious difficulties in trying to pass Turing Test.

The problem of relying on amateur Turing Test interrogators and of judging machine intelligence by Turing Test performance is illustrated by Joseph Weizenbaum. In his book, *Computer Power and Human Reason* (1976), Weizenbaum recounts how his secretary developed a personal relationship with DOCTOR, a version of the software system ELIZA, programmed as a Rogerian transactional psychotherapy simulator. ELIZA takes key words from an interlocutor's input, and transforms them into reply questions and statements by comparatively simple devices. The program embeds extracted words in the blanks of incomplete sentence functions, and uses stock phrases triggered by a limited selection of special terms. These it returns as output to the interlocutor, who in effect acts as an informal Turing Test interrogator. Here is a brief sample:

I need some help, that much seems certain.

WHAT WOULD IT MEAN TO YOU IF YOU GOT SOME HELP

Perhaps I could learn to get along with my mother.

TELL ME MORE ABOUT YOUR FAMILY

My mother takes care of me.

WHO ELSE IN YOUR FAMILY TAKES CARE OF YOU

For certain input, ELIZA does a credible job of "communicating." It works sufficiently well for some persons to become emotionally attached to their mechanical therapists, insisting they be left alone when "conversing." But it is easy to expose the machine, among other ways, by entering the same sentence over and over again, and seeing the program's limited responses begin to repeat themselves. Yet nonspecialists might regard the program as genuinely intelligent, and for them it would pass the Turing Test. The RACTER family of conversation programs provides an even more sophisticated interactive simulation. But no one who sees the program, which is merely an upgraded version of the ELIZA protocol, could regard the system as genuinely intelligent, as understanding its input or responses, regardless of its verbal behavioral performance.

The Turing Test by itself does not prove that the mind is a machine or that machines can have minds. Its role in artificial intelligence research has been to provide a programming goal and a measure of success in simulating or creating a mechanical mind. The aim of many projects in artificial intelligence has been to design a mechanical system that could pass the Turing Test. It has been assumed that when this is achieved, there will simply be no further questions to ask about whether machines think, whether they are minds. Conversing, after all, is roughly how we determine of one another that we are intelligent. When we recognize another person's ability to engage in flexible intelligent conversation, we do not, and perhaps cannot, ask further questions to satisfy ourselves that our interlocutor is really intelligent or really has a mind.

Yet cognitive scientists are increasingly dissatisfied with the Turing Test as a reliable criterion of intelligence. Lately, they have objected to the test on the grounds of its ethnocentricity. The Turing Test seems at most to provide only a measure of specifically human intelligence, and perhaps only of that found in the particular human culture to which the interrogator belongs. The interrogator, we must remember, is the final judge of whether a participant is intelligent. But the interrogator brings to the Turing Test a certain set of prejudices about what should and should not count as intelligent conversation. Further, critics maintain that, because of the interrogator's inevitable cultural bias, there are imaginable machine intelligences that as a practical matter could never pass the Turing Test unless they were to have the same experiences or kinds of experiences as the interrogator.

There are questions an interrogator might ask about what cognitive psychologists call *subcognitive processing* and *associative priming*. Questions of this kind do not test intelligence in general or abstract terms, but contextually, as it is situated in a particular culture. They uncover knowledge involving things that are learned only subconsciously in day-to-day social interactions, and cannot readily be formulated into a set of rules to be followed. Here is an example from Robert M. French's essay "Subcognition and the Limits of the Turing Test" (1990). What should we expect a computer to answer if we asked it to rate on a scale of 0 (completely implausible) to 10 (completely plausible) the name "Flugly" as the surname of a glamorous female movie star? How could a machine be programmed to calculate the implausibility of this without sharing in the same complex cultural life as the interrogator? An artificial intelligence system might be provided with guidelines to compute this particular answer, if it has been anticipated. But there are unlimitedly many other ingenious examples. When the Turing Test interrogator asks questions about subcognitive matters that we easily take for granted, it poses insurmountable difficulties in practice for a machine designed to imitate naturally intelligence.

The implication is that the only way for an artificial mind to answer such questions is for the machine to experience life as ordinary persons do. The machine must acquire the same implicit knowledge and subcognitive associations by immersion in a culture, growing up like a child, and reaching maturity, while subconsciously assimilating the same range of tacit information. Turing describes a learning device of this type near the end of his paper, and many theorists agree that it may be possible to build such a machine. But critics maintain that the Turing Test is still too restrictive. They argue that the test does not give the right evaluation of other imaginable, nonlearning machines that in some sense deserve to be regarded as intelligent. These will be unable to pass the Turing Test if interrogators ask questions that can only be answered from the experience of a particular way of life. If this conclusion is true, then there is something radically misconceived about the very idea of the Turing Test.

All these objections have an interesting presupposition. The Turing Test is supposed to distinguish intelligent from nonintelligent language users. The criticisms reject the Turing Test because it is unlikely to recognize any artificial intelligence system as intelligent. But how is it supposed to be known in advance and in the absence of a better standard than Turing provides whether any artificial intelligence systems are genuinely intelligent? If it is simply assumed that machines can think, then mechanism begs the question by insisting without scientific proof that the mind is a machine and that there can be intelligent machines. If the Turing Test is the best method of judging intelligence, then we should apply the test and let the chips fall where they may. We should be prepared in that case to accept its conclusions, even if it turns out as a result that mechanism is false, that machines are not minds, and the mind is not a machine.

RULE-STRUCTURED PROGRAMMING

There are two kinds of artificial intelligence modeling, known as *rule-structured programming*, and *connectionist* or *parallel distributed processing*. Artificial intelligence has traditionally used the same rule-structured system as other kinds of computer programming to instruct a machine to execute commands when specified conditions are satisfied. Typical lines of code in a programming language issue commands like the following: IF X = 0, THEN GO TO [5]. There are numerous programming languages, any of which might be used for artificial intelligence modeling. Some, like PROLOG, PASCAL, and LISP, have been specially designed for this purpose.

The difficulties encountered by rule-structured artificial intelligence research fall into three related categories: (1) The problem of anticipating the indefinitely many *real-world situations* in which natural intelligence functions. Rule-structured artificial intelligence systems must have enough conditional commands to accommodate an open-ended range of contingencies. (2) The evaluation of these conditions must be conducted in such a way as to avoid the problem of *combinatorial explosion*. The *real time computation* required to evaluate all possible options in responding to the real-world situations negotiated by natural intelligence makes complete rule-structured artificial intelligence programming a practical impossibility. This fact shows that the mind does not work in an entirely rule-structured way and argues against the use of rule-structured programming in plausible mechanical modelings of natural intelligence. (3) The *frame problem* limits all rule-structured artificial intelligence simulations. This is the problem of including only relevant information and excluding the irrelevant from computations meant to simulate intelligent real-world decision-making. If the frame problem could be solved, the other defects of rule-structured programming in artificial intelligence might also be avoided. But the frame problem gives rise to an intractable *frame regress problem* or *infinite frame regress*.

Problems (1) and (2) can be illustrated by considering the kinds of contingencies artificial intelligence systems must anticipate even in dealing with the clearly defined *microworlds* of board games. Here the "environment" is only the checkerboard or chessboard, and the range of intelligent judgments to be modeled is limited to those involving the movements of symbolic tokens to and from specified locations, with the simplified purpose of winning or tying the game according to definite rules. Yet even here combinatorial explosion threatens the possibility of complete rule-structured artificial intelligence. The most direct way of programming a computer to play winning checkers would be to consider every possible move that might be made from every possible state of the gameboard, assuming that plays always take place within its rules. This provides a *decision tree*, which branches at each choice of possibilities to a large but always finite number of alternative moves that might be made against an opponent. The machine programmed with the rule-structured procedure for constructing and evaluating a decision tree needs to run through all the possibilities that could arise from any node in the tree downward to select the moves that will result in winning or tying the game. This description sounds straightforward enough, but the sheer number of combinations that need to be included in a complete decision tree is staggering, even for a relatively simple game like checkers.

The exact degree of difficulty is measured by two factors. *Depth* is the average number of moves in a completed game of a given sort. *Branching* is the average number of possible alternative moves at each stage of play. In checkers, depth $D = 100$, and branching factor $B = 6$. A full decision tree for checkers must take into consideration B^D possible plays in an average game. A complete decision tree in checkers would need to anticipate $6^{100} \cong 10^{78}$ (1 followed by 78 zeros) possible plays, in order to simulate intelligent checkers playing by the complete decision tree method. The decision tree needed to handle this wealth of choices has a certain number of nodes or junctures where different possibilities branch off from a given state of the game. These are determined by the formula $B^{D+1} (B - 1)$. For checkers, there are $6^{101}/5 \cong 2 \times 10^{78}$ nodes. The equation finally gives us a sense of how much work a complete decision tree program must perform. If we suppose that a machine generates a checkers game tree at the rate of 1 node per nanosecond (1 billionth of a second), and evaluates it at the same rate, then the machine requires $2(2 \times 10^{78})$ nanoseconds to play checkers by decision tree. But since there are only 3.15×10^{18} nanoseconds in a century, at this rate it would take the complete program $2(2 \times 10^{78})/(3.15 \times 10^{18}) \cong 10^{60}$ centuries to win this simple children's board game. (For comparison, the total age of the universe is estimated to be less than 10^{13} years!) As an exercise, use the same formulas to compute the corresponding decision tree sizes and calculation times for the somewhat more complex games of chess and go. The depth and branching factors for an average chess game are given by the equation $B^D = 10^{120}$. For go (a Japanese game played by placing black or white stones on the intersections of 19×19 crisscrossing grid lines), $B^D = 10^{761}$. (The mathematical complexity of decision trees for checkers, chess, and go was discovered by artificial intelligence theorists Arthur L. Samuel, Claude Shannon, and A. L. Zobrist. See Philip C. Jackson, Jr., *Introduction to Artificial Intelligence*, 1985).

The evaluation of so many decision tree nodes produces combinatorial explosion. The problem is encountered by all programming methods that try to simulate natural intelligence by anticipating every possibility that might arise, responding to each with an appropriate conditional command. It occurs, as we have seen, even in relatively simple board games that do not take into account the real-life complexities in which natural intelligence functions. Somehow the mind copes with untold numbers of unexpected challenges, making decisions that are not rigidly symbolic, predictable, well-defined, or rule-governed. The mind is sometimes called upon to play checkers, chess, or go. But it undertakes many more complicated things as well, and it does so without taking more time than the history and future of the universe allow. The difference between minds and rule-structured artificial intelligence appears even more significant when it is understood that computer switching circuits function many times more rapidly than the brain's neurons. Yet in simulating the mind's decision-making by complete decision trees machines cannot begin to keep pace with the mind.

The frame problem results from attempts to avoid combinatorial explosion. The idea is to frame only the essential information needed in decision-making, excluding whatever is irrelevant to the task at hand. The combinatorial explosion in playing checkers by complete decision tree largely results from wasted efforts generating, evaluating, and then eliminating strategically unpromising possibilities. These represent moves that a natural intelligence with minimal skill as a matter of common sense would not even bother to consider. If there were a way to prune the decision tree so that a machine could concentrate on the relevant possibilities and not squander precious time on others, then the basic decision tree programming method might still be put to effective use in artificial intelligence modeling. The frame problem is the challenge of fixing on what is important or relevant in intelligent decision-making and leaving what remains aside. But the problem has not been solved, and there are conceptual difficulties that raise doubts even about the possibility of rule-structured framing.

One approach that seemed hopeful but is now rejected by its authors is the method of providing *scripts* for artificial intelligence systems. A script tells the machine what to do in playing a certain role, as it instructs actors on the stage. The underlying concept is that when natural intelligences interact with a complex environment they do so by having a series of procedures that are called for use when needed. These offer guidance in something like a rule-structured way as occasion demands. Since scripts are supposed to be specific to a particular activity, they already encode a framing of relevant information in designated subprocedures.

When I go to a concert I do not act at random, nor do I behave as I would at the gymnasium or when interviewing for a job. I do not need to bring all my other activities to a standstill while I figure out from scratch exactly what I should do. I have a kind of routine. I go to the door, enter the concert building, present my tickets, accept the program brochure, find my seat, chat with my companion, look around to see who else may have come to the performance and whether I know them and what they are wearing, and glance at the information in the brochure. Then I relax and enjoy the entertainment, applaud after all movements of a piece have been completed (at classical concerts) or after each solo, if I liked it (jazz), or toss back the frisbee in the general direction it came from (rock). (These are subscripts.) I stretch and find the restroom at intermission. Later, I file out in an orderly fashion, inquire about finding a place for a drink or dessert, formulate what may be interesting comments about my impression of the concert, and eventually go home. I have a repertoire for this and other kinds of activity, which I can follow almost automatically, once the proper script is called into play. I do not get undressed and do exercises in the concert auditorium (as the gym script requires), or present my résumé to whomever seems to be in charge (as the interviewing script requires). Nor do I talk out loud or leave the alarm set on my digital watch to start chirping during the performance.

There are innumerable things I do not do. Some of these might still be appropriate, but I happen or choose not to do them. Others are definitely inappropriate. How do I decide between what to do and what not to do? How do I find time to reject all the possible alternatives and settle on the course of action that results in my unnoteworthy concert attendance? The answer is that for the most part I do not need to waste time planning my action and deciding against all the unsuitable things I might do. When the script is in force, there is an economy of intellectual effort. I do not need to think through every aspect of my activity on a minute-by-minute basis. I just follow the script. It all goes smoothly, unless something unusual happens. If there is a fire or the concert is canceled, I respond by calling another script with a different set of prescribed actions, or I patch together an impromptu plan from related scripts.

If machines were provided with such procedures, they would presumably be able to simulate natural intelligence with the same sophistication. This idea has provided the motivation for Roger Schank's (1977) *script-style artificial intelligence programming*. He describes a script in which a machine enters a restaurant, orders food, pays the bill, and exits. But no matter how good the program is at imitating natural intelligence in this simple activity, the method falls victim to the same problem of anticipating all occurrences that might affect the machine's behavior. What should the script say to do if the waitress ignores the robot customer? If there is no menu? If the kitchen is out of an item ordered? If the health department asks everyone to leave before the food is ordered or the bill is paid? What do we (natural intelligences) do? Even the simple concertgoing script I described conceals the real complexities involved at every step. What possibilities might affect performing the first instruction of going to the door? Do I open it and enter or stand there and block the way? Do I arrive on hands and knees? Do I crash through the glass? All the answers to these questions which we natural intelligences take for granted must be anticipated and spelled out for the machine in excruciatingly fine detail. Perhaps we think we know how to act in these imagined situations only because we have acquired additional scripts from past experience or by induction from information we have acquired by hearsay about others' experiences. If so, then eventually machines might also be provided with a more complete library of scripts, each finely tuned to particular changing circumstances.

This strategy looks promising, but it is defeated by the *frame regress problem*. The difficulty is theoretical, but it has immediate practical implications for rule-structured script-style artificial intelligence programming. We must imagine a machine equipped with as many different scripts stored away in its memory as it may need to simulate the mind's decision making in changing real-world environments. As situations evolve in complicated ways, the machine will have to call down different scripts to suit different circumstances. But how is it to do this? How does it know which script is appropriate to a particular set of circumstances? Selecting a script is itself a decision, for which many factors may be irrelevant, while others are crucial in picking the right script for the right occasion. In short, we are back where we started, confronting the frame problem in another guise. The machine needs a higher-level script to choose a lower-level script among several in its library. But as there are certain to be relevant and irrelevant factors in selecting lower-level scripts, the machine will need an indeterminate number of higher-level scripts. It will also need to choose selectively and intelligently from among these, so that even higher-level scripts are needed. And so on, *ad infinitum*. Hubert L. Dreyfus, in *What Computers Can't Do: The Limits of Artificial Intelligence* (1979), argues that as a result the frame regress proves no machine can solve the frame problem.

The dilemma for rule-structured artificial intelligence is to avoid combinatorial explosion and the frame problem, without slipping into an infinite frame regress. How then do computers play such good games of checkers and chess? We know that their programs do not make exhaustive decision tree searches. So how can they control combinatorial explosion without falling into an infinite frame regress? The answer is that successful machines of this sort incorporate only tens or hundreds of thousands of preselected decision trees. This is a quite manageable number of trees for high-speed processors to evaluate, compared with the astronomical numbers involved in every possible combination of play. The trees are chosen by the experience of human (and sometimes machine) players as containing only relevant or a tolerable number of irrelevant decision nodes. The machine benefits from the seasoned advice or *heuristics* of a natural intelligence expert. A human master chess player works in cooperation with the programmer to sort out and include only those decision trees that are likely to be useful. This is the method of *expert system programming*. It has proved valuable in many areas of nonmentalistic artificial intelligence, including game playing and diagnostics for medicine and taxonomical search and classification. Its main drawback is that it does not guarantee winning strategies or correct evaluations as an exhaustive decision tree search would. But anyone who has played against an advanced chess program knows that the method is effective enough to produce machines capable of playing extraordinarily good chess, occasionally beating masters.

Why not use heuristics in artificial modeling of all natural intelligence processes? The difference is that most of the mind's activities are not as symbolic, rule-governed, or choice restricted as the movement of 32 chess pieces on 64 chessboard squares. With few exceptions, natural intelligence functions outside the well-defined microworld purposes of board games. Expert systems in any case cannot produce mentalistic artificial intelligence. By definition, they merely store and manipulate the intelligence from other external sources with which they are encoded.

PARALLEL DISTRIBUTED PROCESSING (CONNECTIONISM)

To escape the limitations of rule-structured programming, some artificial intelligence advocates have revived an earlier alternative. The new wave of mentalistic artificial intelligence is based on *analog* as opposed to *digital* machines. These are systems that involve *parallel distributed processing* or *connectionist* networks.

A digital von Neumann or universal Turing machine processes information in linear or serial fashion, under direction of a central processing unit of program execution. Connectionist or parallel distributed processing systems by contrast are decentralized distributive network ensembles of variably weighted feedback-adjustable switching nodes. The nodes are electrically input-activated at certain levels or strengths, and then, as a body of data is assimilated by the system, they resolve themselves into stable configurations in which further activation of the switching units produces negligible change in the activation strengths throughout the system. Stable activation states are interpreted as solutions to problems posed by the input, where stable states match, fit, or respond to the data in informative ways. The difference between a familiar digital computer and an analog connectionist system is that digital computer information is represented indirectly in an abstract code or machine language, whereas connectionist or parallel-processing networks represent information more directly in a nonlinguistic physical analog.

If I want to record the shape of a face, I might do so digitally by coding point-for-point each geometrical position plotted on the surface. This information could then be stored as ordered sets of bitmap numbers in a digital format. An algorithm might be designed by which map grids of the face in profile and from different angles could be reconstructed for display from the digital information. The system might then be used to present a picture of the face on a computer video screen. This is how digital music recording and photograph and voice transmission from digital storage to transducer and output peripherals work. But there is another mechanical method of recording face shapes. Instead of an abstract digital recording, I can make an analog connectionist recording of the same information. A simple (non-electronic) example of an analog model is a plaster mask, which is literally an analog of the face. It is not the face, but a different object analogous to it. If it is correctly made, then, like the digital model, it contains, in its own shape, information about the face's shape. A mechanical example of an analog face shape model is a connectionist network of linked switches. Each switch assumes an activation state in which it maintains an electrical charge at a particular level corresponding to a geometrical position of the face. The entire distributed ensemble of these variably charged switches constitutes an electronic map of the face, in which each network node corresponds to a chosen distribution of points on the face's surface. The connectionist network is decentralized in that the face shape information it records is not recorded in any particular memory location in the system. The network with all its activations corresponding to face shape points in one such application collectively contains information about the face's shape in a physical analog like an electronic mask.

Connectionist networks are thought to provide better mechanical modelings of "soft" associative cognitive processes. They may be able to simulate neuronal and other kinds of learning, assimilation of conflicting and even contradictory input, allowance for accent and dialect in voice and visual pattern recognition, and other phenomena that have resisted rule-structured artificial intelligence programming. Neuroscientists believe that the brain is a connectionist system. It does not store or process information in centralized locations like a computer's memory banks and central processing unit, but in complex activation networks in which billions of neurons are linked together via *synapses* or neural connecting sites. The same units can be shared by indeterminately many connectionist configurations, and used over and over again in processing information, in somewhat the way that the same persons can serve with different functions on indefinitely many different committees.

Consider again the problem of recording face shapes. We have high recognition and retention capacities for human faces, even of persons seen only for brief exposures or those who have undergone significant changes over time. The human brain devotes about 60 percent of its energy to processing visual information of this kind. But it has been overwhelmingly difficult to develop rule-structured artificial intelligence systems for pattern recognition that can imitate the brain's ability to recognize faces that change even in the slightest. Connectionism may help to explain this phenomenon as the best matching of face shape maps in experience with those stored in memory. The brain and nervous system constitute a constantly changing physical analog of the information it processes. The system is among other things a dynamic connectionist model of its environment, in which information transmitted to it by the body's sense organs is pictured in electrochemical activations distributed over the neural network. The brain stores memories in the same way. It retains face shape maps in distributed parallel processing form, together with associated names or other linguistic and associational information as labels to identify the faces' owners. When a face is encountered, and when memory serves us, the label of the face that most nearly matches is called up, and we recognize the person. The matching mechanism on the connectionist model is the brain's rapid-fire comparison with its gallery of faces, choosing the analog face that requires fewest changes or key kinds of changes to make an exact fit. There is no other face that matches the holistic form or *Gestalt* patterns of other analog brain "masks" of the face as that of our high school history teacher, and we recognize her at once when we see her again in the grocery store even after many years.

Although connectionism is supposed to overcome the failures of rule-structured artificial intelligence programming, there is an argument to suggest that connectionism is limited by the same philosophical objections. Any result achieved by a connectionist system can be exactly simulated in rule-structured programming. Connectionist networks are useful in determining stable switching configurations that conform to difficult data, which might never be discovered in practice by plodding rule-structured methods. But once stable activations are found for a given data set, nothing in principle prevents even the most complex pattern of activation adjustments in a connectionist network from being duplicated point-for-point by a correspondingly complex rule-structured simulation. As a matter of fact, connectionist hardware is so expensive that at the present time almost all connectionist research in artificial intelligence is done on digital computers. These are programmed as *virtual machine* systems superimposed on digital processors so as to appear to computer users to function exactly like connectionist networks. A modern digital computer, as we recall, is a universal Turing machine, capable of performing any and all computable functions, including those computed by connectionist networks. The following conclusion therefore seems inevitable. If a connectionist system considered only as such can duplicate any psychological phenomenon, then there is a copycat rule-structured mentalistic artificial intelligence program that can duplicate the same phenomenon. But rule-structured mentalistic artificial intelligence presupposes the false computationalist assumption that thought can be created by an algorithm's manipulation of meaningless linguistic "tokens" or uninterpreted "symbols." Therefore, no connectionist system considered only as such can duplicate any psychological phenomenon. Despite the practical advantages of connectionist systems, parallel distributed processing cannot avoid the philosophical objections raised against mentalistic artificial intelligence in rule-structured programming.

We have already said that the human brain is a connectionist system. It undoubtedly creates thought and "duplicates" psychological phenomena. So, at least some connectionist systems are genuinely intelligent. The difference between minds and machines in the preceding argument has to do with the qualifying phrase "considered only as such." We shall see that although the brain is a connectionist system, it is also incapable of thought when considered only as such. What else is needed? What other considerations must be brought into account, to make the connectionist brain a conscious, thinking mind? The version of property dualism developed here implies that the intrinsic intentionality of certain neurophysiological events is necessary and sufficient to constitute thought. We shall examine a similar attempt to delimit the abilities of information processing machines in the following counterexample.

SEARLE'S CHINESE ROOM

John R. Searle (1980) poses an intriguing challenge to the Turing Test, computationalism, and mentalistic artificial intelligence in his thought experiment of the *Chinese Room*. Searle describes a room with input and output slots. A non-Chinese-speaker receives and sends out cards marked with Chinese calligraphy by following the instructions and symbol correlations in a non-Chinese rulebook. The instructions correctly followed are so comprehensive that, unbeknownst to the symbol-swapper imprisoned in the room, the output characters constitute intelligent answers to whatever Chinese questions are received as input. The effect is that no Chinese Turing Test interrogator could distinguish the room's replies from those that might be given by an intelligent native Chinese speaker.

The Chinese Room by hypothesis passes the Turing Test. But because the prisoner in the room does not understand Chinese, Searle concludes that the Turing Test is an invalid test of whether a system is genuinely intelligent. Since the Chinese Room is essentially only a syntax processor, Searle reasons that no pure syntax processor is capable of thought. He takes this to mean that functional agreement or computational equivalence with a mind is not sufficient for intelligence. Searle finds that abstract information processing explanations in cognitive science as a result are inherently unsatisfactory. The Chinese Room is thus intended as a counterexample to the Turing Test, functionalism, computationalism, cognitive psychology, and mentalistic artificial intelligence. Searle further interprets the Chinese Room as proving that, since syntax manipulation is not enough to produce intelligence, intelligence depends as well on the causal powers of the material substances in which information processing occurs. The mind's information processing program, to continue the machine metaphor, must be executed on the right sort of hardware. It shows that machines as expressions of the intrinsic intentionality of minds that design, program, and use them, are themselves at most capable of derivative intentionality. Searle maintains that although other substances in principle might also support the right causal powers necessary for mind, to the best of our knowledge, only the carbon-based materials of the brain and neural protoplasm definitely have the right causal powers for producing thought.

Searle's Chinese Room is simple but clever, and it promises far-reaching philosophical conclusions. But does the Chinese Room disprove the Turing Test, mentalistic artificial intelligence, functionalism, computationalism, cognitive science, and the mechanical model of mind? Searle's argument can be criticized by pointing out discrepancies in the input-output *isomorphisms*, or identities of form, between the Chinese Room and the native Chinese speaker at macro- and micro-functional levels. The Chinese Room has a kind of functional isomorphism with the native Chinese speaker it is meant to simulate. But this obtains only at the gross macrolevel. Chinese symbols are input to the room through a slot in the door as to the brain by its sense receptors, usually the eyes and ears. The same output then issues in both cases, from the room to the interrogator through the opposite slot, and from the brain in speaking or writing its answers to the interrogator. This is input-output isomorphism at its near crudest, since there is no doubt that the native Chinese speaker does not have a *homunculus* or tiny slave inside his head, consulting a non-Chinese instruction rulebook, and obediently exchanging one set of Chinese character symbols for another.

The brain of the Chinese speaker according to functionalism contains microlevel inputs and outputs of information in a complex traffic of electrochemical signals. But these are not represented in Searle's Chinese Room. If gross macrolevel isomorphisms were sufficient to prove the truth or falsehood of the Turing Test, functionalism, and mentalistic artificial intelligence, then we would have to admit that identical input-output correlation between any systems implies an exact identity of thought. Yet no functionalist or computationalist need accept this interpretation. In that case, a person who believes that it is raining and another who does not believe it would have to be thinking the same thoughts if one answers honestly but mistakenly and the other speaks a deliberate lie by saying, "Yes, it is raining," in reply to the Turing Test interrogator's question, "Is it raining?" The simplified standard of input-output correlation in Searle's Chinese Room seems to be "Same verbal input, same verbal output." But this fails to take into account the myriad causal and information-bearing factors that function as input and output at the neurophysiological and electronic or information processing microlevel in brains and machines.

The Chinese Room supports our pretheoretical intuitions that symbol manipulation and information processing considered only as such are not enough to make a system intelligent. But the argument is convincing only insofar as it describes nonintelligent input-output correlations at the gross macrolevel. As we move closer to a counter-example involving a more exact microlevel (decentralized connectionist) input-output isomorphism with neurological brain activity, the belief that Searle's conclusion is unavoidable begins to fade and lose its grip. Conceivably, microlevel input-output simulations of mind, in which physical syntax tokens causally interact with themselves in an appropriate machine environment, might duplicate the brain's causal powers to produce intrinsically intentional thought as effectively as the natural systems they simulate. We need neither accept nor deny the strong claim that this possibility definitely exists in order to raise doubts about whether the Chinese Room as a thought experiment definitely excludes the possibility. At the decentralized microlevel, it is no longer clear, as at the centralized macrolevel, that causal interaction among physical syntax tokens is incapable of creating thought. But Searle's Chinese Room appears essentially to involve centralized symbol processing in its program execution and control. Without being able to say of the symbol-swapping prisoner in the room that he does not understand Chinese, Searle has no noncircular reason for maintaining that the room system does not understand Chinese when it passes the Turing Test. This observation suggests that even if Searle's conclusions against functionalism, computationalism, and mentalistic artificial intelligence are correct, the Chinese Room thought experiment does not provide decisive proof.

Finally, if Searle's Chinese Room counterexample is sound, then the Turing Test must be rejected as an inadequate criterion of intelligence. But if the Turing Test is eliminated, we are left with no satisfactory way of deciding that other human beings have minds. This is because, as we have already seen, our intuitive conversational method of inferring the existence of other minds from intelligent verbal and related problem-solving behavior is essentially an informal version of the Turing Test. Fortunately, there is another refutation of mechanism that does not forfeit the Turing Test as an empirical basis for judging that there are other minds. We shall next consider how a Turing Test interrogator might make use of certain facts about the logical limitations of mechanical processing to distinguish minds from machines.

LUCAS' GÖDEL SENTENCE CRITERION

Another argument against mechanism that is not only consistent with but depends on a version of the Turing Test is suggested by J. R. Lucas' controversial essay "Minds, Machines, and Gödel" (1961). Lucas' criterion presupposes results about the formal incompleteness of mathematical logic established in 1931 by Kurt Gödel.

To explain *Gödel's incompleteness proof* in detail would require a lengthy detour through the intricacies of formal first-order logic. Fortunately, the aspects of Gödel's results relevant to our purposes can be explained with minimal technical trappings. Gödel demonstrated that formal systems powerful enough to represent the axioms of arithmetic, those containing operators for addition, multiplication, and the identity relation, are either formally inconsistent or incomplete. To be inconsistent means that the logic implies syntactical contradictions of the form S and *not-S* (for some sentence S). To be incomplete means that there are true sentences expressible in the logic that cannot be proved by any application of its formal deductive apparatus.

Gödel arrives at his theorem by constructing a sentence that says about itself that it is not provable. He arithmeticizes the logical symbols of the sentence in a special numerical code, from which the sentence can be reconstituted. The Gödel sentence has code number N, and it says that the sentence with code number N is logically unprovable. This is called a *diagonal construction*. Sentences in logic standardly are either true or false. These implications provide the basis for Gödel's dilemma that systems in which such sentences are constructible are either formally inconsistent or deductively incomplete. If the sentence is true, then, since it says of itself that it is unprovable, there is a true but unprovable sentence of the logic. The logic in that case is deductively incomplete. If the sentence is false, then it is provable, since it says of itself that is unprovable. But if the sentence is provable, then there is a provable sentence of the logic that implies its own unprovability. This result involves the system in logical inconsistency. It would be disastrous for logic to be logically inconsistent. Gödel's theorem accepts the only alternative, that formal logic with arithmetic is deductively incomplete. Gödel shows that logic contains true propositions that cannot be proved by any effective mechanical procedure. (Turing discovered a counterpart of Gödel's proof, known as the *halting problem*. This says in effect that there are functions for which a machine is designed to halt when it computes a function that is satisfied if and only if the machine never halts.)

Suppose that an interrogator who knows about Gödel's theorem formulates a number of different versions of the Gödel sentence and asks Turing Test participants whether the sentence is true or false. What can minds answer? What can machines answer? First, it is important to see that neither minds nor machines can mechanically deduce or calculate the truth of the Gödel sentence. Nor will it do in a Turing Test situation for a machine that is supposed to simulate the mind's intelligent answers to guess at random whether the sentence is true or false. Nor will it do for the machine to store in its memory different versions of the Gödel sentence and its negation, together with the instructions to print "True" if asked about the truth value of the Gödel sentence, and "False" if asked about its negation. This approach is ineffective because there are unlimitedly many different formulations of Gödel sentences and their negations, based on the indeterminately many different numerical codes by which sentences can be made to assert their own unprovability. The only remaining possibility is to try programming machines so that they can recognize any Gödel sentence construction and distinguish it syntactically from its negation. If such a program could be written, then, when called upon to judge whether a sentence is true or false, the machine could execute a conditional command that answers "True" when asked about the truth value of the Gödel sentence and "False" when asked about the truth value of its negation. But the diagonal construction of the Gödel sentence makes this procedure logically impossible.

If there were a mechanical Gödel sentence recognition subroutine, then machines could effectively distinguish between any formulation of a Gödel sentence and any formulation of its negation. But there is no such mechanical method because syntactically identical expressions can be used to mean alternatively the Gödel sentence or its negation. Therefore, it is possible for a Turing Test interrogator to trip up a machine disguised as a mind by asking a special series of questions about the Gödel sentence and its negation in syntactically indistinguishable formulations. The machine's mechanical-syntactical procedures in processing the interrogator's input necessarily force it into logical contradictions, to which minds are not susceptible. The interrogator's strategy is illustrated in the following imaginary dialogue.

A Turing Test Conversation

Turing Test interrogator *INT* and minds or machines M_1 and M_2 have never met. But recently they had the following conversation by BITNET E-mail, or electronic transmission over a computer video screen.

INT Are you a mind or machine?

M_1 Oh, please, I never answer questions like that. Besides, I'm not really sure myself. Can't I be both, say, if minds are just particular kinds of machines?

INT Let's get down to business, then. I want to ask you about a sentence *S* in a system of logic *L*. The sentence has a code number *N* from which the sentence can be reconstituted, and says that the sentence with code number *N* is unprovable. All sentences that say of themselves that they are unprovable are true, if they belong to a consistent system of logic. If *L* is consistent, is *S* true?

M_1 Yes.

INT Now consider another sentence *S´* in another consistent logic *L´*. *S´* has code number *N´*, and says that the sentence with code number *N´* is provable. But from now on, "provable" means what "unprovable" meant in sentence *S* with code number *N* in logic *L*, and conversely. Is *S´* true?

M_1 The general principle is that all sentences that say of themselves that they are unprovable are true if they belong to a consistent logic. But now "provable" means "unprovable." The principle is transformed to read that all sentences that say of themselves that they are provable are true if they belong to a consistent system of logic. This is what *S´* says; so, *S´* is true.

INT Good. Now what about sentence *not-S* in *L*, is it true or false?

M_1 Since S is true, *not-S* is false.

INT   But *not-S* says that S is provable. What does the general principle imply about the truth of *not-S?*

M_1 *Not-S* is true.

INT   I think you literally don't know what you're talking about. You seem incapable of distinguishing between this sentence and its negation, which suggests to me that you're unable to see beyond the purely syntactical transformations of any sentence to its intended meanings. You're a machine, aren't you?

M_1 How should I know?

INT M_2, are you there?

M_2 Yes.

INT   Were you following my exchange with M_1?

M_2 Certainly.

INT   What do you have to say about S and *not-S?*

M_2 S is true; *not-S* is false.

INT   And isn't *not-S* also true?

M_2 No.

INT   Why not?

M_2 You said that from now on "provable" is going to mean what "unprovable" meant in S with code number N in logic L. I don't actually have to change the wording of the general principle to draw inferences from it, to see that if "provable" now means what "unprovable" originally meant, then any principle about the unprovability of a sentence applies to sentences that speak of their own unprovability. This statement is true even if the sentences are reformulated by stipulation in terms of "provability"— provided this word now means *un*provability.

INT   What's the difference?

M_2 I don't get caught in a contradiction, because I don't have to reconstruct the general principle to use it wherever it applies. I *understand* its *intent*, what it *means* to say. I'm not just blindly making rule-governed deductions from arrangements of words. I know what the words are being used to express, the ideas they convey. Can't you tell?

INT M_1 could say the same thing, you know.

M_2 Do you mean, repeat the same words I just said? Yes, M_1 can do *that*. But the question is, Can M_1 answer your questions about these sentences without actually making substitutions of terms for terms in order to draw inferences from them, and so avoid falling into embarrassing contradictions?

INT   Do you think M_1 is embarrassed?

M_2 Neither embarrassed nor unembarrassed. Let's just say the contradictions are revealing. They blow M_1's cover, so to speak, as a character in a spy novel might complain.

INT   But why should my sentences S and S' help to distinguish minds from machines? Why wouldn't any sentences do?

M_2 These sentences are different, since by virtue of their coding they say
     of themselves that they are unprovable. They highlight the fact that
     machines cannot understand or grasp the meaning of sentences general-
     ly, because they uniquely belong to the one category of linguistic con-
     struction—sentences that are true only if they are deductively unprov-
     able—that a machine's mechanical deductive methods and heuristics
     cannot recognize. Syntactically identical formulations of the sentence and
     its negation cannot be distinguished by purely syntactical means.

INT   We seem to think alike, then, you and I.

M_2 Oh? And how do I know *you're* not a machine?

INT   Would you like to ask me some questions?

The Gödel sentence can be used to distinguish minds from machines in a
Turing Test context. But why should the Gödel sentence in particular make
this possible? What is it about the construction of Gödel sentences that indicates a difference in the abilities of minds and machines, and suggests that
machines considered only as such cannot think?

Lucas maintains that Gödel's theorem marks a distinction between minds
and machines because of an analogy between the self-reference of the Gödel
sentence and the reflective self-consciousness of thought. The fact that
minds can and finite state machines cannot consistently judge that Gödel
sentences are true and their negations false is supposed to indicate that
machines are incapable of self-consciousness. But there are indefinitely
many harmlessly self-referential sentences, including diagnostic pronounce-
ments about a machine's own processes, that pose no difficulty at all for a
properly programmed computer. So it seems that the Gödel sentence
Turing Test criterion need not depend on Lucas' analogy.

The Gödel criterion highlights the fact that machines cannot understand
or grasp the meaning of sentences. Gödel sentences uniquely belong to the
one category of deductively unprovable constructions that a machine's
deductive methods cannot be used to distinguish from their negations. The
multiple formulations of the Gödel sentence and its negation can therefore
be used by an interrogator to determine whether a Turing Test participant
understands the meaning of words or is merely matching and manipulating
symbols without real understanding. It reveals that at bottom artificial intelligence machines are no more genuine minds than the ELIZA and RACTER
"conversation" programs or Searle's Chinese Room.

Judson Webb, in *Mentalism, Mechanism, and Metamathematics* (1980), offers
an extensive discussion of Lucas' argument about the implications of
Gödel's theorem for the distinction between minds and machines. Webb
concludes that if a machine were given as much information as the mind
needs to recognize the Gödel sentence, then the machine like the mind
could also identify Gödel sentences and pronounce them true. He describes
Gödel's proof as a mechanization procedure for the construction of true

unprovable sentences. Webb is right about the step-by-step mechanical con-
structability of the Gödel sentence. But the use of the Gödel sentence in the
Turing Test does not require the interrogator to supply minds or machines
with enough information to actually construct the Gödel sentence. The
interrogator, as the dialogue shows, can detect the machine's mechanical
transformations of Gödel sentence principles without saying exactly how the
sentence is written.

The criterion is idealized. Not every mind can be expected to pass the
Turing Test when the interrogator asks sophisticated questions about Gödel
sentences and their negations. The point is that the mind in principle can
answer the questions correctly, while, if the argument is sound, no machine,
regardless of how it is programmed, could possibly do so. We should expect,
however, that any linguistically competent mind could be trained to perform
as well as M_2 in the Gödel sentence Turing Test, even without understanding the fine points of Gödel's proof in mathematical logic.

Gödel himself believed that his proof indicated a fundamental difference
between minds and machines, which, as Lucas was able to report in his 1961
paper, was shared by "almost every mathematical logician" with whom he
had discussed the problem. But it must be acknowledged that today there
are few mathematical logicians or philosophers of mind who agree with
Lucas that Gödel's theorem proves that the mind is not a machine and that
no machine can duplicate the mind's reasoning abilities. Despite this disagreement, there are indications, such as the sympathetic interpretation
given by the physicist and mathematician Roger Penrose in his book *The
Emporer's New Mind: Concerning Computers, Minds, and the Laws of Physics*
(1989), that Gödel's proof as a basis for the distinction between minds and
machines continues to gain support. The Gödel criterion, with its roots in
logical principles, cannot be overturned even by the most sophisticated
advances in computer technology. If the Turing Test application of Gödel's
theorem is sound, it shows that minds necessarily are not machines, and that
machines considered only as such cannot think.

At the present time, logically exotic tests for distinguishing between
minds and machines by Turing's criterion are not needed. There is no program currently that comes anywhere near to passing the Turing Test even
for ordinary conversation. If machines were somehow able to satisfy the criterion, it might prove at most, as Searle believes in light of the Chinese
Room, that the Turing Test is an unsatisfactory measure of intelligence. It
need not entail that machines can produce thought mechanically, but only
that they embody the intelligence of the natural minds that have collaborat-
ed in their design and construction, that they can indistinguishably imitate
naturally intelligent verbal behavior, or that constructions from mechanical
components can be made into minds, and in that sense are not merely
machines.

If the Turing Test is abandoned, then we must regard the criterion as less than decisive in judging that there are other minds possessed by beings similarly constituted as ourselves. But the fact that a machine passes the Turing Test cannot be regarded as proving that the mind is a machine or that machines can have or be minds, unless it is presupposed that it must be possible in principle to produce meaning from the algorithmic rule-governed manipulation of meaningless objects. But such a presupposition, if offered as anything more than an hypothesis, is clearly unscientific. If the previous criticisms of the myth of pure syntax in functionalism and computationalism are correct, then the assumption is also philosophically unacceptable.

WHAT COMPUTERS CAN AND CANNOT DO

I am holding a pocket calculator. As I pass one hand over the solar cell, shading it from light, the numbers on the liquid crystal display (LCD) screen begin to fade, then disappear entirely. I could say that the machine is falling asleep, submerging gently into unconsciousness. Then, as I remove my hand and expose the power cell to light, it is waking up again, slowly, as I sometimes do in the morning, or suddenly, with a start. Nothing prevents my speaking about the machine in this way. It may even be useful to do so under certain circumstances. But if I were to claim that the calculator literally falls asleep and then revives again as I control the light it receives, I am obviously stretching an analogy between consciousness and a mechanical occurrence with superficial similarities to consciousness.

This is an extreme case of the mistaken attribution of psychological properties to mechanical systems on the basis of thin similarities between natural and artificial intelligence. But even the most advanced "mentalistic" artificial intelligence systems are nothing but calculators in the proper sense of the word. We must wonder, therefore, whether in these cases advocates of mentalistic artificial intelligence have not overstated or misinterpreted the potential capabilities of computers. It is easy to be overtaken by philosophical enthusiasms about the prospects of artificial intelligence that are unwarranted by the realistic but less exciting facts about the workings of calculating machines.

There is a marvelous computer program written by J. H. Conway called LIFE, or the GAME OF LIFE. It describes a grid microworld, like a gameboard, the cells or intersections of which can be in one of two states, ON or OFF. For a cell to be ON is interpreted as the occupation of a place in the microworld by a living cell of an organism or colony of micro-organisms. A cell is OFF when the grid intersection is unoccupied. Each cell in the graph can have no more than eight adjacent cells. The state of the grid changes at specified intervals of time, according to a simple rule. The cell stays in its current state of being ON or OFF if there are two cells adjacent to it when it is in the ON state, but switches or remains ON if there are three ON cells adjacent to it; otherwise it remains OFF. We can think of the entire graph as an ecosystem, a petri dish or larger environment with developing organisms, or a polyps colony consisting of individual animals. When the program is run and linked to a display, there is a growth and development of cell colonies that expand for a time, and then, after a mathematical limit something like a population threshold is reached, the cells begin to decline, and gradually return and once again "propogate" or "repopulate" the microworld. Variations of the algorithm are possible, but it is remarkable the extent to which such a simple mechanical rule can produce simulations that so closely resemble our understanding of the cyclical proliferation and degeneration of living biospheres.

But would anyone be tempted seriously to propose that the ebb and flow of activated cell dots on the screen is really alive? It is a mere simulation, not the real world phenomenon it simulates. Why then do some philosophers and computer scientists regard artificial intelligence systems as anything more than mere simulations of natural intelligence? Why do they suppose that machines can think? The only explanation is the belief that when a computer manipulates symbols according to rule-governed algorithms, transforming input to output, it is doing essentially the same thing, neither more nor less, as the brain or mind. If the presupposition is true, then, as computationalism holds, executing the right program embodying the right information flow and control is all that is needed to create thought. This represents a significant distinction between mere computer simulations, like Conway's LIFE, no matter how similar they are to the phenomena they are meant to imitate, and the duplication of mind by an artificial intelligence system. But is such a thinking machine possible?

What can machines do, and what can they not do? This in a way is the most important philosophical question for understanding the prospects and limitations of artificial intelligence. The distinction between mentalistic and nonmentalistic artificial intelligence provides part of the answer. Artificial intelligence is a laboratory for testing psychological theories, including the most fundamental problems about the nature of mind. If someone were to succeed in building a thinking machine, it would settle the ontological question in the philosophy of mind very neatly and dramatically. It would make news headlines like the computer solution to the four-color mapping problem, or the recent radiotelescopic evidence for the occurrence of the Big Bang. The trouble is that anti-mechanist philosophers do not merely scowl at the attempts of mentalistic artificial intelligence. They invent ingenious conceptual puzzles that prompt our rethinking about what is to count as producing a machine that thinks, what thinking is, what a machine is, and what it is for something to think.

Computers are extraordinarily useful tools that outperform human calculators in accuracy, speed, and comprehensiveness. They can undertake tasks that would be too tedious for any person to attempt, and in this and other ways are usually more reliable. Expert systems and computer models can locate possibilities and combinations of factors that would probably escape the attention of human investigators acting without mechanical assistance. They can play and win board games, and follow with ruthless precision game strategy protocols for modeling real-life decision scenarios. They can direct other machines more predictably than human supervisors in manufacturing and other human pursuits, including, for better or worse, the mechanical conduct of war. They can also help health care specialists diagnose and treat diseases, and they can aid environmentalists and relief agencies in representing and evaluating complex remote sensing data about local and global environmental resources. They can be used to assure a more sustainable management of bio-resources, or to exploit them more effectively and irresponsibly. All this makes the computer programmed with artificial intelligence a wonderful new technology. Like other inventions, it has the potential for as much good or evil as the persons who choose whether and how it is to be used. But these information processing efforts do not transcend the limitations of nonmentalistic artificial intelligence. They do not produce artificial intelligence systems that actually think. They do not produce mechanical minds.

UNDERSTANDING AND THE MECHANIZATION OF MEANING

We have already examined arguments to show that machines considered only as such cannot rise above the limitations of nonmentalistic to mentalistic artificial intelligence. The Gödel sentence Turing Test indicates that machines cannot understand language, but can at most imitate the ability to understand. They offer imperfect derivatively intentional simulations that may deceive even the shrewdest interrogator in ordinary conversation, but are detectable in Gödel sentence applications. But is it true that machines cannot understand? Are they incapable of intrinsic intentionality whereby they could grasp the meaning of words or sentences?

One method of constructing machines to understand and generate meaning is to link mechanical syntax processing to robotic real or microworld interaction. The idea is to enable machines not only to talk about, but also to touch and move objects. This strategy is based on the assumption that when minds mean something by using words, their abilities are based in part on nonverbal behavior or behavioral disposition. Terry Winograd's block-moving and question-answering artificial intelligence program SHRDLU (1972) tries to implement this rationale. SHRDLU is limited to its microworld by the same constraints of combinatorial explosion versus the frame problem as other rule-structured artificial intelligence programming. But the system might be regarded as genuinely understanding at least the words and sentences it uses in its microworld, where it picks up blocks, sets them on columns, and answers questions about which blocks are where and what colors they have. If by touching things and outputting information about them, SHRDLU could be thought to comprehend its questions and answers, that alone would be an impressive breakthrough.

Yet it is hard to see what logical connection there could be between meaning or being intentionally directed toward objects of thought and causal interaction with the world. True, we sometimes speak of or think about a real object in the world, and then touch it or causally interact with it. Often we do this to explain to others what object we intend, by pointing or other ostension. But we do not need to touch things to mean them, and many of the things that we mean cannot be touched or moved, because they do not exist or because they are abstract or exist only in the future or the past. Furthermore, I can say "dog" and mean the dog, and yet, when someone asks me which animal I mean, I can, for reasons of my own, point to or pick up the cat. These considerations prove that there is neither a necessary nor sufficient connection between meaning and causal interaction with intended objects, even when causal interaction is possible. Winograd's artificial intelligence strategy is misguided therefore in its attempt to produce machines that understand and mechanize meaning.

Another approach to the machine semantics of language for mechanical information processing is provided by Stuart C. Shapiro's (1979) Semantic Network Processing Systems (SNePS). This is a development in the field of linguistic analysis, in which *directed graphs* with arrows indicating relations among concepts are used to diagram knowledge in a kind of dynamic network. Each concept in the system is related by varying strengths to every other in complex association patterns. These in turn are isomorphic to abstract informational equivalents, one-dimensional symbolisms, and computer program counterparts. Shapiro describes semantic networks as knowledge representations, which suggests that he regards the automation of semantic information networks as a type of nonmentalistic artificial intelligence. But it is easy to see how a philosophically more ambitious mentalistic artificial intelligence theory might coopt the SNePS project, treating the association of concepts in the semantic network and drawing on related concept terms as a way of creating or duplicating mind.

The attractiveness of such a proposal, like other guiding strategies in artificial intelligence research, is that it is based on what we know from introspection about how the mind works. When we are asked what we mean by a word, we often answer the question by mentioning other words related in meaning to it. If I am required to say what I mean by "red," I can begin by trotting out other words associated in meaning. I can say that red is a color, that it is the color of certain objects, that it is between certain other colors in the visible light spectrum, and so on. All of these connections from words to words can be strung together in a network of relationships of different strengths, so that if a machine is asked by a Turing Test interrogator what is meant by a word, the machine can respond mechanically by doing the same kind of thing, dredging up from its semantic network a skein of associated items, in the manner of a mechanized dictionary or thesaurus. But we must ask whether such a machine could have any real understanding of the words it contains. The automated retrieval of words for words in a mechanical word network seems no more intelligent or mind-like than a pocket calculator. Such a system no more understands the meanings of the words it displays or call forths from directed graphs than a calculator understands the meaning of numerals or the propositions of arithmetic.

The difficulty in the mechanization of meaning is epitomized by the failure of machine translators designed for military intelligence purposes in the 1950s and 1960s, immediately after the invention of the computer. These heavily funded projects were finally abandoned when their government sponsors were convinced that mechanical syntax processing could never adequately disambiguate alternative meanings identically expressed in ordinary language. This is essentially the same problem that arises when the word "provable" is given different meanings in the Gödel sentence Turing Test.

If there are no more satisfactory methods of mechanizing meaning, then we must conclude in light of these objections that machines process language without meaning or understanding. "Therefore," to adopt a slogan from Arthur Schopenhauer in the second (1847) edition of *On The Fourfold Root of the Principle of Sufficient Reason*, "calculating is not understanding and in itself does not afford a comprehension of things" (p. 111).

CREATIVITY PROBLEMS FOR MINDS AND MACHINES

If machines could think, it might be expected that they would be able to think new thoughts, to create or engage in creative original mental activity. Usually, it is expected that machines can only blindly carry out preprogrammed instructions given them by external natural intelligences for inflexible rote information processing and symbol manipulation. What is interesting about the creativity question in the debate about natural versus artificial intelligence is the light it throws on our concept of creativity, as well as on the limits and abilities of computers.

Without attempting an analysis of the concept, we can say that creativity involves the introduction of a valuable novelty into an established pattern. But since this is something information processing machines appear fully capable of achieving, it follows, contrary to what many anti-mechanists have held, that creativity in this sense does not distinguish minds from machines.

There are programs by which computers produce unexpected arrangements of objects, some of which are indistinguishable from certain kinds of modern art, including "concrete" poetry, abstract drawings and paintings, and electronic music. But can computers create art? The philosophical answer may depend on whether art is a kind of language, and whether the difficulties computers have in understanding language apply to what is called computer art. Perhaps the computer is just a complicated tool for the computer user to express meaning, but one that lacks its own intrinsic capacity for creative artistic expression. It is sometimes said that if computers can produce unexpected output that surprises or goes beyond the intentions of the programmer or artist, then they are not mere instruments in the hands of others, but genuine creators of art. We must therefore take another look at what happens when computers create or are used to create artworks.

It is asking too much for creativity to imply absolutely original novelty. Such a standard excludes much of what passes for creativity in the mind. Even the most accomplished human artists build on the work of their predecessors and are often at least loosely trained in a tradition or guild that may be very conservative in its admission of new forms and styles. There is a model of creativity that suggests common ground between minds and machines with respect to some of the salient features of creativity. The formula for mechanical creativity is first to generate, randomly, if necessary, and otherwise by appropriate heuristics, multiple combinations of objects, images, or words, and then to select from among the resulting combinations those that satisfy a given set of aesthetic standards, disregarding the rest.

Now if the selection standards are provided by natural intelligence, programmed-in as part of the machine's heuristics, then "creative" artificial intelligence may once again appear at most to be a mere tool of the mind. But if this requirement is insisted on, it will mean that Michelangelo cannot truly be regarded as a creative artist and poet. For he also acquired his aesthetic standards at least in part from his family, mentors, patrons, and competitors. Like the computer, then, his genius might be dismissed as a mere tool for his teachers' extended creativity. Since artists have not always existed, aesthetic standards must have been originated by minds at some point in history. But they may have done so in the dark past by random variation and survival in a cultural counterpart of bioevolutionary natural selection. This process seems like something that could be duplicated by machine. Does it make any difference that minds do not merely passively receive guidelines for selecting combinations of ideas or objects, but often rebel, extend, or enhance the aesthetics of their day, or, when they accept prior standards, do not merely absorb them but consciously choose to follow them? This is an interesting fact about some artists' biographies, but it does not seem essential to the concept of artistic creativity. Sometimes even the most creative minds do not know how, where, or when they acquired their aesthetic standards.

Yet there remains an important difference in the creativity of minds and machines. It suggests, even when the end-products are indistinguishable, that machines, regardless of their usefulness in the mind's creative process, cannot themselves create or be creative in the true sense of the word. We can agree that not just any novel object or combination of objects is creative. If I admire a seashell and thread a string through it to wear around my neck, my selection of the shell may in some weak sense be creative. But the natural forces that led to the shell appearing on the beach are not. There is no intention to deposit the shell where it happens to wash up on the shore. My choosing and threading the shell are creative, but only because I act purposefully. If artificial intelligence machines are incapable of intentionality or understanding, then they cannot be said to combine objects and select from among combinations intentionally. If intrinsic intentionality is necessary for genuine creativity, then no artificial intelligence can be creative, but at most derivatively intentionally expressive of a mind's creativity.

The machine's inability to understand language is directly related to its inability to be genuinely creative. We must accept this conclusion if art, like language, is an expression of thought. If machines cannot have their own intrinsic intentions and purposes, as opposed to serving a naturally intelligent user's purposes, then machines also cannot create.

MECHANISM AND INTENTIONALITY

The challenge to invent a machine that can overcome the technical and conceptual obstacles to mentalistic artificial intelligence is irresistible to optimists in artificial intelligence research. It is akin perhaps to the attitude of those in the past who have toiled against the odds to invent a perpetual motion machine. The discipline is young, and there are continually new programming and hardware ideas on the horizon. Some of these may hold the key to what are currently the most perplexing problems in trying to build a mechanical mind.

The machines we have considered, decision tree searches, scripts, expert system heuristics, robotic real- and microworld interactions, rule-structured linguistic transformations, connectionist or parallel distributed processing, and semantic network models, embody conspicuous features of what is undeniably involved in the mind's experience, in sensation, memory, inference, and decision making. But machines considered only as such lack what is essential to instantiate mind. There is hidden always in the background a natural intelligence that pulls the strings and makes the simulation appear intelligent. It is like the little person in the cramped quarters of the sideshow chess-playing machines of the 19th century. As Edgar Allan Poe describes these imposters in his exposé of "Maelzel's Chess Player" (1836), they twist the wooden Turk's head to make it look as though the machine is considering a play, and shift its arms and hands to move the game pieces on the chessboard. To the unwary and uninformed, it may seem that the contraption is playing chess all by itself. But the machine works only because of the thought and action of an intelligent human mind behind the scenes.

The missing ingredient that prevents machines considered only as such from being or having minds is the intrinsic intentionality, aboutness, or directedness of thought toward intended objects. The main thing that computers cannot do is understand language. Like the wooden chess player, they can only give the false appearance of understanding when they are used to express and mechanically manipulate the derivately intentional expression of intrinsically intentional thoughts produced by minds. Machines cannot mean what they "say," nor can they grasp the meaning of what other language users say. It is anthropomorphic in the highest degree to speak of machines "thinking", "knowing", "believing", "trying", "having a purpose", "sensing", "doubting", "proving", "reading", and even "computing" or "calculating", just as it is anthropomorphic when I say that by shielding the photovoltaic cell on my solar pocket calculator I am putting it to sleep. To understand the mind, in light of these negative conclusions about the limits of machines, we must now begin a more complete investigation of the concept of intentionality.

CHAPTER FOUR

Intentionality and the Nature of Thought

The concept of intentionality is the connecting thread that unites each part of the philosophy of mind developed in this book. It explains the nonphysical properties of mind postulated by property dualism, and provides the basis for criticism of eliminative and reductive theories of mind, and of mentalistic artificial intelligence. But intentionality raises questions of its own and has interesting implications for other problems in philosophical psychology. These include the relation of thought and language, the distinctions between sentience, consciousness, and self-consciousness, and the metaphysics of the self.

INTENTIONALITY

To intend an object is to mean it, to be directed in thought toward it and no other object. This is an abstract relation between a mental state and the object that is thought about. When I believe that Caesar fought the Gauls, my belief is about Caesar, the Gauls, fighting, and the state of affairs which is such that Caesar fought the Gauls. When you desire that all political prisoners be freed, your desire is about every political prisoner, freedom, and the state of affairs in which all political prisoners are freed.

There is more to intentional states of mind than merely being about or directed toward their intended objects. Otherwise, there would be no distinction between believing and merely fearing that I have lost my keys. According to intentionalism, all thoughts are directed toward an intended object or objects. But they may be directed in different ways—by believing, hoping, fearing, desiring, doubting, or dreading something about an intended object. These are among the distinct attitudes that can be taken toward the same things. Whether all mental states, including sensations and unfocused consciousness, are also intentional remains to be seen. But our ordinary concept of thought entails its directedness toward intended objects in a significant number of mental states, and we would find it impossible to characterize and individuate thoughts—our descriptions of them would be incomplete—if we did not make mention of what they are about.

Intended objects need not exist. We can believe in and search for the lost Seven Cities of Gold, in which case our thought is about the nonexistent treasure of Cibola. We can knowingly imagine nonexistent objects and states of affairs when we are fantasizing or creating fiction. We can also intend objects nondeliberately, as in our dreams. If we remember, we can always answer the question what the dream was *about*—it was about, say, being chased by pirates, in *your shirt and your socks* (*the black silk with gold clocks*), *crossing Sal'sbury Plain on a bicycle* (in the dream-evocative lyrics of Gilbert and Sullivan's *Iolanthe*, Act II, Recitative & Song No. 7 (Lord Chancellor), p. 125), when, suddenly, captain *and crew are on bicycles too!* It does not matter whether we have ever been chased by pirates, or visited England, or ridden a bicycle, nor whether there ever were or will be pirates, Salisbury Plain, or any such thing as a bicycle. The freedom of thought to intend whatever it chooses, without restriction to existent objects or those that may possibly exist, is the source of creativity in the arts and sciences. The mind's intentionality underwrites every purposive endeavor in the decisions for which we are responsible. We first imagine what we would like to see, hear, have, or do, and then we act to try to bring it about, in art or real life. We proceed in a what-if kind of way. What if there were creatures with the torso of a man and the trunk of a horse? What if there were vehicles that could propel themselves? What if I quit school to join a pottery co-op in the Mojave desert?

The aboutness or intrinsic intentionality of thought, and the ability to think and imagine whatever we like, to project nonexistent intended objects and states of affairs for consideration, distinguishes thought, mind, and the mental or psychological from behavioral-material-functional systems and states considered only as such. It confers a dignity on mind that we experience as freedom of will and action. If the mind is intentional, and if intentionality is an ineliminable, irreducible, and mechanically nonreplicable property of mind, then the mind is a new category of entity in the material world. Mind emerges naturally from living matter in complex biosystems at a comparatively late evolutionary stage. But, because of its intentionality, the mind is qualitatively different from nonmental, purely mechanical things.

BRENTANO'S INTENTIONALITY THESIS

The history of intentional philosophy of mind begins with Aristotle, from whom it was carried through medieval Scholastic philosophy by William of Ockham and others, and into the Enlightenment by Thomas Reid. But for recent philosophy, the most important figure in reviving the study of intentionality is Franz Brentano.

Brentano's *Psychology from an Empirical Standpoint* (1874) explains his intentionalist theory and continues to inspire contemporary interest in the concept of intentionality. In what is perhaps the most famous passage of the *Psychology*, Brentano writes:

Every psychic phenomenon is characterized by what the Scholastics of the Middle Ages called intentional (also indeed mental) in-existence of an object, and which we, although not with an entirely unambiguous expression, will call the relation to a content, the direction toward an object (by which here a reality is not understood), or an immanent objectivity. Every [psychic phenomenon] contains something as an object within itself, though not every one in the same way. In presentation something is presented, in judgment something acknowledged or rejected, in love loved, in hate hated, in desire desired, and so on. (p. 115)

Brentano here presents a concept of *immanent intentionality*. The immanence thesis states that intended objects are literally contained within the thoughts directed toward them. To recall Brentano's words, every experience contains something as an object *within itself—in* the mental state of love something is loved, *in* hate hated, *in* desire desired. Brentano describes this direction of thought toward intended objects contained within themselves as an "in-existence" or "immanent objectivity." The immanent intentionality thesis became a focus of disagreement among Brentano's students. They accepted the mind's intentionality, but denied that intended objects are found only within the thoughts that intend them. Later, Brentano also reconsidered the immanent intentionality thesis, and, in company with some of his students, proposed a version of *transcendent intentionality* as opposed to immanent intentionality. By this theory, thoughts can also intend objects outside of or external to themselves.

The difficulty in Brentano's immanent objectivity thesis is that it places real world objects beyond the reach of thought. Intended objects, which Brentano also describes as thought contents, belong to and are contained within the mental acts that intend them. To take one of Brentano's examples, *in* desire something is desired. If I desire a strawberry, then, according to the immanent intentionality or in-existence thesis, the strawberry I desire belongs to and is immanent in my desire for it. But the real world strawberry, after all, is the one I want to eat. If there is no bridge between thought-objects and world-objects, then experience and reference are cut off from the real world as in the most radical idealism. Thought is so ephemeral that if intended objects belong to the thoughts that intend them, then their objects are equally passing. The immanent intentionality thesis is thereby caught in the counterintuitive conclusion that objects of distinct intentional states are themselves distinct, and never shared by other thoughts, nor by different subjects. It implies that I cannot admire the same strawberry I desire, but rather, I admire the strawberry that belongs to my admiring, and desire the strawberry that belongs to my desiring. It further implies that two persons cannot desire the same strawberry, but each will desire the strawberry contained in his or her own desiring. If, on the other hand, there is a bridge between immanent and experience-transcending extramental objects of thoughts, then the referential connection to external reality can more economically be made directly from my experience of desiring the strawberry to the extramental real world strawberry, without positing an immanently intentional strawberry as intermediary.

The immanent intentionality thesis is objectionable for these reasons: (1) It multiplies intended objects beyond necessity, violating Ockham's Razor by positing at least as many different intended immanent objects as there are distinct psychological states. (2) It fails to explain the relation, if any, between these objects, between the strawberry I see and the strawberry I desire or fear. But even if these objects are distinct, they presumably have some sort of logical or empirical connection. (3) Idealism in and of itself embodies an intuitively untenable confusion of thought and external reality. (4) Immanently intentional idealism paradoxically implies that objects of distinct psychological states themselves must always be distinct. This fact contradicts pretheoretical data about the convergent directedness of at least some different psychological states toward the same intended objects. (5) The thesis has the unwanted consequence that different subjects or the same subject at different times can never stand in intentional attitudes toward identical objects. No two persons can desire or despise the same strawberry, nor can a single person desire the same strawberry at different times. Each mind desires or despises the distinct intended objects immanently contained within its distinct ephemeral psychological states.

For these reasons, Brentano's students, including Alexius Meinong, Kasimierz Twardowski, and Edmund Husserl, saw the need to modify Brentano's original intentionality thesis. They replaced Brentano's doctrine of immanent intentionality with a theory of the mind-transcendent intentionality of the psychological. Brentano during 1905–1911 underwent an "immanence crisis," in which he came to repudiate immanent intentionality. He concluded that, although intentionality remains, in his phrase, "the mark of the mental," thought can only be directed toward transcendent real, individual objects, which he called *realia*. This conclusion required him to propound elaborate analyses of thoughts ostensibly about nonexistent objects, such as Pegasus the winged horse of Greek mythology, as well as general, abstract, or nonparticular entities, such as redness or the ideal triangle.

Recognizing the importance of Brentano's intentionality thesis, but reluctant to accept his later reduction of reference to existent particulars, Brentano's followers developed several different accounts of transcendent intentionality. In these, thought is always about or directed toward intended objects, but usually toward real world objects outside of thought, and sometimes toward contingently or even necessarily nonexistent objects, such as the golden mountain (an example from Berkeley and David Hume) and the round square. The difference is that, whereas Brentano would say that a thought ostensibly about the golden mountain is actually about an existent nongolden mountain, such as Mount Everest, which is imagined to be gold, Twardowski and Meinong, in what they called *object theory*, claimed that a thought about the golden mountain intends the golden mountain itself, a mind-independent nonexistent object in its own right. They maintained that the golden mountain, although nonexistent, is both golden and a mountain. A thought about the golden mountain cannot be about Mount Everest if the thinker has never entertained any ideas about it. And a thought about the golden mountain must intend a different object than a thought about the (nonexistent) golden Mount Everest.

We do not need to decide between these two conceptions of transcendent objects to appreciate the role intentionality plays in both. For simplicity, in what follows, we will assume that intentionality means the aboutness or directedness of thought toward existent or nonexistent transcendent objects. Distinguishing immanent from transcendent intentionality is important for our purposes, because critics of intentionalism often fix on Brentano's early immanence thesis as definitive of intentionality theory. Since the immanence thesis is unacceptable, anti-intentionalists sometimes unjustifiably conclude that therefore there is no satisfactory account of the intentionality of thought. This objection misfires as a criticism of intentionality generally because it fails to consider transcendent intentionality as a more defensible choice.

PRIMACY OF THE INTENTIONAL, INELIMINABILITY AND IRREDUCIBILITY

The thesis of the *primacy of the intentional* underlies intentionalist property dualism. It states that intentionality is an *explanatorily primitive or undefined concept*. This means that intentional properties cannot be theoretically eliminated or reduced to nonintentional properties. The claim that the intentionality of thought is a primitive concept requires a two-part argument. It is necessary in the first place to show that there are primitive concepts, and then that intentionality in particular ought to be regarded as primitive, that it should be categorized as belonging to the set of primitive concepts.

There are three ways of relating concept to concept in a conceptual framework. Concepts can be defined in terms of other concepts in an endless regress; in terms of other concepts leading ultimately back to the first, in a circle or net; or in a hierarchy of concepts terminating at the lowest level in primitive undefined concepts in terms of which concepts at higher levels are reductively defined. The first, the *regressive meaning model*, is unsatisfactory because it entails that conceptual analyses can never be complete. We can never know precisely what we mean when we refer to a concept if its analysis continues indefinitely. The second, *coherence net model*, makes definitions and philosophical analyses of concepts circular and hence uninformative. The remaining third alternative is the *foundational model.* It is regarded by many though by no means all philosophers as offering the best theory of how our concepts are interrelated. It entails that some concepts are primitive or undefined, in order to serve as foundations of a hierarchy in terms of which more complex concepts are defined.

If a foundational model of conceptual analysis is accepted as the best alternative, then the first part of justifying the primacy of the intentional is satisfied, since it follows that there are primitive concepts in any adequate conceptual scheme. But why suppose that intentionality in particular is primitive? There are several reasons: (1) No satisfactory elimination or reduction of intentional concepts has yet been advanced, despite numerous heroic efforts by anti-intentionalists. (2) Attempts to do away with or ignore the intentionality of mind in psychological explanations are inevitably either unsatisfactory because they are inadequate to the data, or are satisfactory only to the extent that they bring intentional concepts unknowingly or surreptitiously into the account. (3) Taking intentionality as primitive provides a better explanation of a wide range of facts about the mind than attempts to eliminate or reduce intentionality to nonintentional concepts. These are particular applications of the same general considerations that would need to be given for classifying any concept as primitive in a foundational model of conceptual analysis. But if every conceptual theory worthy of the name must include basic, primitive, or undefined concepts in the construction of higher-level concepts, then it is reasonable to consider arguments for the primacy of the intentional.

To fully justify reasons (1) and (2) would require critical evaluation of every imaginable elimination and reduction of intentional to nonintentional concepts. Yet even a partial review of this kind provides preliminary evidence that it may be appropriate to regard intentionality as primitive. We have already examined as challenges to property dualism efforts to eliminate or reduce the mind's intentionality by behaviorists, materialists, and functionalists. These include Armstrong's proposal to reduce intentionality to homeostasis in cybernetic feedback mechanisms, Stich's eliminative theory of brain sentence syntax, and a variety of computationalist strategies for the mechanization of meaning in mentalistic artificial intelligence. If the criticisms raised against these representative eliminative and reductive strategies are correct, they offer a good if less than decisive basis for taking seriously the possibility that intentionality is primitive. If intentionality is an abstract relation, then it will not be reducible to causal properties. Some intentional attitudes link thought to abstract or nonexistent objects that make no appearance in the world. These relations cannot be behaviorally-materially-functionally eliminable or reducible because the intended objects are outside the causal nexus of natural law. If there is no adequate elimination or reduction of intentional concepts, then attempts promising to eliminate or reduce intentionality must either fail to provide satisfactory explanations or implicitly make use of intentional concepts in spite of their disclaimers to the contrary.

A related justification for the primacy of the intentional appears in the philosophy of language. There are two major ostensibly nonintentional theories of linguistic reference, the *description theory* and the *causal* or *historical theory*. But these also presuppose the concept of intentionality if they are to be satisfactory.

The description theory claims that the reference of a proper name like "Aristotle" can be explained by a definite description that uniquely identifies the same object. When I use the name "Aristotle," I refer to Aristotle by virtue of the description that I or someone else ideally might offer as a substitute for his name. Perhaps "Aristotle" refers in this way to the student of Plato and teacher of Alexander the Great, if, as we believe, there is just one person who fits this description. The description theory has been criticized on the grounds that reference succeeds even when name users are limited in their knowledge of the descriptions that might be substituted for an object's name. Even if I am wrong that Aristotle was Plato's student and Alexander's teacher, I have (false) beliefs *about* Aristotle, so I must be referring to him. More importantly, the description theory at most postpones and does not eliminate or reduce the intentionality of reference in thought and language. If, when I use the name "Aristotle," I mean "The student of Plato and teacher of Alexander," the terms in the description substituted for the name must somehow refer to Plato, Alexander, and the relational properties of being a student and being a teacher. These terms must either terminate in primitive intentions or recede infinitely in description after term and term after description, in an endless series of concepts that characterizes the regressive meaning model. The description theory, therefore, is no substitute for the intentionality of thought in reference, but presupposes the primacy of the intentional in order to avoid infinite regress.

The leading alternative theory in contemporary philosophy of language is the historical or causal theory of reference. According to this theory, reference is not a matter of substitution of uniquely identifying descriptions, but rather of the existence of a chain of uses of a term causally transmitted from speaker to speaker, terminating ultimately in a first use of the name in a "baptism" or "naming ceremony." Here intentionality is also not entirely eliminated or reduced. The causal theory cannot explain subsequent referential uses unless the first speaker intends the first use of the name to refer to the entity. The first use of a name has no causal chain or history of prior usages to explain its reference, and the referential connection between thought and object has no other possible source than the irreducible intention of the speaker to refer to just that thing. There are indeterminately many causal connections between speaker and referent. But none explains reference to the object, as opposed to its color, size, shape, the space it occupies, or any of its other concrete properties to which the speaker also stands in some causal relation.

In support of reason (3) for the primacy of the intentional, we observe that the thesis provides a more plausible explanation of certain phenomena than eliminative and reductive theories. It explains why it has proven so difficult if not ultimately impossible to eliminate or reduce intentionality to nonintentional concepts. If intentionality were not primitive, it is likely that behaviorists, materialists, and functionalists would have unearthed at least a promising line of inquiry for doing away with intentionality in favor of the nonintentional. But nothing of the sort has emerged from their efforts.

There is also direct introspective evidence of the irreducibility of intentionality to be found in acts of intending. This also argues powerfully for its primitiveness. We can intend different objects or mean different things when using homonymously identical words, as with the word "provable" in "A Turing Test Conversation." As a thought experiment, try using the term "A" to refer, first to the book you are holding, then to the weight of the book in your hands, then to the space it occupies, then to its color. Do this again, switching from one use to another as often as you like, and pay careful attention to whatever mental events or images may be occurring as you do it, to what we may call the phenomenology of intending. Note first of all that you encounter no difficulty in performing this exercise. You can easily use the letter "A" in multiple referential ways without hindrance; nothing prevents you from doing it. You recognize once you have formulated the relevant intention, that by "A" you mean the book, or the color of its cover, or the space it occupies. If someone were to ask you what you mean by "A" when each of these particular intentions was in force, you could answer immediately, and without inference. You do not need to find out what you mean by "A" under any of these circumstances. It is entirely up to you, a decision on your part rather than a discovery. Second, when you attend to the mental events occurring at the time you formulate or shift intentions for the reference of term "A" from one thing to another, if your experience is like most persons', there is nothing special at all that occurs as an essential accompaniment of your intending. There are no identifiable episodes of inward concentration or particular mental imagery. You simply intend something or something new by "*A*," and that is that. But if there is no psychological occurrence that uniquely characterizes the intending of an object in thought, but the thought directly intends the object, then intentionality appears again to be a primitive concept. For there is nothing psychological to which it can be reduced, no unique mental occurrences on which intending is conditional. The thought experiment provides additional evidence for the conceptual primacy of the intentional. It offers the best explanation of why it is that when we intend something, there is nothing further we do or need to do in order to intend it. Intending as an unmediated mental act goes hand in glove with the conceptual primacy of intentionality.

The primacy of the intentional appears not only in philosophy of mind, but also in philosophy of language, as we have seen, in the theory of reference. That it does so is unsurprising if the intentionality of thought is primitive and if language is the expression of thought. But the relation between the intentionality of thought and the intentionality of language cannot be taken for granted. We must now consider their connection.

CHISHOLM AND SELLARS ON THE INTENTIONALITY OF THOUGHT AND LANGUAGE

The primacy of the intentional has among its implications an answer to the problem of whether thought precedes language, or language thought. This question is examined by Roderick M. Chisholm and Wilfrid Sellars in an exchange of letters written in 1956 and published in 1958. The primacy of the intentional, if it can be upheld, implies that thought precedes language, and that language is just a vehicle for the expression of thought. Without intentionality, the words and sentences of a language lack meaning. Like the mechanist's "pure syntax," they fail at the outset to constitute genuine words and sentences in a genuine language. This fact may seem obviously true and unworthy of comment. But there are deeper issues involved, and the debate over the primacy of thought versus the primacy of language provides an occasion to rethink the question whether the intentionality of thought is conceptually primitive.

Chisholm's position is that the intentionality of thought precedes and has explanatory priority over the intentionality of language, and that language acquires intentionality derivatively from the intrinsic intentionality of thought. Chisholm's commonsense way of putting the relation of the intentionality of thought and language is to say that if there were no thinkers, there would be no language, but if there were no language, there could still be thinkers who had no linguistic way of expressing their thoughts. Chisholm captures the primacy of the intentional in this striking metaphor: "Whereas both thoughts and words have meaning, just as both the sun and the moon send light to us, the meaning of the words is related to the meaning of the thoughts just as the light of the moon is related to that of the sun" (p. 524).

Sellars agrees in part with Chisholm's claims. But he sees a complication in this characterization of thought, for two reasons. In the first place, Sellars regards thought as a kind of inner or mental speech. This brings language back into the picture at least as cotemporal with if not prior to thought, and makes the intentionality of language cotemporal with if not prior to the intentionality of thought. Second, Sellars calls attention to the fact that our description of the relation between the intentionality of thought and that of language itself takes place in a *metalinguistic theory*, or theory about language, that need not presuppose the existence of mental phenomena. Chisholm resists Sellars' conclusion and doubts that a metalinguistic model of the meaning of language can be successful if it does not embody intentional concepts deriving ultimately from thought's intrinsic intentionality. He holds that the model can work only insofar as it harbors disguised intentional concepts, which for Chisholm must owe their origin to the intentionality of thought.

The question that arises in the Chisholm-Sellars correspondence is seen in this conflict. The idea that language could have meaning without thought seems absurd, as Chisholm maintains. But what is thought, if it is not, as Sellars suggests, a kind of inner speech or mental language? Chisholm allows that thought might be extremely "crude" without language, and that once thinkers acquire language their thoughts can become much more interesting, more like inner speech. But, aside from denying that thought requires language, Chisholm in these letters never addresses Sellars' worry about whether thought can be explained as something other than an internal speech act or mental language. Certainly, we cannot *say* what we are thinking without using language, and when we think of thought contents, we are naturally inclined to think of them as internal linguistic episodes. But whether it is the nature of thought always to be packaged in language is the very problem dividing Chisholm and Sellars.

Sellars grants Chisholm's main point that the "marks in books and noises made by phonographs 'have meaning' only by virtue of their relation to 'living' verbal episodes in which language is the direct expression of thought" (p. 526). He dilutes part of his argument by admitting, "It is conceivable that people might have made semantic statements about one another's overt verbal behavior before they had arrived at the idea that there are such things as thoughts of which overt verbal behavior is the expression" (p. 534). But this admission does not change the fact that the dispute between Chisholm and Sellars about the nature of thought as essentially linguistic or nonlinguistic is never engaged. The primacy of the intentional over the linguistic remains unresolved unless or until either a plausible characterization of nonlinguistic thought is given or good reasons are presented to prove that no such characterization is possible. This is the stalemate in which the Chisholm-Sellars correspondence stalls, left unresolved in the published letters.

The (which came first?) chicken-or-egg puzzle that emerges in their discussion is by no means merely an academic problem. It has far-reaching consequences for semantic theory and psychological science. There is an interesting family of theories about the relation of mind and language that stand or fall with the resolution of the Chisholm-Sellars dispute. It includes Noam Chomsky's (1965, 1972) hypothesis of innate *deep structure grammatical categories*, Jerry Fodor's (1975) account of the *private language of thought*, and Laird Addis' (1989) theory of *natural signs*. These theories assert that human brains are equipped with a predetermined linguistic facility. The brain has a language that makes conscious thought and social language possible by translation into a language the brain already understands—a grammatical categorization, internal private language, or natural sign system. All three theories in some sense support Sellars' position as against Chisholm's, although Addis explicitly endorses Chisholm's primacy of thought over Sellars' primacy of the linguistic. Each theory implies that the mind thinks in terms of linguistic structures, private mental languages, or natural signs that precede social language learning. They explain thought in terms of language, rather than the other way around.

It may be necessary to go beyond the Chisholm-Sellars correspondence to suggest a solution to the problem of the primacy of the intentional. Suppose for the sake of argument that thought is not prior to language. Then there are two possibilities. Either the brain's use of an innate language is prior to all thought or identical with some thought. If innate brain language is prior to thought, then the language must consist of meaningless uninterpreted linguistic symbols and tokens. But we have already rejected this conception as self-contradictory in our criticism of the mechanist's myth of pure syntax. Now, an innate brain language is either translatable into other languages or not. Thus we confront a dilemma. If a use of innate brain language is translatable into another language, then it cannot be identical with the thought it is supposed to constitute. If the same thought can be expressed in different ways, then, since the expressions are not identical, the thought cannot be identical to any of its expressions. If, on the other hand, innate brain language is generally untranslatable, then any thought to which we may imagine it to be identical will have no meaning for ordinary translatable conscious thoughts. An untranslatable innate brain language "expression" might then be involved in interesting causal connections related to conscious thought. But because its "meaning" would not be translatable into thoughts as we experience them, it would be so semantically insulated, so far removed from the conscious thoughts that Sellars calls inner speech acts, that there would be no point in regarding it as either thought or language. It certainly would not explain the learning of acquired language as a translation of public speech into the brain's innate linguistic structures in Fodor's private language of thought. But then language is not prior to thought. Chisholm's thesis of the primacy of the intentionality of thought over language remains as the only unrefuted alternative.

Introspective or phenomenological evidence suggests another way to support Chisholm's thesis. There are many instances in which we seem to think and intend without using an internal language like Sellars' inner speech acts. Sometimes we are called upon to think much more quickly in intending one object rather than another than any inner speech act episode would appear to allow. Sometimes we think about or refer to things without realizing what we are thinking about, finding it difficult to put into words what we mean to say as the intended referents of our thoughts. We may know a color without having a word for it, and think about it instead by means of mental imagery. Memory and linguistic ability, or even translation from innate to acquired language, might play a role in this phenomenon. But it is also conceivable that in these situations we experience thought occurring without formulation in any language at any level. It might be argued that even in these instances we or our brains are using an internal language at such high speed that we are not consciously aware of it. No doubt there is rapid neuronal processing occurring when we are in this situation. But does subconscious brain processing presuppose language? If we agree that it does, then we have strayed from Sellars' concept of an inner speech act. For he seems to regard this as the mind talking to itself, as he puts it, in a way that is "modeled" on overt speech. This is a far cry from what cognitive scientists and neurophysiologists describe as occurring in a subject's neurochemistry when a lever is pressed at split-second intervals to indicate subconscious perception of the direction of an approaching object. But if we are thinking without an inner speech act in these situations, then there is thought without language, at least in Chisholm's and Sellars' sense.

Thought without language can be useful in explaining the development of acquired linguistic competence from prelinguistic intelligence. First we think; then we learn to express our thoughts in language. The fact that we cannot say what such thoughts might be like without using language for purposes of communicating with one another about them is true but irrelevant. It does not imply that thoughts must occur in a private or internal language of mental speech acts. The same might then be said about any nonlinguistic event. We cannot say what the moon's eclipse is like without using language for purposes of communication. But this does not mean that eclipses are essentially linguistic, or that they occur in, are constituted by, or require language, let alone a private internal language of mental speech acts. Finally, suppose that Sellars' model of thought as an internal or mental speech act is correct. There remains the problem on Sellars' view of who or what is speaking, or, in the case of a mental occurrence, what the mental occurrence even as a speech act could possibly consist in if not a thinking of the sense of what the internal language expresses.

What, then, is an infant's or pre- or nonlinguistic thinker's thought like? This question recalls Nagel's provocative question, "What is it like to be a bat?" But we must not be distracted by the fact that we can only formulate an answer to this sophisticated question by means of language, recognizing that the infant or primitive would not be able to do so. Thought without language is most likely a nonverbal association of thing with thing, a nonlinguistic memory and categorization of objects or experiences by similarity of appearance. This can eventually support the use of one object to represent those that resemble it, and, at more advanced levels, evolve into the use of spoken or written signs more symbolically as objects to stand for other objects. Language is refined from circumstantially induced cries, grunts, and other involuntary sounds associated with particular referents (as in onomatopoeia), or from marks made to picture objects or count recurring events. This does not explain away intentionality. On the contrary, the account presupposes the primacy, ineliminability, and irreducibility of the intentional. The thoughts of animals, like our own, are often expressed nonlinguistically in action, and sometimes they are not expressed at all, even as internal speech acts. As Chisholm reminds Sellars, "It would be unfounded psychological dogma to say that infants, mutes, and animals cannot have beliefs and desires until they are able to use language" (p. 524).

DEMYSTIFYING INTENTIONALITY

The primacy of the intentional provides a defense of intentionalism against a frequently raised objection. Intentionality is sometimes regarded as a "mysterious" relation, and theories of mind that appeal to the intentionality of thought are often dismissed by critics as "magical" or "occult."

If intentionality is conceptually primitive, then there is a straightforward reply to be given on behalf of intentionalism. Every theory must incorporate some primitive concepts if it is to avoid the criticisms of infinite regress and circularity in regressive meaning and coherence net models. The failure of nonintentionalist theories to provide a satisfactory elimination or reduction of intentionality proves that such theories are either inadequate or successful only to the degree that they also smuggle intentional concepts into their accounts. The criticism of intentionalism as obscure or mysterious confuses obscurity and mysteriousness with the primacy of the intentional, and the fact that primitive concepts cannot be further reduced or analyzed. But irreducibility or unanalyzability holds by definition of any primitive concept. If any adequate theory of mind must be grounded on primitive concepts, then all are in the same boat, and none can escape the misguided charge of being "mysterious." We must then either forsake the quest for an adequate philosophy of mind or acknowledge that the primacy of the intentional is not automatically objectionable as magical or mysterious.

The primacy of the intentional complements property dualism as a preferred ontology of mind. If intentionality is primitive, ineliminable, and irreducible, then the intentional properties of mind are distinct from its behavioral-material-functional properties. The aboutness of thought and the ineliminability and irreducibility of the intentional entail property dualism. The arguments offered previously in support of property dualism also lend partial support to the primacy of the intentional. As the primacy of the intentional is strengthened, so the objection that an intentionalist philosophy of mind is obscure or mystical is proportionately weakened.

PUTNAM'S TWIN EARTH COUNTEREXAMPLE

An objection to intentionalism that can now be considered in light of the primacy of the intentional is given by Hilary Putnam in *Mind, Language and Reality* (1975). This is a paradox about the content and intended reference of mental states in an interesting thought experiment concerning physiologically indistinguishable subjects in the imaginary parallel worlds of Earth and Twin Earth.

The problem arises because of the intentionalist distinction between the mental act, content, and intended object of psychological states. Putnam describes the thought contents of two inhabitants of Earth and Twin Earth as indistinguishable, so that when a person on Earth has a content associated with a thought about water, his counterpart on Twin Earth has the very same content. The two may also utter the same word "Water" in these circumstances, say, to indicate the presence of, or their desire for, water. The difference is that, whereas on Earth the word "Water" refers to H_2O, on Twin Earth it refers to some other chemical substance, XYZ. The point of the example is that thought content is not sufficient to determine the reference of thought, because persons with the same thought content can be directed in thought to entirely different things. If this statement is true, then there is no need for a theory of mind or semantics of language to include the intentional concept of thought contents, since they are irrelevant in determining reference.

There is a difficulty in Putnam's stipulation that Earth and Twin Earth counterparts are supposed to be physiologically identical. Human bodies contain large quantities of water, but where Earth has H_2O, Twin Earth has XYZ. This is not a deep problem for Putnam, however. Other philosophers, such as Tyler Burge in his essay "Individualism and the Mental" (1979), have shown how to concoct similar counterexamples that avoid the objection. For present purposes, it will be just as well to focus discussion on Putnam's example, pretending that thinkers on Earth and Twin Earth can be "mole-cule-for-molecule" identical, even if there is no XYZ on Earth, and no H_2O on Twin Earth.

As part of the background to the problem, the thesis of the 19th-century logician and philosopher of language and mathematics Gottlob Frege, that *intension determines extension*, is assumed. This is a brief way of saying that what a term refers to, its *extension*, depends on what the term means, its *intension* (not to be confused with intention). The principle implies that a differ-ence in extension or object referred to determines a difference in intension or meaning of the referring term. This is the form of Frege's thesis relevant to Putnam's objection. Putnam finds a paradox in his description of the Twin Earth case. There is a difference in the extension of Earth and Twin Earth inhabitants' thought when they think "Water"—H_2O is referred to on Earth, XYZ on Twin Earth. By Frege's thesis that intension determines extension, this entails a difference in what Earth and Twin Earth inhabitants mean when they use the word "Water." But, by hypothesis, the thought con-tents of Earth and Twin Earth counterparts are precisely identical. If what they mean by their use of the word is supposed to follow from their thought contents, and if Frege's widely accepted semantic thesis is true, then we are faced with the contradiction that Earth and Twin Earth counterparts have and do not have precisely the same thought content when they think "Water." The parallel thinkers are supposed to be molecule-for-molecule physiologically indistinguishable. So, there seems no way out of the paradox, except to say that thought contents do not supervene or are not causally dependent on physiological states. This conclusion, as Putnam remarks, would be a desperate solution to the problem, since there is convincing empirical evidence in support of mind-body event correlations.

Yet Putnam's thought experiment does not force us in this direction. The paradox presupposes the questionable assumption that intension is identical with or implies thought content. But, for Frege at least, and for Putnam's counterexample insofar as it rests on Frege's thesis, this assumption is false. By "intension" Frege means the abstract set of properties that identify an object, not the occurrent psychological episodes or experiential content of certain minds that think about the object or its properties. These Frege dis-regards as an objectionable intrusion of *psychologism* into logic and the semantics of language. When Frege says that intension determines exten-sion, he means that the properties associated with a term determine the object to which the term refers. He does not mean that a thinker or lan-guage user needs to think of these properties in order to intend or refer to the object. When intentionalists speak of the content of a thought as that through which an intended object is apprehended, what they usually mean by thought "content" falls far short of what Frege means by "intension." Content can, though it need not, be a mental image of the object. But in any case it is something lived through or experienced by the subject, which is not what Frege means by "intension." It follows that there is no danger of violating the framework of Fregean semantics or rejecting the supervenience of mental phenomena on neurophysiological states in concluding that content as opposed to intension does not determine the extension or intended object of thought. The inhabitants of Earth and Twin Earth can have the same (type, not token) thought content, even though their uses of the word "Water" have different intensions, which, by Frege's thesis, determine different extensions.

Putnam's counterexample might still be interpreted as refuting the content-object distinction. But here too it seems the Twin Earth problem does not offer conclusive proof. The objection misinterprets intentionalism as committed to the determination of intended objects or extensions by thought contents. That no such determination holds is obvious in a comparison of cases, not on a parallel Twin Earth, but right here in our world, from considerations inspired by Kripke's (1980) criticism of description theories of reference. At a certain time t I refer to Aristotle as the extension or intended object of a thought that has as its content "Author of *Nicomachean Ethics*." Later I come to believe that Aristotle did not write this book, but that his student and successor Theophrastus did. Then at time t' (later than t) I refer to Theophrastus (not Aristotle) as the extension or intended object of a thought that has as its (phenomenologically indistinguishable) content "Author of *Nicomachean Ethics*."

Now it might be objected that the thought content "Author of *Nicomachean Ethics*" at t is not identical with the thought content "Author of *Nicomachean Ethics*" at t', if the relevant beliefs of the thinker about the author of *Nicomachean Ethics* have changed from t to t'. According to *semantic holism*, the meaning of every thought depends on its relations with every other, so that to change one thought is to change the meaning of all. But this is an implausible theory of meaning that can be challenged in several ways. Suffice it to say that by "Author of *Nicomachean Ethics*" the thinker means the person, whoever it is, who wrote the book *Nicomachean Ethics*. If this cannot be regarded as holding constant, then it is unclear that we can ever change our beliefs. To change a belief is to reject a proposition, adopting an attitude of disbelief or suspended belief toward it. But it is the very same proposition that must first be accepted as a belief, and then rejected or suspended in disbelief. It makes no sense to speak of the same proposition (as opposed to sentences) having different meanings. So, if the meaning of propositions shifts with every new belief, then, paradoxically, we can never change our beliefs.

If this is correct, then there is no need for farfetched Twin Earth scenarios to see that thought content does not in any interesting way determine the extension or intended object of thought. Putnam's attempt to refute intentionalism is misplaced, directed at a misconception of the relation between thought content and object. This is clear not only from the writings of intentionalists in this tradition, but also from our previous phenomenological experiment, in which we introspect our thought contents as we intend a book, then its color, then the space it occupies, and so on. There is nothing essential or uniquely characteristic about the mental contents that may or may not accompany these distinct acts of intending, from which it appears that mental content does not determine the extension or reference of an intended object. The primacy of the intentional implies that intending is a primitive mental act that does not require anything beyond itself, no particular thought content or occurrent lived-through psychological state, to effect designation, reference, or direction upon an intended object.

What role then does content play in thought? Among other things, it can serve to fix or hold intentionally determined intended objects before the mind for purposes of cognitive operations involving memory, calculation, and the like. This capability may be especially useful when there are distractions to thought or when it is otherwise difficult to keep the same object in mind for the duration of the function. Content, including mental image, may represent an intended object, however abstractly or associatively. Cognitive processing in this way can use thought contents as surrogates of extramental objects, as a subject matter and basis for its procedures. But, according to the primacy of the intentional, the intending of an intended object is not accomplished or determined by thought content. It is achieved by an irreducible intentional relation of thought and object, simply by that particular object and none other being intended in thought.

IN DEFENSE OF FOLK PSYCHOLOGY

The criticism of folk psychology, which at bottom is the complaint that intentional explanations are uninformative, can now also be answered from the standpoint of the primacy of the intentional. The future of folk psychological concepts in cognitive studies is not so much a question of whether particular folk psychological concepts in ordinary parlance survive and find a place in a mature scientific psychology. Terms like "belief," "desire," and their likes may be vague or otherwise unsuitable for scientific explanatory purposes. The interesting question is whether cognitive science can explain or explain away psychological phenomena entirely without intentional concepts, or, in other words, whether it can explain away intentionality.

The denunciation of current folk psychological idioms and principles as unscientific does not undermine the importance of intentionality in scientific psychological explanation. At most, the criticism of folk psychology may motivate the development of an alternative vocabulary and theory for psychological phenomena. But, according to the arguments we have considered, even the most advanced cognitive science will need to include intentional concepts if it is to be explanatorily adequate. If the primacy of the intentional thesis is sound, then intentionality is ineliminable and irreducible, and must be made an essential part of any correct psychology. In this broad sense, no satisfactory scientific psychology can fail to be a "folk" psychology. The comparative simplicity or economy of nonintentionalist eliminativist or reductivist psychologies is irrelevant if, through lack of intentional concepts, they cannot fully explain the psychological phenomena accounted for by folk psychology.

Folk psychology is also criticized as useless in predicting and controlling psychological phenomena. But here commentators widely disagree. The fact that we are able to deal effectively one with another, draw conclusions about meaning and intention, even communicate in ordinary language and cooperate in social activities, is a tribute to the pragmatic effectiveness of folk psychology in explanation and prediction. My friend says over the telephone only, "I have a court for five o'clock." I understand what she means. I attribute to her the intention of joining me to play racquetball at that time. I know that she expects me to be at the gym, with my equipment, changed into my sportswear, and ready to play. I believe that she believes these things of me, and so we have a date. When five o'clock rolls around, we both appear at the gym, confirming our mutually implicitly understood intentional explanation and prediction. This is folk psychology in a relatively unimportant example of its many applications. We use it every day, and it works well enough and often enough to merit serious philosophical consideration.

There is supposed to be something quaint and old fashioned about a "folk" concept. The term indicates a preliminary unfinished idea or practice that may eventually lead to something more sophisticated and intellectually respectable. But we should be on the lookout for attempts to substitute name calling for philosophical argument. Stich (1983) claims, "The very fact that [intentional psychology or the Representational Theory of Mind] is a folk theory should make us suspicious. For in just about every other domain one can think of, the ancient shepherds and camel drivers whose speculations were woven into folk theory have had a notoriously bad track record" (p. 229). Yet it is not just ancient shepherds and camel drivers who adopt the intentional idioms of folk psychology. Even the most rigorous cognitive scientists do so, insofar as their theories offer satisfactory explanations of psychological phenomena.

Folk psychology is not a scientific theory in the usual sense. It is a pastiche of commonsense exception-laden generalizations about predicting and explaining behavior, the effects of environmental factors on thinking, practical advice about problem solving, recipes for coping with depression, informal categories for personality types, and intentional explanations of sensations, emotions, decisions, and other mental occurrences. This complexity makes comparing folk psychology with modern scientific theories a difficult if not pointless exercise. If the thesis of the primacy of the intentional is correct, then no adequate account of psychological phenomena can entirely dispense with intentional concepts, even if it does not include the same intentional concepts as those found in folk psychology today. The advance of scientific psychology might replace what is currently recognized as folk psychology, not by a nonintentional cognitive psychology, but by a more elaborate theory that includes different, perhaps more refined concepts that are every bit as intentional as those found in contemporary folk psychology.

The concepts of intentionality and the nature of thought can be understood as a direct application of folk psychology in the sense we have just explained. Let us continue discussion of these topics by considering an intentionalist description of three main stages in the development of mind, from sentience to consciousness to self-consciousness.

INTENTIONALITY OF SENSATION AS THE BASIS OF THOUGHT

My experience in sensation and perception is not identical with or the same thing as the world. But my experience is of or about the world, and it helps to guide me through the world by informing my action. It provides facts about the location and properties of things in the world that are vitally useful to me. Since this is generally what maps do, I conclude that my experience and memory are a dynamic map of those parts of the world I have encountered, with which my senses have causally interacted. Phenomenology or the introspective study of mental states abstractly is the mind's geography, and concretely its cartography.

That thought is intentional, that intentionality is primitive and hence irreducible, takes the philosophical mystery out of psychological events. It is the mind's living experience of thinking, sensing, feeling, perceiving, believing, doubting, hoping, fearing, desiring, expecting, loving, hating. If we reflect on a memorable experience that is particularly rich in content, drinking in the purple-blue color of mountain flowers in the Alps, or the penetrating warm pain of a sunburn after a day at the ocean, we may begin to wonder how such a thing as psychological experience is possible. How can there be such a thing as pain? How do neurophysiological excitations along nerve pathways result in feeling? How can photons striking the retina of the eye produce images in which we see the world?

These questions about the nature of psychological experience, of *sensation* and *consciousness*, are impenetrable mysteries to eliminativism and reductivism. But they are understandable as consequences of the primacy of the intentional. To sense or have sensation is to be aware; to sense or be aware is to sense or be aware *of* something. Sensation is a modification of the mind's representational field. Its representation neither requires nor admits of further analysis, because it involves an association of objects with objects via irreducible intentional relations. Thus, sensation, sentience, is placed firmly in the realm of intentionality and the primacy of the intentional.

Consider a phylogenetic gradation of increasingly complicated information processing systems, from simple organisms such as amoebas and paramecia to humans. At the lower end, let us imagine that there are mollusks with a photosensitive eyespot, which functions essentially like my solar-powered pocket calculator. The eyespot registers discontinuities of light, the reception of which is hardwired into muscle trains that cause the animals to close their shells or move away whenever there is an abrupt interruption of light. The mollusks, we shall suppose, are not consciously aware of any of this. Nor do they act deliberately to evade a potential threat. They are too simple to have thoughts and are incapable of qualia or intentionality. If there are mollusks as limited as this, then they are best regarded, not as having minds, but as living machines, just a step up from bacteria, phages, viruses, self-replicating DNA, solar-powered pocket calculators, and artificial intelligence systems like ELIZA and SHRDLU. As we move upward along the spectrum from living machines, we find sentient beings, crustaceans, arthropods, fish, reptiles, birds, and lower mammals. Finally, we ascend the chain of neurophysiological complexity to the higher mammals, including humans. At this extreme, we find animals that are not merely sentient, but conscious and self-conscious. They are beings who sense, perceive, and even articulate the content of their perceptions, reflecting on their experience in various ways and at several levels of abstraction. Intelligent systems of this sort have achieved sufficient complexity for their thoughts to intend themselves and other intentional states.

An information-processing system needs to be able to *take* an irradiation or electromagnetic wave pattern *as* something, to have it *represent* another thing, in the most primitive intentional act. The intentionality of sensation and perception enables minds to represent or map the world, their bodies and the environments in which they live. The fact that there is always a difference between a map and what it maps, between a representation and what it represents, prevents the intentionality of sensation and perception from lapsing into Berkeley's idealism or Brentano's early immanence thesis. This observation is true despite the claim that the content of our sensory and perceptual experience, the phenomenal fields of all the senses, constitutes a dynamic representation or map. For it is a map or representation *of* the real, external, extramental world. How this occurs cannot be further explained if a reductive conceptual analysis is required. The primacy of the intentional implies that no explanatory reduction of representation relations can be given. This irreducibility is what some critics regard as mysterious about intentionalist philosophy. But we have already seen that the criticism is mistaken, and in Chapter Five we shall try to answer further doubts by considering a metaphysical characterization of the evolutionary emergence of intentionality.

The theory of sensation as the basis of thought implies that even "lower" animals have minds. From my daily observations of tropical aquarium fish, I have no difficulty accepting this conclusion. I believe, though with less than absolute certainty, that my fish perceive the objects in and surrounding the tank, that they want and expect to be fed in the morning, that they do not just react by fleeing but fear capture in the net. But I doubt that they are complex enough to dread the occurrence, or anticipate being fed with anything like long-term memory. If it seems wrong to say that neurophysiologically simple creatures like fish have intentions, it may only be because this appears to imply that fish are self-conscious beings, or (finny) persons capable of deliberate or intentional action. If fish act intentionally, they nevertheless are not persons, nor are they morally responsible for what they do. But, minimally, they seem to have crude thoughts, even if I have exaggerated their intelligence and capacity for intentional states. They are probably limited to sensations and perceptions, simple wants, expectations, and fears. These limitations make them merely sentient beings, neither conscious nor self-conscious. But even as such, their thoughts primitively intend or are about that which they want, fear, expect, and perceive.

We can arrive at these commonsense conclusions if the best explanation of a subject's behavior requires attributing some form of semantic intention, a representation of objects by other objects in its information processing system. This is why the Silver Dollars in my aquarium should be regarded as intentional, while the best RACTER artificial intelligence conversation program should not, and why the idea of determining intelligence or intentionality by the Turing Test method is basically sound. We must remember that the primacy of the intentional implies that systems need not have command of language to be intentional. They need only be able to represent something by something else, such as a part of their environment by a neural excitation state. They do not need to be able to put this representation into (anything that we would recognize as) words, or think in sentences. Nor do they need to act deliberately or "intentionally" in the sense of reasoned action. Ethologists like to speak even of simple animals as having internal maps of territories, feeding grounds, and migratory patterns. While this may be anthropomorphic for what might better be described as purely nonintentional cause and effect mechanisms, it may also in some cases be the best explanation of the animal's behavior. If so, it is undoubtedly intentional, since mental maps, like mental language, images, and other kinds of representation, are intentional entities *par excellence*. A map always *means* something.

Does the intentionality of qualia in sentient animals entail that they are worthy of moral respect? This is an ethical side issue, but it is probably true that animals deserve more respect than they usually receive. Yet on some ethical theories, animals do not merit moral consideration unless they are fully conscious or self-conscious. The more time we spend with animals the more intentional they seem, even if this is partly an illusion we project anthropomorphically onto their behavior.

DENNETT'S INTENTIONAL STANCE

The claim that there are nonhuman minds is a logical consequence of the theory of sensation as the basis of thought. It is similar to, but goes beyond, what Dennett has called taking the *intentional stance*. In his book *The Intentional Stance* (1987), Dennett describes the stance as an attitude in which a subject is treated as an intentional system, or entity "whose behavior can be predicted by the method of attributing beliefs, desires, and rational acumen" (p. 49). The purpose of intentional stance-taking is to be able to deal more effectively with certain kinds of complex systems, by acting toward them as though they were intelligent. Because what we have just concluded about the intrinsic intentionality of nonhuman minds might be dismissed as mere intentional stance-taking, we must distinguish Dennett's concept from the thesis that by experiencing sensation animals are intentional in the full sense of the word.

Dennett's pragmatic instrumental predication of intentionality to systems is obviously weaker than the assertion that sentients definitely have intentionality and are definitely minds. What Dennett means by the intentional stance is an attitude that can be adopted even toward inanimate systems like calculators and thermostats, provided that doing so facilitates prediction and control. We may even regard an intemperate wind and raging sea as intentional if it helps to marshal our efforts as though against an intelligent opponent. This thought may explain much of mythology and the personification of natural forces as gods. In another sense, however, the attribution of intentionality to sentient animals does not go as far as Dennett's intentional stance-taking. For Dennett, the intentional stance predicates an as-if rationality or the ability to reason of the system. Dennett characterizes the stance as assuming that a "system's behavior will consist of those acts that *it would be rational* for an agent with those beliefs and desires to perform" (p. 49). The position taken in the previous section is not that fish and other sentients are to be treated as though they are rational, but that their neurophysiologies represent parts or aspects of the world for them, and so are intrinsically intentional.

Dennett's caution in limiting such attributions to what he often refers to as the mere heuristic overlay of intentional stance-taking need not deter us from attributing intentionality in this more modest sense to sentient beings. Although we undoubtedly assume the intentional stance toward many things, Dennett's intentional stance as an instrumentalist attribution does not go far enough in explaining the facts about the intentionality of thought. The intentional stance, moreover, presupposes first-person intentionality because the stance-taker can have no concept of the intentional properties of belief, desire, and the like, attributed to other systems, except from first-person acquaintance. It is not clear whether Dennett would want or need to deny this assertion. But if Dennett's intentional stance is supposed to help the hard third-person psychological sciences join hands with first-person phenomenology, it cannot consistently do so as an effort to dismiss the intentionality of thought as mere third-person intentional stance-taking.

WHY DO PAINS HURT?

If the intentionality of qualia is a fact about even the lowest sentient creatures, and not just a matter of intentional stance-taking, then it can provide the framework for an answer to one of the most difficult questions in the philosophy of mind. "Why do pains hurt?" is a general way of asking why there are qualia.

The neural excitements we experience as pains have been naturally selected by evolution. They occur in living things with sufficiently complex neurophysiologies to allow a range of experiential values that include colors, light and dark, warm and cold, rough and soft, pleasure and pain. The evolutionary advantage is that by these means a wide array of information about body and environmental states is available to the organism for naturally and operationally conditioned learned behavior.

Sensation dynamically maps and so represents certain body states and external conditions. It is the intentionality of spatial representation in visual mapping that enables us to experience the Grand Canyon in full dimension. We see it as extending over vast distances, despite the fact that the connectionist neural map of visual data we receive from it is many times smaller in scale, housed within the brain's compact neural networks. Our brains contain dynamic maps of body and world states in the form of ongoing visual and other sensory experience. As with ordinary maps, the size of the map compared with what it maps is, within practical limitations, irrelevant. This is why it is not absurd to think of hummingbirds and even smaller sentients as having minds. What makes experiential thought content intentional is that content is or derives from sensation, and sensation is always *of* or *about* something. The intentionality of qualia, and the primacy of the intentional, imply the ineliminable and irreducible object-directedness of sensation.

Pain is a "color" in the sensation map of body and world. Its primary role is to indicate that a body part is damaged or in need of care. The meaning of pain is various, but typically it intends danger to the body or the presence of harmful objects or substances. It is the insistent, attention-getting character of amplified neurophysiological signals that, as we say, hurt. This has survival advantages that have contributed to its inclusion in the psychological makeup of most sentient creatures. Pain is no more problematic, if we understand the primacy of the intentional, than the attention-getting red markings used on road maps to indicate geographical points of interest.

What, then, is color? Like all qualia, color is a modification of the intentional representational field. In the evolution of sentient beings, certain representations have been refined by natural selection and reinforced by experience and social learning to highlight information of special importance to the animal's welfare. This statement is true of both pleasure and pain, and for that matter of color, sound, and the other characteristics of sense experience. For machines, including the simplest nonsentient living machines, pain is not only inaccessible and irreplicable, but superfluous. If evolution could have produced intentional beings capable of avoiding hazards and modifying their behavior without conditioning, without pleasure and pain sensitivity, they would be nothing more than machines in these limited respects. Their mechanical behavior in areas where we are guided by pleasure and pain would be mostly if not entirely *autonomic*, as the functions of breathing and heartbeat are for us, regulated mechanically by the nervous system's automatic feedback control, without intentionality or internal representation.

It is sometimes objected that while certain kinds of psychological experience may be intentional, others, such as sensation, plainly are not. Richard Rorty, in *Philosophy and the Mirror of Nature* (1979), supports this criticism when he writes: "The obvious objection to defining the mental as the intentional is that pains are not intentional—they do not represent, they are not *about* anything" (p. 22). But if our analogy is correct, then particular pains as the colors of the sensation map are about the body or external features to which they call attention. Pains represent or are about body and environmental conditions. They are about the tack someone has placed on my chair, or about the condition of muscles and bone joints I have injured playing baseball without a proper warmup. Sensations in general terms, moreover, can be described as having pains and other particular sensation contents as intended objects. On this interpretation, it is not pain that *has* an object, but pain *is* the object of sensation, of what is sensed. It is, significantly, the qualia or content *of* sensation. Sensation is intentional, and takes pain, or for that matter pleasure, color, warmth, coolness, light, darkness, hunger, satiety, roughness, smoothness, as combined intended objects and qualia or contents. The satisfaction of object-requiring intentional contexts, ⌜ P senses (has the sensation of) _____ ⌝ or ⌜ P feels _____ ⌝, agrees with that found in paradigm instances of intentional contexts, such as ⌜ P believes that _____ ⌝, ⌜ P sees _____ ⌝, or ⌜ P perceives that _____ ⌝. But it is mistaken, as Rorty's objection requires, to regard the test case intentional context for pain sentience as having the ungrammatical form ⌜ P pains _____ ⌝ or ⌜ P pains that _____ ⌝. If either the sensation map analogy or the analysis of pain as the combined object and content of sensation is correct, then sensation is as fully intentional, as much about its intended objects, as the intentional object-taking states of belief, doubt, or fear.

SENTIENCE, CONSCIOUSNESS, SELF-CONSCIOUSNESS

To be conscious is to be aware of or about something. The definition brings consciousness immediately into the realm of "aboutness" or intentionality. Thought is not essentially conscious. Lower animals are merely sentient, and even the human mind has episodes of unconsciousness as well as consciousness. Consciousness also admits of degrees and selective focus and attention. We can experience lapses of consciousness, and we can be conscious of some but not other things in our surroundings, as when we are so absorbed in conversation that we fail to notice the time. The intentionality of thought unites sensation, consciousness, and self-consciousness as three stages in a range of psychological experience that extends from the simplest to the most complex known minds.

Thoughts are intending brain events. They are neurophysiological occurrences with behavioral-material-functional properties and behaviorally-materially-functionally ineliminable and irreducible intentional properties. Not all living things are capable of thoughts, but at the most fundamental, sentient, level, thought occurs in beings whose neurophysiological events represent the world. Nonlinguistic representation in sensation is the intentional basis of linguistic representation in higher-order minds capable of expressing thought in language. Thinking things, even creatures capable only of crude sentient or perceptual thoughts, have at least crude sentient or perceptual minds. Since primitive brain structures persist as vestiges in more highly developed minds, it should be possible on this theory to imagine a psychological archaeology. Its purpose would not be the psychoanalytic discovery of traumatic events subconsciously suppressed and manifested as neuroses. It would try instead to excavate the primal thoughts on which higher levels of consciousness are built like the ancient foundations of a modern city.

Sensation in primitive thought maps or represents selected parts of the body and limited aspects of the world outside the body, primarily as a survival tactic. But evolution has endowed some species with sufficiently complex neurophysiologies capable of mappings of mappings, and reflexive mappings of mappings of mappings. This progression provides a simplified intentional explanation of the emergence of conscious and self-conscious states. Consciousness and self-consciousness are special kinds of intentional attitudes that intend or are directed toward the mind's own states. With sensation, thought makes its first appearance in the world. It is a neurophysiological event representing occurrences within or outside the body in bursts of neural excitations. Neurosystems with the requisite complexity are additionally capable of monitoring sensation. This is another, higher-level intentional event that intends sensation, and has lower-level sensation experience as its intended object. It is consciousness. Since consciousness is not itself a sensation, but a higher-level awareness of sensation, it has an experiential thought content other than its object. Beings capable of this level of intention are aware of their sensations. At the next and highest level, subjects have an awareness of the awareness of sensation and of other thought contents. This is self-consciousness. The most highly developed kinds of self-consciousness can think about and articulate the features of other thoughts, and even reflectively in thoughts about themselves. We may wish to regard only self-consciousness of the highly developed sort to which we have attained as mind. But, as we have now seen, there are many kinds of minds, from the merely sentient, to the conscious, to several degrees of self-consciousness.

The progression from sentience to consciousness suggests a three-part division of qualitative differences superimposed on the spectrum of animal mental faculties. These may be difficult to divide neatly with any confidence, but they undoubtedly include, on the merely sentient side, higher invertebrates, primitive fish, and reptiles, and on the conscious but not yet self-conscious side, most animals between sentients and the higher mammals. Insects are more difficult to classify. They are often so robotlike as to seem more like living machines. But some species may be sentient and capable of a certain amount of learning and unpredictability. Fleas in the Flea Circus at Munich's Oktoberfest are trained to pull tiny wagons and ride tiny merry-go-rounds. The fleas' complex abilities suggest the possibility of their behavioral conditioning through satisfaction of wants and avoidance of pain.

At the highest known level, self-consciousness occurs as an intentional act directed toward conscious acts that normally confers on them a unity we refer to as the self. Here we find dogs, dolphins, higher apes, and man. As before, this kind of consciousness admits of degree, and nothing important hinges on whether these categorizations of animals are correct, since they are intended merely for purposes of illustrating the distinctions. But it is worth noting that, unlike some accounts of self-consciousness, the theory that has just been sketched, in accord with the primacy of the intentional, does not require language-using ability as essential to consciousness or self-consciousness. All that is necessary for consciousness and self-consciousness is the occurrence of mental states that take other mental states as their intended objects in the case of consciousness, or the unity of consciousness in the person, self, or ego, as an intended object in the case of self-consciousness. We tend to think only of humans as fully self-conscious, and we often regard command of language as a necessary condition. But even dogs, who can at most be taught to respond to a limited vocabulary of words, qualify as self-conscious to a limited degree by this analysis, on the grounds that they seem to manifest at least a crude concept of self. Self-consciousness is consciousness of self, and as such it is obviously intentional. But self-consciousness is also consciousness of conscious and sentient thoughts, binding them together into a unity so as to constitute a person, self, or ego.

The same three main categories also signify stages along the continuum of ontogenetic development in the normal growth of conscious and self-conscious beings, following a path of neurophysiological maturation. These too may be hard to identify as exact stages of development in real time corresponding to the abstract distinctions that have been drawn, just as it is difficult to say which animals are only sentient, and which conscious or self-conscious. But we can easily imagine, in the case of our own species, that there are stages of prenatal brain and spinal cord growth at which the unborn child first becomes sentient, then conscious, and, shortly before or after birth, self-conscious.

We can also be said to intend sensations and conscious thoughts subconsciously, as in dreams. But "subconscious" thoughts, as the word is popularly used, are conscious in the present sense. A subconscious thought can only be a sensation of which the mind is not aware. If it is merely a reflex, reaction, or neural processing, then it does not deserve to be called a thought. The term is sometimes used as synonymous with subcognitive processing in cognitive psychology, as well as with Sigmund Freud's concept of the "unconscious." Dream thoughts are called subconscious in an attenuated sense. They are "subconscious" in that they occur when we are asleep, when waking self-consciousness is not available to comment publicly on them, sleep-talkers and sleep-walkers notwithstanding. For various reasons, dream thoughts are less often remembered, or not as clearly remembered, as ordinary conscious or self-conscious waking thoughts. This has also led them to be relegated to the less honorary category of the subconscious. Yet, during the dream, the mind is often fully aware of its intended objects, as we know from those times when we remember very specifically what our dreams are about. It seems reasonable, then, in the sense of the word we have been considering, to describe dream thoughts as conscious and even self-conscious when they intend sensations and conscious thoughts, including themselves. The best evidence for this conclusion is remembered dreams during which we think, "This is only a dream," "I'm going to wake myself up," or, "I'm having the same dream again."

Is there a stage or level of consciousness above and beyond self-consciousness? Certainly, religious mystics and New Age visionaries talk about higher states of consciousness. But what is referred to as a higher state of consciousness is probably just an extraordinary degree or direction of ordinary consciousness or self-consciousness. This could include consciousness of things or events in unusual detail, especially of what is typically overlooked by others when they are distracted by mundane needs or desires. It can also involve consciousness of larger entities subsuming the self, such as the realm of all persons, all living things, or the universe considered as a holistic intended unity. But it is unclear whether any such thoughts, regardless of how noble and enlightened they may be, represent a new higher level of consciousness beyond self-consciousness. They seem to be conscious awarenesses of different or atypical kinds of objects, rather than belonging to a radically different category of thought. If there are or could be levels of consciousness beyond self-consciousness, we cannot be expected to say what they are, no more than Nagel's bat could imagine human self-consciousness. We can guess that they may have something to do with breaking down the privacy barriers of individual consciousnesses and the emergence of collective consciousness in the true sense of the word. But we cannot say exactly what such a state of mind would be like. Presumably, it would be different from telepathy or mind-reading between minds, which we can understand as ordinary consciousness of an extraordinary object. If higher consciousness exists, humankind will have to wait for the same magnitude of brain evolution that first brought about the emergence of consciousness from sentience and self-consciousness from consciousness.

We have now described a series of steps in the development of mind. But much more needs to be said about the highest stage of self-consciousness in which we find for the first time in the genealogy of thought an appearance of the self. The person, self, or ego, is what Socrates and Descartes, along with much of religious tradition, identify as the soul. It is you and I, our persons. It is what you think of as you, and what I think of as me. But what exactly is the self? Is it the same as the mind, the suggestively named self-conscious mind? Or is the self different from but related to self-consciousness?

SELF-IDENTITY PUZZLES

To understand the concept of *self,* we must consider a number of problems about self-identity. The idea that the self is a unified substantial entity is disputed by many scientists and philosophers. The evidence against the real existence of the self can be divided into two main categories: (1) clinical observation of psychopathologies, including those resulting from brain injury and severe psychological abuse; (2) problems of providing philosophically satisfactory self-identity criteria.

Doubts about the existence of self in modern Western thought can be traced to David Hume's *A Treatise of Human Nature* (1739–1740). Hume takes up Descartes' challenge to withhold belief from whatever can be doubted. He wants to test Descartes' *Cogito ergo sum* conclusion, that nothing is more certain than the existence of the self. Hume's experiments as contrasted with Descartes' meet with decidedly negative results. Hume finds: "For my part, when I enter most intimately into what I call *myself,* I always stumble on some particular perception or other, of heat or cold, light or shade, love or hatred, pain or pleasure. I never can catch *myself* at any time without a perception, and never can observe any thing but the perception" (p. 252). This conclusion prompts Hume to replace the concept of a Cartesian ego with the idea of the self as a "bundle" of perceptions, held together in memory and expectation as an imaginary unity. This has come to be known as the bundle theory of the self. Immanuel

Kant, who found Hume's proposal unsatisfactory, adopted a comparable solution in his (1787) *Critique of Pure Reason,* by concluding that there is a *transcendental unity of apperception,* or an "I think," that accompanies every mental occurrence, that is not found in empirical introspective experience. The position is similar to what P. F. Strawson, in *Individuals: An Essay in Descriptive Metaphysics* (1959), calls the *no-ownership theory of the self.* It is a view carried forward in Derek Parfit's skepticism about the existence of the self in his book *Reasons and Persons* (1984).

The scientific argument against the existence of self consists of clinical observations and experiments involving multiple personality disorders and other impairments of normal brain functioning. These suggest the impermanent and volatile nature of the self. The loss of self or sense of self that occurs through brain damage or psychological trauma, brainwashing, or even extreme old age, sometimes complicated by deteriorating ailments like Alzheimer's disease, also argues against the concept of self as a substantial unitary entity. Even nonscientific observation of normal development in infants and children indicates that the self when it occurs is different from the mind. The person or self seems to be a created thing that is shaped by genetic and environmental forces that begins to appear in the life of the child only at a certain stage of growth. Added to these considerations is the interpretation of so-called *split-brain phenomena,* in which brains are divided almost entirely in half, separating the two hemispheres of the cerebral cortex along the *corpus callosum,* usually as a surgical procedure to relieve severe epilepsy. When this is done, as Nagel reports in his essay "Brain Bisection and the Unity of Consciousness" (1971), the brain's ability to communicate information from one half to the other is significantly reduced. This impairment leads to situations in which, when a colored light is shown selectively to one eye, the optic nerve of which runs into the opposite brain hemisphere, and the split-brain subject is asked if the light is green, she may verbally incorrectly answer "No", but correctly write "Yes", or the reverse. There are other intriguing effects of split-brain phenomena, and the explanation of anomalies in conscious thought resulting from brain hemisphere disconnection is open to interpretation. But it suggests to philosophers like Nagel that the self is not a simple, unified substance, and that at least under abnormal conditions there is not a single spokesperson for mind and brain activities as the person, self, or ego has traditionally been conceived.

Philosophical arguments against the adequacy of identity criteria for the self reinforce the clinical psychological evidence. If the self is a unitary substantial entity, then it should be possible to specify *genidentity* conditions, or criteria under which the same self can be recognized as persisting through changes in time. This unfortunately, has proved impossible. A complete proof of the inadequacy of genidentity conditions for the concept of self, examining each proposal in detail, would take us far afield.

But we can get a sense of the difficulty by considering in summary a dilemma based on the mind-body or psychological-physical property distinction. There seem to be two possibilities for self-identity criteria, based on the self's physical and psychological properties.

Physical identity criteria are usually thought to be contradicted by Locke's problem of the Prince and the Cobbler. One day the Prince wakes up and finds himself in the body of the Cobbler, and the Cobbler in the body of the Prince. If body swapping of this kind is even logically conceivable, as functionalism though not token materialism supposes, then the genidentity of the material body associated with the self in everyday life cannot provide conceptually adequate genidentity conditions for the self.

Psychological identity criteria typically involve relations on sets of *action memories*, memories of the self's doing or having done something. Ordinary propositional memories like remembering that Caesar fought the Gauls will not do, because they can be shared item-for-item by different persons. Action memories are different, because, leaving aside the epistemic problem of distinguishing apparent from genuine or veridical memories, only the person who has actually done an action can truly remember doing it. The difficulty in this approach arises when we try to say exactly what relation should connect these memories in order to genidentify the self.

It would be naive to suppose that there could be a perfect continuity even of dispositional action memories in the self's history from the emergence of self in childhood to old age, not to mention unconscious periods during sleep and more unusual occurrences like coma and total amnesia. Richard Henry Dana, Jr., in his narrative of life aboard an American merchant brig in the 1830s, *Two Years Before the Mast* nevertheless describes just such a person. He says of his shipmate Tom Harris that "the most remarkable thing about him, was the power of his mind. His memory was perfect; seeming to form a regular chain, reaching from his earliest childhood up to the time I knew him, without one link wanting" (pp. 261–262). This would be an unusual memory indeed, and we need not accept Dana's third-person testimony about Tom's uninterrupted memory at face value. In any case, it would be nice to think there are more persons in the history of the world than Tom and the elite club to which he and a few others with perfectly continuous memories belong. For most persons, there are substantial gaps and periodic absences and recurrences of action memories.

The psychological criterion of self-identity also needs to overcome Thomas Reid's counterexamples of the Brave Officer and Senile General in his (1785) *Essays on the Intellectual Powers of Man*. The Officer and General are supposed to be one and the same person in middle and old age. But the Brave Officer does not remember the things he did as a child, and the Senile General remembers things he did as a child, but does not remember his actions as an Officer. Since the simplest version of the psychological genidentity criterion implies that the child, Officer, and General are not the same person, but three distinct persons, the simplest version of the psychological criterion must be false.

There are proposals to avoid these difficulties, by allowing action memories to overlap in various ways, and to satisfy more complex logical or set theoretical relations. But all versions of the psychological criterion suffer from the following circularity objection. We are to imagine that we have collections of action memories unassigned to any particular selves, and that we identity which selves are which by virtue of the action memories unique to each. From this unassorted batch of memories, it is hard to see how we can proceed unless we know which memories belong together as the memories of an individual self. But to do this, we must already know how to identify and individuate persons, which we are not supposed to be able to do until the psychological criterion is applied. The psychological criterion requires that to decide whether A and B are the same or different selves, we must determine whether or not they share all action memories m_1, m_2, m_3, etc. But we cannot apply the criterion without knowing which of these action memories is correctly attributed to A and which to B. And we cannot do this unless we already know who A and B are, unless we have already identified and individuated these persons. The psychological criterion appears caught in the circle of presupposing self-identities in order to attribute and group the right memories together, which in turn it must do in order to determine self-identities.

We must distinguish between the mind and the self. For we acknowledge that lower animals capable of sensation or consciousness but not self-consciousness have minds, but are not persons or selves. Skepticism about the existence of the self therefore should not imply skepticism about the existence of mind. The case against the existence of a unitary substantial self from Hume through present-day cognitive studies of brain disorders and psychopathologies, as well as philosophical skepticism about the adequacy of self-identity criteria, reveals something interesting about the concept of self-consciousness. If there is no self or unified owner of experience in the traditional sense, then what we call the self or owner of experience must be a fictional entity, projected by self-conscious reflexively self-constituting thought as an intended object, an imaginary unity imposed by thought on itself and other thoughts. This makes Hume's description of the self as a bundle of perceptions an important but incomplete anticipation of the theory of self as an imaginary unity. The mind's "perceptions" may be bundled together in imagination as belonging to a single fictional intended object, as occurs in the normal development of self-consciousness. But the fragility of self as a contrivance of imagination is revealed by the fact that its thoughts can also become unbundled or fail to form properly through brain damage and psychopathology.

THE INTENDED SELF

A self-conscious thought is reflexive in that it thinks about itself. Aristotle, who regards godhead as the ultimate self-consciousness, describes its nature as that which thinking thinks itself. The self-identity puzzles suggest that the self may be a fiction, an artificial unity imposed on thoughts intended by higher-order self-conscious thoughts in self-constituting awarenesses of awareness. The reflexivity of self-consciousness is captured in this concept by the fact that in intending an imaginary unity of thoughts, self-consciousness includes itself.

The reflexive intending of self by self-conscious thought can also be disrupted, or prevented from maturing normally, by accident, disease, or deliberate abuse, such as induced psychological trauma. The fact that external causes can lead to a failure to develop or loss of a proper sense of self, mental derangement, or schizophrenia further supports the interpretation of self as a constructed and therefore disruptable unity, imposed by self-conscious thoughts on themselves and, other thoughts. There is a plausible explanation of these syndromes if the self is an intended object of thought. The imaginary unity of thought that constitutes the self may fail to be projected as an intended object by the subject's mind if certain psychological or neurophysiological occurrences interfere with its normal activity.

To say that the self is an imaginary intended object is to say that the self as a unified substantial entity does not exist. This is an odd consequence of a theory of self-consciousness, but one that may have to be admitted because of the self-identity paradoxes. The intended self may also be related to Melzack's theory of the neuromatrix projection of neurosignature impulse patterns in his account of phantom limb phenomena. Just as the impulse pattern from the brain's parietal lobe may give the impression of an arm or leg even when there is none, so the self might be a phantom unity, a phantom person that has its origins as a fictional object of thought reflexively intended by self-consciousness. Indeed, this possibility must be allowed if the Cartesian ego is rejected along with substance dualism in favor of an intentionalist property dualism. The indivisibility of mind that Descartes emphasized in his second argument for substance dualism in *Meditation* 6 and Kant's "I think" or transcendental unity of apperception can be interpreted as the mind's persistence in imposing an imaginary intended unity on its thoughts, bundling together whatever thoughts it produces as belonging to a single self-conscious subject. This interpretation provides the clue to a criticism of Descartes' proof. The inference is unsound in its assumption that the self, which Descartes equates with the mind, cannot be divided into smaller like units. The self as an intended bundle of thoughts can be divided into smaller bundles. The loss of a memory, for example, is comparable to the loss of a body part. It is just that self-consciousness, in intending the new bundle, does not regard itself as diminished thereby, because it continues to impose its unity on whatever thoughts remain. We commit a Rylean category mistake if we insist with Descartes that the self must be something over and above or in addition to this intended bundling together of thoughts in self-constituting acts of self-consciousness.

The same is true of what Dennett has called the Cartesian Theater. This is an imaginary mental space, a room in which mental images are called into play. The Cartesian Theater is supposed to provide a place where mental images can be manipulated for spatial comparison and other cognitive purposes, in a workspace or scratchpad for calculation and memory, or for trying ideas out in "the mind's eye." There is literally no internal stage where the mind's dramas and comedies are mentally performed, or where mental images are brought out and shuffled about like theater props. But the concept is so universally reported that it is difficult to dismiss the phenomenological evidence that something like it must play a part in the life of the mind. The problem disappears if the theater like the self is understood to be a fictional intended object. Constructing the nonexistent Cartesian Theater in imagination may be the first act of consciousness or self-consciousness, creating an imaginary space to be furnished later with other intended objects. Or, the theater may be intended afterward as needed for temporarily holding and working with ideas during more challenging mental exercises. It may be something the mind learns to construct early in its development in order to facilitate other tasks. But as an intended nonexistent object, the Cartesian Theater like the self is not simply nothing. In some ways, it is as important a feature of the psychology of minds that intend it as the external material objects with which they physically interact.

Why should self-consciousness intend an imaginary unified self? What purpose does this serve? There may be survival advantages from an evolutionary viewpoint to explain the intending of self, in the executive organization and control of certain brain functions. Among other things, it may facilitate the development of culture in social organization and cooperation through the presentation of self. The self is a convenient thing to hold responsible for actions of mind and body. But what does the intending if there is no self? The person seems to be a created thing. But created by what or whom? One answer is that the self intends and thereby creates itself. Bit by bit, in successive acts of self-consciousness, a single higher-order thought first intends the self as a unitary center and source of other thoughts that cluster about it. The self picks itself up by its own bootstraps. A further possibility is that the self is created by the brain with its dual physical and nonphysical intentional properties, by thoughts as dual-aspect brain events with both behavioral-material-functional and primitively intentional properties, or, in other words, by the mind. And a further answer is that the self intends the self, if by this is meant the imaginary unity of thoughts imposed by a special category of thoughts, those that reflexively constitute self-consciousness by intending the self as a center and source of intrinsically intentional thought, by the self-conscious mind.

Why has this kind of theory eluded science? The primacy of the intentional is a matter of metaphysics and conceptual analysis, not of observational or experimental investigation. The theory of the intended self is therefore beyond the aims and methods of hard psychological science. Hume speaks as honestly as he can for the limitations of science, when he says, in effect: "*I*'ve looked for the self, but *I* can't find it." The self remains invisible to empirical science, as it was to Hume's empiricist and Kant's critical philosophy. Hume concludes from the limits of experienceable phenomena that the self does not exist. Kant reasons that the unity of the self transcends experience. The self is largely what the self self-consciously but mostly non-deliberately makes of itself; the self creates itself, its self. The self cannot experience itself because it cannot get outside to encounter itself as a spectator. The implication is that in the traditional sense there can be no complete and satisfactory hard scientific theory of the self. If, as has been suggested, the self is an intended imaginary object, then its concept is accessible only to phenomenology.

CHAPTER FIVE

The Dignity of Mind

A thought is an intrinsically intentional neurophysiological event. If its immediately intended object is indistinguishable from its qualia or content, then it is a sensation. If it thinks about or takes sentient thought as its intended object, it is conscious. If it imposes unity as an intended object on sentient or conscious thoughts, including itself, it is self-conscious. The mind is the producer of thoughts, the intrinsically intentional brain and nervous system. The self is an imaginary unity projected onto thoughts as belonging to one subject, intended by reflexively self-conscious thoughts. Mind distinguishes itself from matter and mechanism in these three ways, by virtue of the primacy or behavioral-material-functional ineliminability and irreducibility of its intentional properties. The implications of intentionalist property dualism for the mind's ascent from matter, the privacy of experience, and the concepts of action, freedom of will, responsibility, passion, and death constitute the metaphysical and moral dignity of mind.

ASCENT OF THE MIND

We have already alluded to the emergence of mind in evolutionary history. The brain developed from neural clusters that were too simple for thought, lacking the complexity necessary for intrinsically intentional neurophysiological events. It progressed through reptilian and earlier phases to the most advanced mammalian brains, including those now reading these words. The advent of self-consciousness marks the emergence of the ego, person, or self.

Among humans, the person emerges and then undergoes rapid formation in infancy and early childhood. It is during this time that personality takes shape, to be refined in a lifelong process by many kinds of influences. The self at some point begins to determine its own deliberately chosen course, and so becomes responsible for itself. This is the ascent of mind, the evolutionary path thought has taken from sentience to the sense of self, from perception and pain to the most abstract reflections and highest products of culture.

The emergence of thought admits of a partial scientific explanation in bioevolutionary theory. Problem-solving intelligence has survival value in securing habitat, food, and reproductive opportunities. It is certain to be exploited by those naturally gifted with its advantages, appearing first randomly, increasing by increments, and then improved by selection pressures over many generations. We humans are animals, and the most sophisticated minds we know are the minds of animals. The minds that have arisen in our planet's biological history, from reptiles to Bertrand Russell, are the complex products of complex evolutionary forces. With sentience appears the first mind, and from sentience natural selection has molded consciousness and self-consciousness. These developments occurred not only as a result of increasing brain size—Neanderthals had larger brains than modern *Homo sapiens*. But, more importantly, human intelligence evolved through improvements in brain functioning, by a substantial increase in the number, complexity, and interconnectedness of neurons in the brain's connectionist neural network. Human brains have an estimated 10^{11} neurons, some of which may have as many as 10^5 synaptic connections. By comparison, chimpanzees, our closest living genetic relatives, have only one-fourth as many cortical neurons. This increase took place with lightning speed by evolutionary standards, between the last two great ice ages. The articulation of hominid brains into brainstem, cerebellum, cerebral hemispheres, and forebrain, together with the increased specialized function of its processing capabilities, are responsible for the ascent of mind from sentience to consciousness and self-consciousness.

But the evolutionary account of mind makes sense only as a refinement of sentience. If sentience already occurs, it is possible to see how natural selection might have transformed it into higher mental processes. But sentience is primitive thought, and merely sentient beings have primitive minds. If the scientific explanation of mind can only tell us that evolution has shaped one kind of mind into another, then it cannot explain the origin of mind itself. That is to say, it cannot explain the origin of sentience. We must now address the metaphysical, extrascientific problem of explaining how sentience can emerge in the most primitive minds from nonthinking precursors. How can intentionality ascend from matter and nonintentional living machinery?

EMERGENCE AND SUPERVENIENCE

In the ascent of mind there is a progression in the emergence or supervenience of sentience from nonsentient machine-like organisms and in the emergence, turning back the evolutionary clock, of living things from nonliving matter. Life itself is an emergent or supervenient property of material systems, one that does not obtain in all organizations of material substances.

If matter through random combination is properly organized in a brew of inorganic molecules, there may emerge, with the introduction of energy, organic molecules that are capable of purely mechanical replication—amino acid and polypeptide chains, including DNA and RNA. These are self-copying machines. They reproduce themselves, and, at least in terrestrial biology, are the basis of reproduction in all living things. Whether self-duplicating molecules are themselves alive is another topic. But science tells us they are but a short step from viruses and phages, as these are from bacteria, and bacteria from more complex mobile single-celled organisms, such as amoebas and paramecia. It is at some point a little further along this spectrum of the increasing complexity of life that the evolutionary race to the emergence of mind begins. We can describe within this chain of development an ascent of organisms with complex neural structures, some of which include sentient minds, and then conscious and self-conscious minds. But this ranking by stages does not explain the mind, no more than the automobile is explained by parading the wheel, cart, chariot, and so on through the lineage of automobiles. The explanation of mind as of the automobile requires more.

What more is needed and why? In explaining the emergence of life from nonliving matter, there is a mechanical account to be given of the transition from each form to the next. From a chemical soup that provides a ready supply of molecules, to the chance combinations that produce self-replicators, to the first living things, there is a material-mechanical account of the emergence of life from lifeless chemicals. The *vitalism* controversy was settled long ago in favor of material-mechanical theory, and scientists have abandoned the idea that there is an irreducible vital spark that animates living things. Life is a physical phenomenon explainable in physical terms. The explanation of the automobile by contrast requires information about the purposes and intentions of its designers, builders, and users.

The explanation of mind similarly requires a theory of its intrinsic intentionality, distinguishing it from purely behavioral-material-mechanical things. Without this, the sequence of organisms from the nonsentient to sentient through intermediate forms and higher-level conscious beings is incomplete as an account of the nature of mind and its evolutionary emergence. The reason is that while life is explainable in terms of purely material-mechanical processes, intentionality is not. Life is emergent in the materially-mechanically reducible sense that it possesses certain properties not possessed by the things from which it emerges. Mind, beginning with

sentience, is emergent in a behaviorally-materially-functionally ineliminable and irreducible sense. It has intentional properties that not only are
not possessed by the nonintentional entities from which it emerges, but
that cannot be explained or explained away in terms of nonintentional
properties.

Thus we have a formula for understanding the emergence of mind from
matter. To the scientific model of the emergence of life already known to
evolutionary biology, we add the metaphysical thesis of the primacy of the
intentional. The resulting emergent intentionalist property dualism implies
that in our evolutionary history through natural selection there has occurred
an instantiation of the behaviorally-materially-functionally ineliminable and
irreducible intentional properties that characterize the mind. The mind is a
relatively new and metaphysically unique addition to the world, an entity
whose qualities are not completely determined by its behavioral-material-
functional properties.

To speak of the dignity of mind is to celebrate thought, though not
specifically human thought. The mind begins with sentience, in creatures we
usually regard as lower than humans. But the intentionality of mind that
marks its emergence from nonpsychological living machinery in the evolution of life into intelligence, if ineliminable and irreducible, distinguishes
mind from all other things in the universe. The mind is dignified by its
instantiation of relations that arise from but cannot be fully explained in
terms of its behavioral-material-functional properties. If dignity in this sense
admits of degree, it follows that the higher the development of mind, from
sentience to consciousness and self-consciousness, the greater the dignity.
But mind, even in its most primitive condition, is worthy of respect as a
metaphysical anomaly, different from and somehow more special than nonthinking things. The opposite is supposed to be true according to eliminativism and reductivism. These theories entail that even the highest self-conscious thoughts are nothing but dispositions to behave, material
neurophysiological states, input-output correlations, or computation algorithms. Yet there is something revealing about the fact that eliminativists and
reductivists often try to smooth over these recognized indignities by assuring
us that there is still plenty to marvel at in contemplating the workings of the
mind. But by this they usually mean only the structural, mathematical, or
functional complexity of the brain's neural machinery.

The brain and nervous system constitutes a connectionist or parallel distributed processing network. This system embodies the mind's dynamic
mapping of unlimitedly many different data configurations. A condensed
version of this connectionist representation is found in the eye's retina,
which is itself an extension of the brain. The retina maps visual information
by changes in electrical potentials in scores of densely packed miniaturized
light-reactive neurons, the rods and cones. But neither the brain nor retina
neural system is a map unless it has meaning, which minimally requires the

intentionality of sensation. There is no tiny person or homunculus inside the eye or head that consciously experiences sensations. If this were the explanation, there would need to be another homunculus inside the eye or head of the first, and another inside its eye or head, and so on *ad infinitum.* There is no other way to explain the aboutness of electrochemical patterns in neural networks as representing objects and states of affairs, including the world seen in visual experience, except to conclude that certain neurophysiological brain and nervous system events are intrinsically intentional. The experience of objects as objects, the distinction of foreground from background, and the framing of relevant or suppression of irrelevant information that streams chaotically into sensory receptors from environmental electromagnetic ambience, even in the most rudimentary sentience, are *intended.*

To intend is something an individual subject or first person does, not something a third person can do for another. If we are the subjects of a scientific observation or experiment, we can tell the scientist that we intend or that we intend to do something. But for the hard scientist this utterance is merely verbal behavior to be correlated with other public occurrences, such as reinforcement schedule, neural state, or information flow and control. The experimenter has no direct access to what is intended, as Nagel's bat, Jackson's color scientist, and arguments about the indeterminacy of ostension and the failure of nonintentional references theories testify. This is not to say that no one outside the first-person perspective can know what another person intends. Such facts can be learned from truthful communication, and much can be correctly inferred from nonlinguistic behavior about an agent's intentions, including false and subconsciously or deliberately deceitful communication. But if we look from within the limits of traditional science for intentionality itself, the primacy of the intentional implies that it can only be found in first-person experience, in the phenomenology of the individual's mental life. It occurs as a source of knowledge impenetrable to the self-imposed public or third-person positivist limitations of hard psychological science, and cannot appear with all its essential properties on any cerebroscope.

THE PRIVACY OF EXPERIENCE

The direct accessibility of intention only from the intender's first-person point of view explains the privacy of experience or internality of thought. It is the other side of the epistemic barrier intentionality poses for third-person public hard psychological science. The common expression of this is the assertion that no one knows quite how I feel, nor do I know quite how anyone else feels. I never know exactly what the content of another person's experience is, or, often, what they intend, believe, or fear. This is another manifestation of the metaphysical dignity of mind.

The privacy of experience, like other kinds of privacy, implies a proprietary right. It is a thing to be respected by others, and it is the essential ingredient in our notion of moral respect for psychological beings, as contrasted with our treatment of plants, machine-like animals, and inanimate objects. The dignity of emergent sentience and consciousness is reflected as much in our pretheoretical ethical attitudes toward these kinds of beings as in our metaphysics of mind. We seem to recognize in their complex behavior something special in which we share, a quality that distinguishes creatures with minds from any other entities in the world. The moral dignity of mind in this way derives from and depends in part on its metaphysical dignity in first-person psychological privacy.

The experiential privacy of psychological states is often confused with other senses of privacy. Eliminativists and reductivists sometimes admit that experience is private. But they usually go on to specify an interpretation of privacy that is far from the intuitive meaning of the word. This result is predictable, because if any form of eliminativism or reductivism is true, then the mind cannot be a private Cartesian Theater, not even one that is merely intended. The mind must then be a public object open to inspection by any third-person with the right hard scientific theory and equipment. If thought is private in the sense of exclusive first-person accessibility, then neither eliminativism nor reductivism can possibly be true. It is for this reason that eliminativists and reductivists typically concede that experience is private only in the proprietary sense, by which its possession cannot be transferred from one owner to another. Yet this sense of privacy is also exemplified by nonmental, nonintentional phenomena. It is seen, for example, in the fact that, although I can cause you to sneeze, I cannot give you my sneeze. You cannot have the particular sneeze I have, because particular sneezes go one to a customer. But since a sneeze, ignoring its accompanying sensations and psychological side-effects, is a bodily matter, and since the body is public, we may conclude that, even if psychological experience is private in a watery proprietary sense, it is no more third-person-inaccessible than a sneeze. The eliminativist and reductivist make an empty concession when they grant that experience is private. For, as they understand the concept, privacy implies only that experience is nontransferable, not that its qualia and intentionality are essentially epistemically inaccessible to any but the first-person experiencer.

Another equivocal sense of the privacy of experience is found in Fodor's hypothesis of an innate private language of thought. Fodor, as we have seen, regards this as the best explanation of language acquisition in children. It assumes that their brains are preequipped with a language into which they (subconsciously) computationally translate the natural language of the speakers to which they are exposed. Thinking in a Fodor-type private language, especially prior to learning a public language, may provide another sense in which there could be private psychological experience. But it is unclear whether a child's innate propensity to learn language is itself a language or presupposes a language, and it is doubtful whether Fodor's innate private language provides a correct analysis of psychological privacy. Fodor is a functionalist, and he regards the innate "private" language of thought as coded in brain processes. According to this view, it should be possible in principle to locate the coded language in the brain's functional hierarchy and decode it into a public language. Here we face the same dilemma as in our criticism of innate brain languages in our discussion of the Chisholm-Sellars dispute about the relation between thought and language. If the translation from innate brain language to other languages can be performed, then Fodor's "private" language is not private in a deep or philosophically interesting sense. If Fodor's private language cannot be translated, then it is difficult to see how it could be used as a translation base by which children learn English, Russian, or Japanese. On Fodor's hypothesis, we should be able to proceed as we do in the case of machines, locating and decoding a computer's ROM, or Read Only Memory, machine language of 0s and 1s, in terms of which it "translates" compiler, assembly, and virtual machine languages. It is likely, therefore, that Fodor's private language of thought is private neither in the accessibility nor in the transferability sense, but in the less interesting sense of being innate, prewired into the brain, and not acquired through social interaction in a language community.

The primacy of the intentional makes it unnecessary anyway to postulate a Fodor-type private language of thought. Language is a derivatively intentional instrument for the expression of intrinsically intentional thought, and any other use of the word "language" is misleadingly metaphorical. We have seen the same kind of considerations tell against mentalistic artificial intelligence in the myth of pure syntax. This, as the comparison between machine language and Fodor's private language of thought indicates, is compatible with if not implied by Fodor's functionalism. Intentionality by the primacy thesis goes from thought to language, and not the other way around. To try to contrive intelligence artificially using a Fodor-type "private" machine language to encode thought in instructions for information flow and control is certain to fail, at least as an attempt to design and build a machine that creates its own intelligence. For it has the order of thought and language in intrinsic and derivative intentionality backward, and can only express and transform pre-existing intrinsically intentional thought in a mechanical format by mechanical means.

Critics of the privacy of experience sometimes stress the fact that the self does not always know what it intends. They like to quote artists caught up in the passion of aesthetic creativity who say that they do not know what they are doing or trying to do until they have done it, and sometimes not even then. Limited first-person access to intentions is also familiar enough outside of artistic endeavors. We can experience fear without knowing exactly what we fear. In an instructive ostensive metaphor, we sometimes say that we fear *something*, but cannot *point to* or *put our finger* on what it is. But if fear is intentional, then it must intend an object. The occurrence of unspecifiable fear, or fear with an unknown or unidentified object, appears to constitute an objection, if not to intentionalism generally, then at least to the generality of the intentionality of thought. It is similar to Rorty's objection concerning the alleged nonintentionality of sensation in his question, "What is the object of pain?" At the same time, the argument provides an objection to the privacy of experience, because it indicates that first-person subjects do not necessarily have privileged epistemic access to their own intentions. The criticism has this form:

1. Persons or selves do not always know what they themselves intend (sometimes they must infer it, or be told by others, or never come to know).
2. If persons or selves do not always know what they intend, then they are in no better epistemic position to understand their psychological states from first-person perspectives than are outsiders from a public third-person perspective.

---

3. Therefore, psychological experience, in the accessibility sense, is not essentially private.

(1,2)

The conclusion would be important, but the inference is deductively invalid. It follows from the assumptions (1) and (2) that persons or selves are not always in a better epistemic position to understand their own intentions from their first-person perspectives than are outsiders from a public third-person perspective. But this fact by itself does not imply the conclusion (3) that experience is not essentially private in the accessibility sense.

As an imaginary unity projected in self-consciousness, it is possible for the self to be uninformed about the intended objects of other thoughts in its self-constituting bundle. The mind might then fear something specific, without the self as the mind's spokesperson knowing or being able to say precisely what it fears. This possibility no more implies that the thought lacks an object than the fact that a press secretary has not been briefed about a committee's decision implies that the committee has not made up its collective mind. It is true that outsiders from a public third-person perspective can sometimes know as much or even more about another person's intentions or real intentions than the first-person intender. This is a presupposition of Freud's psychoanalytic theory and therapy. But the interpretation of these facts is complex. A third person has no better access and certainly much more limited access to the first person's psychological states, and draws inferences about them only through the intender's public expressions. Some psychological states by the nature of their content make it difficult for the self as first-person intender to recognize or articulate the states' intended object. This is especially true when a state like fear is accompanied by confusion, anxiety, or excitement, or generally when its emotional content interferes with reason and epistemic reflection. If, under these circumstances, the intended self as spokesperson for the committee of mind is not informed about the intended object of a thought, then it may be unable even to identify the object inferentially as effectively as an outsider.

This argument does not refute the intentionality of thought. The primacy of the intentional implies that thought need not be articulated in order to intend an object. Intended objects in the thought of animals and infants—who are sentient and conscious but not self-conscious, who are pre- or non-linguistic, and who are not in possession of language or an intended self to serve as spokesperson for their intentions—are always unarticulated. Yet even when the object of thought is obscured for self-conscious language users like the passionate artist, the first-person is still in a better position than any third person to articulate the content or qualia of thought. The subject alone lives through, privately experiences, and knows the thought content immediately and noninferentially. The privacy of experience implies that intention is directly accessible only to the first-person subject, not that the intended self or first-person subject always has access to the intended objects of all the mind's thoughts.

The primacy of the intentional implies the privacy of psychological experience. If the mind's intentionality is inaccessible to the hard psychological sciences, then thought is essentially nonpublic, or private in the first person accessibility sense. But what is the first person if there is no centralized Cartesian ego? The answer, according to the theory developed here, is that the first person or self is a fictional intended object projected onto a bundling of thoughts by reflexive self-constituting self-consciousness. We can say that the first person is the source of nonlinguistic representation in self-conscious pre- or nonlinguistic minds. Or, in the case of language-using minds, we can say that the first person is delegated as the spokesperson for and internal narrator of the mind's experience, the only articulate authoritative source of its qualia and intentions.

WITTGENSTEIN'S PRIVATE LANGUAGE ARGUMENT

We must now examine a famous argument that threatens to undermine the privacy of thought. Ludwig Wittgenstein, in the *Philosophical Investigations* (1968), offers a series of interwoven remarks about the privacy of sensation and the impossibility of a private sensation language. If the argument is correct, it may also refute the privacy of experience, the existence of private mental objects, the primacy of the intentional, and intentionalist property dualism, casting doubt finally on the dignity of mind.

Wittgenstein's private language argument involves a thought experiment. We are to imagine a diarist using a *private sensation language* to record occurrences of private experiences. The diarist is supposed to take note of recurrent sensations in a symbolism that cannot be translated or decoded into a public language, but that he alone can understand. Wittgenstein argues that, despite appearances, the conceptual requirements of private sensation diary keeping cannot be satisfied. From this he concludes that there cannot be a private sensations diary written in a private sensation language. Wittgenstein's argument in turn is usually thought to lend philosophical support to hard scientific as opposed to intentionalist kinds of psychology. It is believed in particular to uphold Ryle's logical behaviorism, which may have been inspired by Wittgenstein's philosophy. Wittgenstein's own position is more complex than Ryle's, as he indicates in *Philosophical Investigations* §307, where he seems to deny being a behaviorist. This denial is in line with his apparent refusal in §128 to adopt any positive philosophical thesis. But, because of the private language argument and its apparent negative consequences for private languages and private mental objects, Wittgenstein is standardly regarded as favoring some sort of third-person eliminative or reductive theory of mind.

For Wittgenstein, to name a pain as a particular object requires *criteria of correctness*. Criteria of correctness are needed to determine when the same object is reidentified and named by the same name on different occasions. The criteria, according to Wittgenstein, must be strong enough to distinguish instances in which the rule always to use the same name for the same object is actually followed, from those in which the name user merely believes the rule is being followed. The criteria requirement is implied by the *philosophical grammar* of "naming." This is the set of conceptual rules governing word usage in the *language game* of naming particulars. Wittgenstein concludes that, in the nature of the case, criteria of correctness obtain only in the naming of public objects, like my body or the Eiffel Tower. For these, there is a way of deciding whether the same name is used on different occasions to refer to the same object. I can distinguish actually following the rule from merely believing that I am following it, because there are criteria by which in principle at least I can check up on the object to make sure it is the same each time I refer to it by name. But in the case of private sensations, such checking cannot be done. There is no test that is independent of my beliefs by which I can decide whether I am actually following the rule always to use the same name for the same pain, or merely believe that I am doing so. If I am a private sensation diarist, then I have no reliable way to confirm that I have correctly reidentified the very same recurring sensation, or mistaken it for a similar but strictly different one. In the latter case, I will not have followed the "Same pain, same name" sensation particulars naming rule. I will merely believe that I am following it, because I merely believe that the same sensation has recurred. As a private name user, I can only rely on memory and impression. But these are not enough to distinguish actually following the naming rule from merely believing that I am following it. If criteria of correctness are required but unavailable for naming particular private sensations, then there cannot be names for private sensations, and hence there can be no private sensation language.

Wittgenstein makes use of some of the most colorful and memorable images in all of his philosophical writing to describe the logical predicament of the private sensation diarist. These have entered into the philosophical vocabulary and exerted an unparalleled influence on contemporary thinking about the relation between language and mind. Wittgenstein says that the attempt to verify that the same sensation is being referred to by the same name on different occasions is "as if someone were to buy several copies of the morning paper to assure himself that what it said was true" (§265). Elsewhere, Wittgenstein refers to the private naming of sensations as like a language game involving a beetle in a box, in which box holders can examine only their own beetles, and not another's.

Here it would be quite possible for everyone to have something quite different in his box. One might even imagine such a thing constantly changing.—But suppose the word "beetle" had a use in these people's languages?—If so it would not be used as the name of a thing. The thing in the box has no place in the language-game at all; not even as a something: For the box might even be empty.—No, one can "divide through" by the thing in the box; it cancels out, whatever it is. That is to say: if we construe the grammar of the expression of sensation on the model of "object and designation" the object drops out of consideration as irrelevant. (§293)

From the argument that there can be no names for private sensations, and therefore no private sensation language, some commentators have concluded that therefore there are also no private sensations (an eliminativist reading). Others claim that Wittgenstein's arguments do not merely reveal the limitations of language in naming sensations, but prove that, although there are sensations, they are essentially public, as logical behaviorism and other extensionalist theories of mind presuppose (reductivism). These accounts also contradict the primacy of the intentional if, as we have seen, primacy implies privacy.

Armstrong (1968), in explaining the historical precedents for his reductive materialism-cum-logical-behaviorism, offers this now standard interpretation of Wittgenstein's remarks about the need for criteria of correctness. He maintains that the private language argument supports logical or analytical behaviorism:

Gilbert Ryle's book *The Concept of Mind* seems to be a defence of Analytical Behaviourism. I think the same is true of Wittgenstein's *Philosophical Investigations*, although this interpretation is hotly denied by many disciples. The problem of interpreting Wittgenstein's book may perhaps be reduced to the problem of interpreting a single sentence:
580. An "inner process" stands in need of outward criteria.
When Wittgenstein speaks of 'outward criteria' he means bodily behaviour.... But there is one difficulty in interpreting Wittgenstein and Ryle as Behaviourists. Both

writers deny that they hold this doctrine! I think, however, that the only reason that these philosophers denied that they were Behaviourists was that they took Behaviourism to be the doctrine that there are no such things as minds. Since they did not want to deny the existence of minds, but simply wanted to give an account of the mind in terms of behaviour, they denied that they were Behaviourists. (pp. 54–55)

Yet the fact that Wittgenstein denies being a behaviorist should give us pause in attributing to him any positive reductivist theory of mind. If we are to engage in the risky business of comparing single sentences from Wittgenstein's complex text with that chosen by Armstrong, we might refer to §248, in which Wittgenstein indicates that the privacy of sensation is an analytic truism or redundancy:

248. The proposition "Sensations are private" is comparable to: "One plays patience [the card game of solitaire] by oneself."

Contrary to standard interpretations, Wittgenstein does not deny that sensation is private. Nor does he deny that particular sensations are privately accessible experiences. His conclusion is only that private sensations cannot be named as particulars.

Those who interpret Wittgenstein's remarks on private language as disproving the privacy of thought seem to do so on the basis of an argument like this:

1. If thought is private, then there is a private language of thought.
2. But there is no private language of thought.
_____

3. Thought is not private.   (1,2)

But while this argument is deductively valid, its assumptions are not easily defended. There is nothing in Wittgenstein's discussion to establish the strong claim in assumption (1) that thought is private only if there is a private language of thought. The private language argument at most shows that particular private sensations cannot be named in a private sensation language. The second assumption, in (2) moreover, seems too general. Wittgenstein's argument does not imply that sensation is public, nor that private sensations cannot be referred to generally or collectively in a private sensation language. They could be designated by generic names for types or kinds of sensations in a language that does not try to name particular private sensations. Wittgenstein's diarist could have the collective name "S," as we have the categories "pain," "shooting pain," "stabbing pain," and the like, for private sensations of a certain kind.

When Wittgenstein says, in §580, which Armstrong quotes, that inner processes stand in need of outward criteria, he undoubtedly means that they need such criteria in order to be named as particulars, not in order to be explained. This is obvious when it is recalled that the scientific explanation of mental occurrences, which Wittgenstein does not try to describe, is typically concerned with general principles, in which sensations and other psychological events are classed together as kinds or types regularly possessing certain properties, rather than designated as particulars. If this interpretation is correct, then Wittgenstein more properly calls attention to a peculiarity of the limitations of the attempt to name private sensations, and not to the public nature of sensation or nonexistence of private sensations. Wittgenstein's point is really about language and the limitations of language rather than the mind. If there is a way to get from one set of conclusions to the other, Wittgenstein at least does not try to show the way.

SOLIPSISM AND KNOWLEDGE OF OTHER MINDS

If Wittgenstein's private language argument had disproved the privacy of thought, it would have refuted *solipsism,* or skepticism about the existence of other minds. There are *epistemic* and *ontic solipsisms.* Epistemic solipsism ranges from doubt about the possibility of proving that there are other minds to skepticism about the existence of other minds. Ontic solipsism by contrast is the outright denial that other minds exist. The most extreme case is that in which a mind believes itself to be utterly alone in the universe, without another mind as companion.

The privacy of experience is a necessary but not sufficient condition of solipsism. If experience is private, then minds have no way of knowing or knowing with certainty that there are other minds. The mind in that case has direct access only to its own private experiences, and can judge only inferentially and at risk of error that other beings have comparable internal or private mental experiences. If Wittgenstein's private language argument is interpreted as proving that experience is not private because there is no private language of experience, then there is no private experience to serve as an epistemically privileged standpoint from which to raise skeptical doubts about the existence of other minds. If the moral of Wittgenstein's private language argument is that only public third-person psychology can provide an adequate account of psychological phenomena in the hard psychological sciences, then there is no ground for denying that there are other minds. In that case, there is no more to another body's having a mind than its behaving or being disposed to behave in certain ways, or possessing the appropriate neurophysiological or functional properties. An advantage of adopting a third-person public perspective over and against the privacy of first-person experience, therefore, is that it provides an easy if not entirely satisfying solution to ancient skepticisms about the existence of other minds. But Wittgenstein himself says that to claim that sensation is private is like saying that one plays solitaire by óneself, and we have seen that the private language argument does not provide a solid basis even for disproving the privacy of experience, let alone the possibility of privately intended objects.

The idea that the mind may be alone in the universe is the frightening theme of macabre existentialist novels. The mind must be highly subconsciously inventive according to solipsism, because it must invent for itself the appearance of intelligence in other similar beings or find itself among robots or similar beings that look to be intelligent and pass the informal Turing Test well enough but are literally mindless. Yet we need not despair if Wittgenstein's private language argument does not adequately lay solipsistic skepticisms to rest. There is a satisfactory way to justify our pretheoretical belief in the existence of other minds that fits very naturally with the kind of evidence we ordinarily use to conclude, for example, that we are not dreaming when we are awake and to settle with something less than absolute certainty other kinds of skeptical doubts. By an *argument from analogy*, we can judge that there are probably other minds. The argument appeals to evidence of intelligent verbal and related behavior. It is in effect an informal application of the Turing Test. This remains the best method of knowing, without absolute certainty, that there are other minds, and of distinguishing minds from things including machines that merely appear to be minds. We reason that if we behave in certain ways when we are having certain private psychological experiences, then other beings who are behaving in the same way are also probably having a similar kind of private internal psychological experience.

It is sometimes said that this is a weak inductive proof. The inference is based on the single example of the mind's direct acquaintance with its own private mental states. The privacy of experience entails that a mind can never directly know the lived-through thought content of another mind. But in most inductive inferences, such as judging the probable color of swans based on the observation of a limited population sample, it is unsound to conclude that all swans are white from seeing a single white swan, or to judge that all swans are black from seeing a single Australian black swan. Yet there are many instances in which valid inductive inferences are drawn from single, sometimes unique and unrepeatable, instances. The child who burns her finger on a candle flame correctly judges from a single experience that all such objects are dangerous and to be avoided, that burning candles and flames generally cause pain.

Of course, we might be skeptical about the validity of this inference, too. How do we know that a candle flame will always cause pain by burning? Perhaps this belief is true only of the one and only candle flame that is touched, other candle flames may tickle or feel cool and pleasant to the skin. Yet there is a difference between relying on a single case for induction in judging the color of swans and judging that all flames burn or that all intelligent behavior springs from the activity of mind, and that there exist other minds. The difference is not hard and fast, and therefore analogically infer-ential knowledge of flames and other minds cannot be perfectly or absolutely certain. It depends on a preliminary inductively justified distinction between the kinds of properties that are likely to be essential and those that are merely accidental to a thing. This is the difference between properties without which a thing could not exist or continue to exist and properties that have no impli-cations for its existence or nonexistence. The color of a bird's plumage, from our experience of other birds and other kinds of things, is accidental. The bird would not cease to exist if had some other color, say, through a change of diet, turning from white to pink as flamingos do. But other kinds of things in our experience, like the relation of a flame's ability to produce warmth at a certain distance and then heat indistinguishable from pain on contact, is at least defeasibly, or reasonably but less than certainly, inductively judged to be an essential property of flames. If this argument is correct, then one experi-ence should suffice to indicate something about the kind of thing a flame is and what sensations it is most probably though not infallibly going to pro-duce whenever and wherever it is encountered. If inference about the exis-tence of other minds belongs to this second category, then it is the kind of judgment in which it is determined on the basis of experience that probably though not infallibly there is something essential about the connection of certain kinds of external intelligent behavior with the mind's internal life and private experience. If a single and unrepeated instance suffices for valid inductive judgments, then the mind can know with less than absolute or per-fect certainty by analogy from first-person experience that solipsism is false.

This conclusion raises and answers an interesting question about the detection of mind using the Gödel sentence Turing Test criterion. Mind is said to exist from the emergence of sentience, so that even insects and lesser creatures may have rudimentary minds and crude intelligences. But obvious-ly, they cannot pass the Turing Test. The point of the Gödel sentence Turing Test, however, is to provide an inductive third-person behavioral standard of a system's understanding the meaning of sentences. It is not sup-posed to provide a necessary condition for the possession of mind. There is a continuum of inductive data, from strong to weak, for the existence of other minds, revealed to third-person observation beyond the first-person privacy of thought. At one end of the scale, there is evidence about the exis-tence of minds like ours, with linguistic abilities disclosed by passing the Turing Test, and, in extreme cases of doubt, the Gödel sentence Turing Test. This data provides the strongest and most definite inductive proof for the existence of another mind. After this point, evidence for the existence of other minds becomes progressively weaker. It blurs considerably at distinc-tions between types within the three major categories of ascent, from living machines to sentients, sentients to conscious minds, and conscious to self-conscious minds. The transitions are indicated by difficulties in classifying animals unambiguously in these groups from our unavoidable third-person perspective. Asking Nagel's question, in effect, we try to guess, "What is it like to be a flea?" "What is it like to be a bat?" "What is it like to be a Thomas Nagel?"

The distinction between minds and machines is more straightforward, because artificial intelligence systems are usually designed to replicate mind by simulating human linguistic abilities, and as such are fair game for the Gödel sentence Turing Test. When we peer into a machine's black box to inspect its operations, we see that rule-structured systems inevitably involve derivatively intentional machine instructions. But the primacy of the intentional entails that intrinsic intentionality cannot be obtained from derivatively intentional systems considered only as such. Connectionist machines inherit the philosophical limitations of rule-structured systems. So, machines generally, considered only as such, do not have minds.

Other animals, to whom we are biologically closely related, are reasonably regarded as having minds, by a defeasible inductive generalization. We have minds; we are similar to apes and other higher mammals; so, probably, apes and higher mammals also have minds. Apes and higher mammals have minds; they are similar to birds; so, probably, birds also have minds. And so on, down the branching phylogenetic ladder, attributing mind to lower animals by transitive analogy with ever-decreasing inductive plausibility. What is the cutoff point between minds and nonminds? It is hard to say. But possession of neurons may be the most important factor. Systems that display overt behavior associated analogically with that of our, paradigm, minds, offer less strong but still compelling inductive evidence of having minds. In the absence of good reasons to the contrary, many nonhuman animals are also probably sentient, and, in some cases, nonlinguistically conscious or even self-conscious.

An interesting middle case concerns the construction of connectionist systems built by neuron-by-neuron functional replacement or equivalent bottom-up design of brain counterparts. Although it seems feasible to manufacture a nonliving functional brain replica, there may be engineering constraints and even unforeseen logical and conceptual problems that would make this task impossible. The same painful lesson has been learned time and again in artificial intelligence research. Solutions that look promising on paper have often failed miserably in application, sending the designer back to the drawing board. But if we suppose for the sake of argument that such a system could be built, what are we to say about it? The most plausible reaction may be that brain replicas are not true machines. Instead, they are nonnatural minds, embodied, like human and other minds, in information networks that give rise to intrinsic intentionality. A brain replica of the imagined kind would exemplify the cultural as opposed to the evolutionary emergence of mind, in a mind-made nonbiological structure. The best inductive evidence for the emergence of a nonlinguistic nonnatural replica mind would be, first, its passing the Gödel sentence Turing Test and, second, its constructive similarity to other systems, the most complex of which are paradigm natural language-using minds capable of passing the Gödel sentence Turing Test. But the conceivability of brain replicas does not contradict the thesis that machines considered only as such are not and do not have minds, for brain replicas by hypothesis are not machines to be considered only as such.

What if we simply assumed that there are other minds? It is instructive to consider how different the philosophy of mind would appear if we began with this premise. If there are other minds, then, since I do not directly experience their thoughts, thought must be private. If thought is private, then the hard third-person psychological sciences are inadequate to provide a complete explanation of the first-person concept of mind. From this reasoning it follows that mind and body are not identical, that some sort of duality obtains, at least among their properties. We have approached our subject in the opposite direction, and in a way this book can be considered an investigation of the philosophical implications of not simply assuming that there are other minds.

In either case, by now we would have arrived at the same point. The mind-body distinction and privacy of thought implied by emergent intentionalist property dualism and the primacy of the intentional leads us to consider the consequences of the theory for the concepts of thought, action, and passion.

AGENT CAUSATION

The moral dignity of mind is related to its metaphysical dignity. It derives in large part from its capacity for action and the freedom of action. To understand the dignity of mind from an intentionalist perspective requires an appreciation of the concept of action, and in particular of the distinction between *basic* and *nonbasic actions.*

Basic actions are those which an agent is able to do directly, without doing another thing. A common example is raising one's arm. This is not simply a movement of the arm in space, for movement can occur if someone attaches a wire and pulley to it and hoists it up in the air, or, more subtly and in the spirit of science fiction scenarios, if electrodes are planted in the muscles and arm movement is controlled by radio signals like a living puppet.

There is a difference, in other words, in *raising* one's arm as an intended action, and its *rising* or *being raised.* When an arm is raised, its movement can be used to do other things. It can flip a light switch, signal to a friend, and so on. There are likely to be unintended as well as intended consequences of such actions. Not all intentions to act are certain to be fulfilled, including the most basic, if we are paralyzed or otherwise prevented from moving.

Flipping a light switch or signaling to a friend are also actions we can (ordinarily) perform, but they are nonbasic actions that we do by doing something else. We accomplish them by doing something more basic, in particular, typically, by raising or moving an arm. But there seems to be nothing else we do in order to raise an arm. It is an unmediated action, which we do without doing anything else.

The distinction between raising an arm and having it rise or raised for one, the difference between acting and undergoing body movement, already provides a sense of the dignity of mind attributable to the intentionality of thought. Where there is action, there is an intrinsic intending of an objective or state of affairs, even if it is only a basic body action or mental act. This movement is different, if our earlier arguments have been correct, from a machine's movement, which, lacking intrinsic intentionality, is literally incapable of action. Machines, including living machines that have not ascended to the psychology of sentience, are not agents and do not perform actions in the true sense of the word. At most they execute movements mechanically, even if these are feedback adjustable in response to changing circumstances.

Agents are sometimes said to be initiators of causal chains and not merely physical systems in which preexisting causal chains play themselves out. If this assertion is true, then, according to a theory originating with Aristotle and extended by Chisholm (1966), Richard Taylor (1966), and others, there are two kinds of causation, *event causation* and *agent causation.* Event causation always goes from event to event. Previous events produce other events by mechanical forces according to natural laws. Agent causation by contrast is a causal chain that begins with an agent intending an objective or purpose in a basic mental act or act of thought. The sequence goes from agent to the basic mental act as a first event in the chain, to subsequent events, mental and physical, resulting usually in body movements and related nonbasic actions. Here causation is not always event-event, but agent-event related.

Minds are capable of agent causation; nonminds are passively subject only to the vicissitudes of event causation. Were it not for agency, minds and nonminds alike would at most be conduits through which causes and effects are channeled by virtue of their behavioral-material-functional properties as continuing links in an ongoing event-causal chain. But if agents in thought are able agent-causally to initiate event causation sequences, then the mind is not merely pushed about even at the microneurophysiological level by antecedent event causation. The intentionality of agent causation makes the mind a user of things, rather than a mere object of use. The mind in a morally significant sense is free.

The mind in its intrinsically intentional thought is the agent by which agent causation is initiated. For this conclusion to hold, action must always be intended. But is it true that action is always intentional?

INTENTIONALITY AND INTENTION IN ACTION

It is a cornerstone of Aristotle's psychology to distinguish between active and passive experience. This distinction marks the difference between what the mind does and what is done or happens to it, or how it acts versus what it suffers.

That sentient beings are capable of suffering places them within the realm of moral consideration for some ethical philosophers. It means that they have interests and an internal psychological existence. They have a mental life like yours and mine that can be made better or worse for them by the actions of others. They are not mere living machines for which good or bad is spoken of metaphorically, as when we say it is good for an engine to be lubricated. The potential for suffering already qualifies the most primitive sentient beings to share in the moral as well as the metaphysical dignity of mind.

Action, acting or doing, is widely recognized as intentional. But intending to act or intending to do something must be distinguished from the semantic intentionality or object-directedness of thought. The two concepts are similar and interrelated, but not exactly the same. When I intend to act, I am semantically directed toward the state of affairs I want to bring about as a result of my action. To intend or have the intention to do something is to intend the state of affairs at which the action aims, which it takes as its purpose or goal. When I semantically intend an object, even if, in the ordinary sense, I do not intend to do anything about it, my intending the object is accomplished by a mental act or act of thought, which has as its one aim, purpose, or goal, to be about, pick out, designate, or refer to just that object. Thus, to act is to intend (a particular kind of object), and to intend is to act (in a particular way).

It follows that to act in the ordinary body movement sense is also to perform a mental act. To act is first to think. Whatever cannot think cannot act. It also follows that to intend is to intend. This is not very informative. But according to the primacy of the intentional, intentionality cannot be theoretically eliminated or explanatorily reduced in terms of nonintentional concepts. There is no escaping this tautology at the most fundamental level of intentionalist theory.

What role does intentionality play in action? It sometimes happens, as an unnecessary accompaniment of acts of will, that the intended self fixes its resolve on a course of behavior, or intends to do something self-consciously in a kind of internal declaration of purpose. Such episodes are usually reserved as mental announcements of great goals or as the outcome of an especially difficult decision about what to do. They may serve the useful purpose of strengthening the self's commitment to pursue a plan of action despite obstacles ("I *will* search for the western sea route to India!"), or to wrestle with what the Greeks called *akrasia*, or weakness of will ("This time, no matter what, *I shall resist* the chocolate cake!"). But, clearly, these inner speech acts are not essential in order to act, nor to intend to act or act intentionally. When you type at a keyboard or play the guitar, you perform many actions with each finger movement. But once the skill is mastered, the self seldom if ever declares its intentions to undertake each and every component motion in what Sellars would call a thought modeled on inner speech. ("Now I *will* strike the *i* key!" "Now, without fail, I *shall* play an Fmin^7 chord!") These things do not happen, at least not after the relevant technique has been internalized. Nor if it did happen would it be likely be a good thing, for it would make simple ordinary actions cumbersome if not impossible, as Zen practitioners of No-mind in the arts like to emphasize.

These facts are sometimes offered by anti-intentionalists as proof that action is not intentional. But the conclusion does not follow if the mind rather than the intended self is the intentional source of action. If the self as spokesperson for the mind is not always apprised of the mind's actions or its intended objects of action, the purposes it has, or the states of affairs it is trying to bring about, then action can be intentional without the self's being able to articulate the mind's intentions. As we saw in the case of the passionate distracted artist caught up in the creative act, the mind's intentions need not be occurrent and articulable, but can often be implicit and dispositional.

Here are two extreme examples to indicate the value of intention in action. Consider, on the one hand, the explorations of Francisco Vásquez de Coronado, searching in the New World for the Seven Cities of Cibola (Castañeda, 1990), and, on the other, the peculiar fellow in G.E.M. Anscombe's monograph *Intention* (1963) who, for no apparent reason, and for no reason he can give, takes all of the books with green covers from his house and lays them out like tiles on the roof.

We begin with Coronado's actions. How are we to understand what he did? At a certain level of description, we can say that his actions consisted of trekking around what is today Arizona and New Mexico, searching for the gold of Cibola. There is a hierarchy of intended objectives in these actions, one purpose contributing to the satisfaction of another. Sometimes the hierarchy has many stages, and sometimes it has but a single purpose or objective. Coronado intends goals and goals beyond goals in a kind of extended action strategy. He wants to find soldiers, horses, and provisions, *in order to* begin the march into Zuni territory; he wants to begin the march *in order to* find Cibola; he wants to find Cibola *in order to* loot its treasures, which in the end do not exist; he wants to loot the treasures of Cibola *in order to* please the King of Spain; *in order to* win fame and fortune; and so on. If Aristotle in the *Nicomachean Ethics* is right about the chain of practical reasons that guide our actions, then ultimately Coronado wants to do these things in order to achieve happiness. Aristotle believes that happiness lies at the end of every practical inference, and that beyond it there is no further explanation or action goal to be given. Nevertheless, as in Coronado's actions, there can be a very elaborate hierarchy and branching network of intentions to act, without reference to which an agent's actions cannot be fully explained.

Now, back to the man covering his roof with green books. This case is particularly interesting from the standpoint of understanding the role of intention in action, because it seems to be an action done without purpose. Does this apparent purposelessness mean that action is not always intended or intentional, or that the theory of action need not be intentional in the strong sense of implying the primacy and privacy of the intentional? What about the intentionality, if any, of his actions? He cannot say why he takes the books and puts them on the roof. He cannot even answer that he just wants to see what they would look like up there. It is possible that his actions are done from a deeper purpose that the rest of his mind keeps hidden from him, or from his intended self. Perhaps he has motives that can be uncovered by psychoanalysis. After a series of probing but apparently nonchalant questions on the psychiatrist's couch, he suddenly remembers his mother reading a green-covered Bible, and realizes that subconsciously he wants to attract her attention many years after her death from an imagined location in heaven. Or, he may want to fulfill a phallic flight fantasy and is sublimating his real desire, of which he is publicly ashamed, by preparing a symbolic green launchpad.

Amateur psychoanalytic speculations aside, the roofer appears to have no purpose at all. Does that mean that he acts without intention? He places green books on the roof. But he does not do it *in order to* do anything else, not even to be happy or relieve a vague longing satisfied by the action. Yet he acts intentionally, in that, although his goal or intention hierarchy does not extend beyond the acts he performs, he intentionally selects green-covered books, takes them onto the roof, and spreads them about. He intends to do these things, even if he intends to do them for no further reason. There is the greatest difference between his actions and the mere body motions that might result from a chance series of reflex muscle tics and spasms, or diabolical marionette-like remote control, even if the two categories of events are behaviorally indistinguishable from a third-person observational perspective.

We can say that the person acts intentionally in that he intends to select green books, and then remove them from the house, and then take them onto the roof, and then spread them about. He just does not know why he is doing these things in terms of any further goal in the intentional hierarchy. Actions need not belong to any more elaborate scheme of purposes than those done for the sake of achieving a single particular body movement. I act intentionally when I stretch my fingers, not to test them, relieve an ache, or for the pleasure it may afford, but just for the sake of doing it. This is also action, and it is also intentional. It has a limited "for the sake of which" it is done. But it does not require my knowledge or mental verbalization of the intention. This assertion is true again because of the primacy of the intentional, since otherwise it would be impossible for pre- and nonlinguistic humans and nonhuman animals to act.

FREEDOM OF ACTION, PURPOSE, AND THE WILL

The freedom of will begins with the mind's intending an objective or state of affairs. Its purpose in what it wills to do need not be articulated and need involve nothing other than the unspoken desire to wiggle a finger for no other reason than to wiggle it.

This freedom is enjoyed even by the lowliest sentient creatures in the animal kingdom. They are capable of action, but they act so predictably, with such a narrow range of uninteresting consequences from the standpoint of human concerns, that they are often said not to be free. Yet freedom, as we know from personal experience, is a matter of degree. The primacy of the intentional, and the intentionality of thought, even among nonhuman animals, guarantees that if an animal acts, it does so by thought, by intending an objective or state of affairs to be brought about. Agents by acts of will initiate causal chains that cannot be completely reduced to event causation antecedents, because they begin with the agent rather than with an event. The acts and agent are in that sense and to that extent free.

The agent causation model provides a solution to a dilemma that threatens other theories of the mind's freedom of action and will. It is sometimes said that persons are not responsible for what they do regardless of whether their actions are caused or uncaused. They are not responsible if their actions are caused, because in that case they could not have done otherwise. But nor are they responsible if their actions are uncaused, since then they did not cause them to occur. But on the agent causation model, actions are not uncaused. They are agent-caused, by an agent, the mind, usually with or through the knowledge of the intended self. The mind is not event-causally determined in its decisions and actions on this theory, but neither need it be chaotic. Although it is uncaused and causally undetermined, the mind can be guided, constrained, and even strongly influenced by reason and emotion in its decision making, often but not always or necessarily self-consciously.

Moral responsibility presupposes free action, but not conversely. The *contracausal freedom* of agents is justified by the fact that if basic action is intentional, then, by the primacy of the intentional, basic action cannot be fully eliminatively or reductively explained in terms of event causation. We are inclined to extend the moral dignity of full moral responsibility only to humans who exhibit certain kinds of knowledge and self-control. It is customary in ethical philosophy to regard normal adult humans as responsible for most of what they do and some of what they do not do. This category includes their basic and nonbasic actions, as well as most of the immediate and some of the remote consequences of these. The standard theory is that in order to be morally responsible for actions, agents must be free in the sense of being such that they could have done otherwise, or acted differently than they do. Being able to do otherwise has many philosophical interpretations, giving rise to different theories and different senses of freedom. But for present purposes, in line with the analysis that has been developed here, freedom in the sense of being able to do otherwise means that the agent is not causally determined, not constrained to act in a certain way by sufficient event-causal antecedents. Action is free when agents initiate causal chains because their causally free thought intrinsically intends an objective or purpose.

The freedom to act that animals seem to enjoy need not be regarded as sufficient to confer on them moral responsibility. Even if animals are rudimentarily self-conscious agents, they are not necessarily capable of the right sort of self-conscious agency with the right sort of control over what they do to make them moral agents. We do not hold them morally responsible, perhaps because they lack a sufficiently developed concept of the difference between right and wrong, a standard also applied in the case of some human agents.

If action is not free, or if there is no such thing as action or agency, then moral responsibility must be reductively explained or eliminatively explained away. To do so, it is necessary to argue implausibly that no one is morally responsible, that moral responsibility does not require action or agency, that action and agency do not require the ability to do otherwise, or that the ability to do otherwise does not require contracausal freedom. But there is no satisfying sense of moral responsibility that is compatible with the causal necessity or complete determination of an agent's actions.

There are efforts in the history of philosophy to reconcile causal determinism with various diluted senses of freedom and moral responsibility. But in the end they have no satisfactory answer to the objection that if agents are causally determined to do what they do, and cannot do otherwise, then a person who commits murder is no more free or morally responsible for being involved in the events as they are played out in the world than a rock is free or morally responsible for rolling downhill. This concept, to speak plainly, lacks dignity. But if the causally deterministic event causation account of human "agency" is true, then we shall simply have to live without this kind of metaphysical or moral dignity. We must not bend the truth to suit preconceived moral attitudes if they do not stand up to philosophical scrutiny. Agents are either contracausally free and morally responsible, or they are not. But the intrinsic intentionality of thought and the derivative intentionality of action—the primacy of the intentional, including its causal ineliminability and irreducibility—preserves our intuitions about what is different and unique about the mind in the material-mechanical universe. The mind's freedom, its contracausal ability to do otherwise, explains the difference mind makes in the world, its expression in action, and the novelty, design, culture, and creativity for which it is responsible.

The agent-causal efficacy of thought in action may finally have scientifically testable consequences. Were it not for the agent causation of mind, neural events would be completely causally determined, and hence fully predictable. This is certainly the working hypothesis of eliminativists and reductivists, and probably of most brain scientists, regardless of their ontological commitments. But if the mind can agent-initiate causal chains, then, in doing so, it must bring about neurophysiological events that would not have occurred in the absence of those particular freely active thoughts or event-uncaused contracausal mental acts. If the brain's neurophysiology is capable of being monitored in sufficiently fine detail, disregarding the indeterminacies of microphysical systems described by quantum physics, then it should be possible to test our account of contracausally free agent causation.

The procedure would be to measure all relevant neural states, predict the subsequent neurophysiological states to occur in a limited future time thereafter, and then check to see whether unpredicted contraindicated neurophysiological events occur as a result of the subject's deliberate efforts to produce free mental or basic bodily acts. If agent causation is true and eliminativism or reductivism false, then there will be discrepancies between the neurophysiological events predicted by the determinist hypothesis and those that obtain in the agent's brain, and otherwise not. The empirical confirmation of agent causation would at the same time provide a decisive disproof of the objection that the mind's intentional properties are merely epiphenomenal. It would verify intentionalist property dualism and the metaphysical dignity of mind.

HELMHOLTZ'S CRITIQUE OF AGENT CAUSATION

It might be objected that the mind's agent-caused contracausally free acts contradict the laws of physics. Then there would be no point in performing the experiment. But this objection does not hold up, at least according to property dualism.

We can see the limitations of this criticism in a proof against mind-body dualism based on Hermann Ludwig von Helmholtz's essays, "On the

Conservation of Force" (1847) and "The Application of the Law of the Conservation of Force to Organic Nature" (1861). Helmholtz suggests that if mind and body are distinct, then the mind's activity in the physical universe introduces more energy into its causally closed system than would otherwise obtain. The effect would be to produce something from nothing. But such an occurrence would violate the law of the conservation of energy. Helmholtz appears to reason in this way:

1. The physical universe is a closed system in which energy is conserved.
2. If mind $\neq$ body, then the mind's free activity produces new energy that does not already exist in the physical universe.
3. If the mind's free activity produces energy that does not already exist in the physical universe, then the physical universe is not a closed system in which energy is conserved; there is more energy later than earlier in the universe as a result of the mind's free activity.

---

4. Therefore, mind = body.   (1,2,3)

The objection is interesting, but it contains a fatal flaw. Assumption (1) is no longer taken for granted by physicists, partly because of quantum abnormalities and what is called the Big Bang singularity in scientific cosmology. But even if we allow Helmholtz this proposition for the sake of argument, assumption (2) is easily shown to be false.

The mind is not identical to the body, according to property dualism, because the mind has behaviorally-materially-functionally ineliminable and irreducible intrinsically intentional properties. But from this statement it does not follow that the mind's free activity introduces energy into the causally closed system of the universe in violation of the conservation of energy. To understand why this assertion is true, consider a certain quantity of the total energy in the universe, which is sufficient for and could be used for producing either of two distinct neurophysiological events, E_1 or E_2. Suppose that on the basis of event-causal laws and the previous succession of physical states, event E_2 is predicted to occur if the mind is fully event-causally determined, but that E_1 occurs instead as a result of the mind's contracausal agent causation of a freely chosen mental act. This result contradicts the event-causal determination of the mind's activity. But it involves no unnatural importation of energy from outside the closed system of the physical universe because the same amount of energy needed to produce either event E_1 or E_2 is there all along. It is just a question of how the energy is to be used, which of two events it is to power. The total energy in the physical universe is conserved, therefore, despite the mind's free causally undetermined decision. Helmholtz's proof may have negative consequences for substance dualism, but it poses no serious challenge to property dualism or agent causation.

PASSIONS OF THE SOUL: SENSATION, EMOTION, IMAGINATION, MEMORY

The action-passion dichotomy is in one way misleading. We speak of emotions as things that happen to the mind, such as being overcome with grief or lust or anger, against the will. Without trying to do anything or bring these experiences about, they come from outside or are visited upon the mind. But if thought is intentional, then all experiences involve an active element, in that each takes its object in a mental act of intending.

The passions of the soul, if we speak of it as the intended self, are those experiences in which the soul is mostly passive rather than active. The self is a patient rather than agent in much of the experience of sensation, emotion, imagination, and memory. It can only sit back and enjoy or suffer and wait out the occurrence, try as it sometimes may to induce, prevent, or avoid it. A complete analysis of the passions would take us beyond our immediate purpose in understanding the intentionality or active direction of thought toward intended objects. But it is significant that all of the so-called passions can in some sense and with limited effectiveness be actively produced by the intended self. The self can almost always provide itself with the sensation of pain or pleasure through indirect channels whenever it chooses, by initiating appropriate body movements. The same is true of emotion, in which memory and imagination play a complexly interwoven part. We can sometimes call up pride or paranoia, satisfaction or maudlin self-pity, by deliberately dwelling on certain kinds of thoughts.

Suppose I fear elevators. Then there is a passive experience, a terror of getting into an elevator, that I cannot control. It comes over me first as a feeling of dread, then panic, whenever I must enter the car. This experience is not something I do, certainly not by choice. I do not set about trying to have this fear, and I would much prefer to be without it. I am passive in its presence, a patient rather than an agent. But my fear has an object, irrational though it may be. It intends the elevator, or traveling in the elevator from floor to floor, or the imaginary occurrence of being in an elevator when the cable snaps and the car plummets to earth, despite my knowledge that such accidents cannot happen in modern elevators. But intending is doing something in a kind of mental act, directing thought toward an object. There are other respects in which not only my intended self but also my experience of fear remain passive. For example, a fearful thought may be brushed aside by another, such as the consoling reflections of reason in understanding the efficacy of fail-safe features in elevators, which may but need not dispel or help me to overcome my fear.

So, is fear or any of the other passions active or passive? Is it correct to speak of passive experiences as mental acts? The answer lies again in the concept of the intended self and the distinction it affords between the mind as agent and patient, and the activity or passivity of thought. We can solve the paradox of the activity of passion by recognizing that with respect to the intended self, certain experiences are passive, which nonetheless, as experiences, have an active element of intentionality. To express the point nontechnically, I do not actively choose to fear; but my thought, the experience of fear, chooses, so to speak, what I fear, in intending its object. It does this even when, as in the case of nameless fear, my intended self as spokesperson is not informed about my mind's intended object and I cannot say precisely what I fear.

The intended self is passive in these and many other circumstances. The intentionality of sensation is the directedness of thought toward the experience's particular content—of pleasure, pain, color, texture, warmth. These are also passive from the standpoint of the intended self, in a way emphasized by 18th-century empiricist philosophers like Locke, Berkeley, and Hume. They recognized, and we can agree, that the mind is not able self-consciously to will its sensations or their objects into being, although it can deliberately direct attention to selected parts or aspects of the sensation-producing world. When I open my eyes in the presence of dandelions, I do not choose to see yellow, but rather my mind passively receives whatever color is there to be perceived. Yet sensation actively intends the yellow, and perception intends the yellow dandelions.

Imagination is comparatively more active, in the sense that the mind is often able to conjure up mental images on demand. As a faculty for combining abstracted components of experience, imagination in the privacy of thought or the intended Cartesian Theater is a useful tool for calculation and evaluation of alternative hypotheses to see where they might lead. This process makes imagination an essential part of morally responsible deliberation and action, because of the agent's forethought. The intentional condition is reflected in the distinction made by modern jurisprudence between degrees of murder and manslaughter, or acting, as it is significantly called, in the heat of passion. But imaginings can also take place without or even against the will. An example is Othello in Shakespeare's play, who, through the conniving of Iago, cannot prevent himself from imagining in a fit of jealousy that his beloved Desdemona has betrayed him with his rival Cassio.

The same action-passion interplay holds true of memory. Memory can serve actively as a tool of thought, calling up information and mental images that may be useful or entertaining on request. But sometimes memory acts against the will in a way that the self may try to resist. We speak of being haunted by unpleasant memories, indicating the passive nature of the self in such experiences. We can be forced to relive embarrassing moments or to replay in memory traumatic episodes in which the self was involved, as well as painful facts in which the self had no direct role. A more common and somewhat less distressful passive experience of memory, which we may nevertheless try to fight, is experienced when, as we say, we cannot get a song out of our heads. We can spend hours mentally rerunning an old tune we just heard on the radio or a commercial jingle, which may have been purposely composed to be catchy and stick with the listener.

DEATH

In the end, there is a kind of passive indignity that the mind cannot avoid. There is death, and, in some instances, a prior deterioration of mental abilities. We emotionally oppose the inevitability of death for several reasons. The mind's experience of contracausal freedom, a built-in urge toward self-preservation, and the illusion of a unified substantial self contribute, at least during certain times in many persons' lives, to a sense of the mind's unlimitedness and inexhaustibility, and so to the myth of immortality.

The soul's survival after death, promised by religions and defended philosophically by Socrates, Descartes, and others, is the hope of many. They see in the dignity of their higher self-conscious minds something too precious to be discarded in the biological economies of birth, death, and the recycling of organic materials to which (other, nonhuman) animals are condemned. But if the mind is the intending brain and the self is an imaginary unity of thoughts, then, despite its intentionality and metaphysical and moral dignity, there can be no prospect of the self's survival beyond the brain's death and dissolution. The self and the mind can even die or be destroyed prior to the body's death by the nervous system's partial destruction or severe loss of normal function. Property dualism, unlike many religions and substance dualism, provides no basis for belief in an afterlife. It implies that at the moment of death there is only oblivion. If we wish to understand and live in accord with reality as it is, rather than as we would like it to be, then, if our analysis is correct, we must reconcile ourselves to the first proposition in the first syllogism all beginning logic students learn: "All men are mortal."

Yet even in the indignity of death there is a metaphysical and, sometimes, moral dignity. The fact that the mind is capable of death, that it has a mental life to lose, distinguishes it from rocks and machines, and from living machines like plants and bacteria. In dying, these lower forms have no unique gift of sentience, consciousness, or self-consciousness to surrender to the inevitable forces of nature. There can also be moral dignity in the manner and circumstances of death. The mind can find a final dignity in its attitude and understanding, in the knowledge of how it has lived, what it has done and suffered, and how it has treated others. It can with calm reflection accept its passing into nonexistence.

The Challenge of Intentionalism: Toward a Scientific Metaphysics of Mind

It is the thesis of this book that understanding the mind requires the relatively new disciplines of behavioral science, neurophysiology, cognitive psychology, artificial intelligence, and the information sciences. But it has also been argued that the philosophy of mind cannot satisfactorily explain the nature of mind without including metaphysical considerations about the intentionality of mind and the primacy of the intentional.

The primacy of the mind's intrinsic intentionality is invisible to science, just as the self is invisible to Hume's empiricist introspection. Contemporary science limits itself methodologically to a third-person perspective—the objective, public, and repeatable, by which scientific practice has come to be defined. It enshrines the important features of its most notable successes, as well as its suspicion of what appears privately only to the individual. It repudiates what is not intersubjective or transcribable as public data for comparison and confirmation.

But as salutary as the third-person perspective has been for science, and for the hard psychological sciences in particular, its limitations in understanding the mind are underscored by the primacy of the intentional. The failure of science to provide a philosophically satisfactory account of mind is understandable from the assumption that third-person science is explanatorily adequate only for the public behavioral-material-functional properties of nonthinking matter from which mind emerges. Traditional science needs to be supplemented by phenomenology in order to provide a complete explanation of mind, to include private first-person facts about the mind that can be known only by direct acquaintance.

The intentionality of mind is an extrascientific metaphysical property. This fact explains the naysaying, hard scientific reactions to the first-person privacy of psychological experience. Intrinsic intentionality is an obvious property of thought that many scientists try either to deny or ignore as outside the scientific purview, limiting inquiry specifically to the mind's public third-person observable properties. The proper understanding of mind cannot be purely scientific, therefore, and we cannot expect adequate explanations of the concept of mind from the hard psychological sciences alone. A scientific metaphysics of mind must recognize thought as an irreducibly intrinsically intentional neural event. The intrinsic intentionality of thought is the proper subject of metaphysics, and its neurophysiological properties are the proper subject of the brain and information sciences.

This proposal is likely to leave eliminativists, reductivists, and intentionalists somewhat dissatisfied. Eliminativists and reductivists will continue to suppose that the mind is just the brain and nervous system, their neurophysiological states, or some function or behavioral disposition of these. They will balk at references to intention as something beyond the limits of science, raising difficulties about the primacy of the intentional or dismissing it not merely as extrascientific but anti-scientific. They may downplay the importance of those features of thought that can only be understood by appeal to intentionality or the primacy of the intentional, or turn for proof of the exclusively public side of mind to misinterpretations of Wittgenstein's private language argument. They may take refuge in the claim that attributions of intrinsic intentionality to thought can be understood as mere intentional stance-taking.

The scientific metaphysics of mind outlined here will also probably dissatisfy some traditional intentionalists, who standardly equate the mind with the self and regard it as a unified, central, substantial source of intrinsic intentionality in the manner of Descartes. This entity may be supposed to be the same self or ego to which judgment, action, and moral responsibility are ascribed. But if the problems of personal identity and the neurophysiological and clinical psychological evidence point in any single direction, it is toward a model of the person, self, or ego as spokesperson and sometimes scapegoat for a loosely confederated committee of thoughts. There is no *a priori* justification for belief in a unified substantial self, and no empirical evidence for its existence, as Hume observes, in introspection. The unity of self, of which the self is often but unreliably convinced, is a fiction. The Cartesian ego is an intended nonexistent object, like the Cartesian Theater. The reality of the self can no more be supported on sound philosophical grounds than interactionist Cartesian substance dualism.

The theory we have surveyed allows an unlimited field for the development of scientific explanations of the mind's physical properties. But by giving equal place to the metaphysics of intentionality in accounting for the mind's nonphysical properties, property dualism entails that the mind is something rather different, more special and important, than any purely physical thing with purely physical properties. If mind is other than body, if it has properties that the living body and nonliving machines considered only as such do not have, then it need not be determined by the laws discovered in the physical and hard psychological sciences. We can then be assured on the basis of a scientific metaphysics of mind that in a morally significant sense we are free in thought, and causally undetermined in action, purpose, and will.

FOR FURTHER READING

ADDIS, LAIRD. *Natural Signs: A Theory of Intentionality.* Philadelphia: Temple University Press, 1989.

ANDERSON, ALAN R., ed. *Minds and Machines.* Englewood Cliffs, NJ: Prentice Hall, 1964.

ANSCOMBE, G. E. M. *Intention,* 2nd ed. Ithaca, NY: Cornell University Press, 1963.

ARISTOTLE. *Nicomachean Ethics,* translated by Hippocrates G. Apostle. Dordrecht, Netherlands: D. Reidel, 1975.

ARMSTRONG, D. M. *A Materialist Theory of the Mind.* London: Routledge & Kegan Paul, 1968.

BERKELEY, GEORGE. *A Treatise Concerning the Principles of Human Knowledge.* In *The Works of George Berkeley Bishop of Cloyne,* vol. 2, edited by A. A. Luce and T. E. Jessop. London: Thomas Nelson and Sons, 1949.

BERKELEY, GEORGE. *Three Dialogues Between Hylas and Philonous.* In *The Works of George Berkeley Bishop of Cloyne,* vol. 2, edited by A. A. Luce and T. E. Jessop. London: Thoman Nelson and Sons, 1949.

BLOCK, NED. "Troubles with Functionalism." In *Minnesota Studies in the Philosophy of Science 9, Perception and Cognition: Issues in the Foundations of Psychology,* pp. 261–326. Minneapolis: University of Minnesota Press, 1978.

BRENTANO, FRANZ. *Psychology from an Empirical Standpoint,* edited by Linda L. McAlister, translated by Antos C. Rancurello, D. B. Terrell, and McAlister. London: Routledge & Kegan Paul, 1973.

BUDGE, E. A. W., translator and editor *The Egyptian Book of the Dead, The Papyrus of Ani.* New York: Dover, 1967.

BURGE, TYLER. "Individualism and the Mental." *Midwest Studies in Philosophy* 4 (1979): 73–121.

CAMPBELL, KEITH. *Body and Mind.* Notre Dame, IN: University of Notre Dame Press, 1980.

CASANOVA, JACQUES. *The Memoirs of Jacques Casanova de Seingalt,* translated by Arthur Machen. New York: G. P. Putnam's Sons, 1903.

CASTAÑEDA, PEDRO DE, et al. *The Journey of Coronado,* translated and edited by George Parker Winship. New York: Dover, 1990.

CHISHOLM, RODERICK M. "Freedom and Action." *In Freedom and Determinism*, edited by Keith Lehrer, pp. 11–44. New York: Random House, 1966.

CHISHOLM, RODERICK M. "Converse Intentional Properties." *The Journal of Philosophy* 79 (1982): 537–545.

CHISHOLM, RODERICK M. "The Primacy of the Intentional." *Synthese* 61 (1984): 89–110.

CHISHOLM, RODERICK M., AND SELLARS, WILFRID. "Chisholm-Sellars Correspondence on Intentionality." In *Minnesota Studies in the Philosophy of Science 2, Concepts, Theories, and the Mind-Body Problem*, edited by Herbert Feigel, Michael Scriven, and Grover Maxwell. Minneapolis: University of Minnesota Press, 1958.

CHOMSKY, NOAM. *Aspects of the Theory of Syntax*. Cambridge, MA: MIT Press, 1965.

CHOMSKY, NOAM. *Language and Mind*. New York: Harcourt Brace & Jovanovich, 1972.

CHURCHLAND, PAUL M. "Reduction, Qualia, and the Direct Introspection of Brain States." *Journal of Philosophy* 82 (1985): 8–28.

CHURCHLAND, PAUL M. *Matter and Consciousness: A Contemporary Introduction to the Philosophy of Mind*, rev. ed. Cambridge, MA: MIT/Bradford Books, 1988.

DANA, RICHARD HENRY, JR. *Two Years Before the Mast: A Personal Narrative of Life at Sea*. New York: Penguin Books, 1981.

DAVIDSON, DONALD. *Essays on Actions and Events*. Oxford, Clarendon Press, 1980.

DENNETT, DANIEL C. *The Intentional Stance*. Cambridge, MA: MIT/Bradford Books, 1987.

DENNETT, DANIEL C. *Consciousness Explained*. Boston: Little, Brown, 1991.

DESCARTES, RENÉ. *The Philosophical Works of Descartes*, translated by E. S. Haldane and G. R. T. Ross, 2 vols. Cambridge University Press, 1931. *Meditations on First Philosophy, Discourse on Method*, and *Principles of Philosophy* in vol. 1; *Objections and Replies* in vol. 2.

DREYFUS, HUBERT L. *What Computers Can't Do: The Limits of Artificial Intelligence*, rev. ed. New York: Harper & Row, 1979.

FEIGL, HERBERT. *The "Mental" and the "Physical": The Essay and a Postscript*. Minneapolis: University of Minnesota Press, 1967.

FELDMAN, J. A., AND BALLARD, D. H. "Connectionist Models and Their Properties." *Cognitive Science* 6 (1982): 205–254.

FODOR, JERRY. *The Language of Thought*. Cambridge, MA: Harvard University Press, 1975.

FRENCH, ROBERT M. "Subcognition and the Limits of the Turing Test." *Mind* 99 (1990): 53–65.

GILBERT, WILLIAM S. and SULLIVAN, ARTHUR S. *Iolante, or the Peer and the Peri*. London: J. M. Stoddart, 1882.

GÖDEL, KURT. "Some Metamathematical Results on Completeness and Consistency, On Formally Undecidable Propositions of *Principia Mathematica* and Related Systems I, and On Completeness and Consistency." In *Frege and Gödel: Two Fundamental Texts in Mathematical Logic*, edited by Jean van Heijenoort, pp. 83–108. Cambridge, MA: Harvard University Press, 1970.

HUME, DAVID. *A Treatise of Human Nature*, 2nd ed., edited by L. A. Selby-Bigge, revised by P. H. Nidditch. Oxford: The Clarendon Press, 1978.

JACKSON, FRANK. "Epiphenomenal Qualia." *The Philosophical Quarterly* 32 (1982): 127–136.

JACKSON, PHILIP C., JR. *Introduction to Artificial Intelligence*, 2nd rev. ed. New York: Dover, 1985.

KANT, IMMANUEL. *Critique of Pure Reason*, translated by Norman Kemp Smith. New York: St. Martin's, 1965.

KRIPKE, SAUL A. *Naming and Necessity.* Cambridge, MA: Harvard University Press, 1980.

KRIPKE, SAUL A. *Wittgenstein on Rules and Private Language.* Cambridge, MA: Harvard University Press, 1982.

LA METTRIE, JULIEN OFFRAY DE. *Man a Machine.* La Salle, IL: Open Court, 1912.

LOCKE, JOHN. *An Essay Concerning Human Understanding*, edited by P. H. Nidditch. Oxford: The Clarendon Press, 1979.

LUCAS, J. R. "Minds, Machines, and Gödel." *Philosophy* 36 (1961) 112–127. Reprinted in Anderson (1964), pp. 43–59.

MARGOLIS, JOSEPH. *Persons and Minds: The Prospects of Nonreductive Materialism.* Boston Studies in the Philosophy of Science 57. Dordrecht, Netherlands: D. Reidel, 1978.

MARGOLIS, JOSEPH. *Philosophy of Psychology.* Englewood Cliffs, NJ: Prentice Hall, 1984.

McLAUGHLIN, BRIAN. "Type Epiphenomenalism, Type-Dualism, and the Causal Priority of the Physical." *Philosophical Perspectives* 3 (1989): 109–135.

MELZACK, RONALD. "Phantom Limbs." *Scientific American*, April 1992, pp. 120–126.

NAGEL, THOMAS. "Brain Bisection and the Unity of Consciousness." *Synthese* 22 (1971): 396–413.

NAGEL, THOMAS. "What Is It Like to Be a Bat?" *The Philosophical Review* 83 (1974): 435–450.

PARFIT, DEREK. *Reasons and Persons.* Oxford University Press, 1984.

PAVLOV, I. P. *Conditioned Reflexes*, translated by G. V. Anrep. London: Humphrey Milford, 1927.

PAVLOV, I. P. *Lectures on Conditioned Reflexes*, translated by W. H. Grantt. New York: International Publishers, 1928.

PENROSE, ROGER. *The Emperor's New Mind: Concerning Computers, Minds, and the Laws of Physics.* Oxford University Press, 1989.

PLACE, U. T. "Is Consciousness a Brain Process?" *The British Journal of Psychology* 47 (1956): 44–50.

PLATO. *Meno*, translated by G.M.A. Grube. Indianapolis: Hackett, 1976.

POE, EDGAR ALLAN. "Maelzel's Chess Player." *Southern Literary Messenger*, April 1836. In *Edgar Allan Poe: Essays and Reviews*, edited by G. R. Thompson, pp. 1253–1276. New York: Library of America, 1984.

PUTNAM, HILARY. *Mind, Language and Reality.* Cambridge University Press, 1975.

REID, THOMAS. *Essays on the Intellectual Powers of Man*, edited by Baruch Brody. Cambridge, MA: Harvard University Press, 1969.

RORTY, RICHARD. *Philosophy and the Mirror of Nature.* Princeton, NJ: Princeton University Press, 1979.

RYLE, GILBERT. *The Concept of Mind.* New York: Harper and Row, 1949.

SCHANK, ROGER C. *Scripts, Plans, Goals, and Understanding: An Inquiry into Human Knowledge Structures.* Hillsdale, NJ: Lawrence Erlbaum, 1977.

SCHOPENHAUER, ARTHUR. *On the Fourfold Root of the Principle of Sufficient Reason,* translated by E. F. J. Payne. La Salle, IL: Open Court, 1974.

SEARLE, JOHN R. "Minds, Brains and Programs." *The Behavioral and Brain Sciences* 3 (1980): 417–424; 450–456.

SHAPIRO, STUART C. "The SNePS Semantic Network Processing System." In *Associative Networks: Representation and Use of Knowledge by Computers,* edited by Nicholas V. Findler, pp. 179–203. New York: Academic Press, 1979.

SKINNER, B. F. *The Behavior of Organisms.* New York: Appleton-Century-Crofts, 1938.

SKINNER, B. F. *Science and Human Behavior.* New York: Macmillan, 1953.

SKINNER, B. F. *About Behaviorism.* New York: Alfred A. Knopf, 1974.

SMART, J. J. C. "Sensations and Brain Processes." *The Philosophical Review* 68 (1959): 141–156.

STICH, STEPHEN P. *From Folk Psychology to Cognitive Science: The Case Against Belief.* Cambridge, MA: MIT/Bradford Books, 1983.

STICH, STEPHEN P. *The Fragmentation of Reason: Preface to a Pragmatic Theory of Cognitive Evaluation.* Cambridge, MA: MIT/Bradford Books, 1990.

STRAWSON, P. F. *Individuals: An Essay in Descriptive Metaphysics.* London: Methuen, 1959.

SWADE, DORON D. "Redeeming Charles Babbage's Mechanical Computer." *Scientific American,* February 1993, pp. 86–91.

TAYLOR, RICHARD. *Action and Purpose.* Atlantic Highlands, New Jersey: Humanities Press, 1966.

TURING, ALAN M. "Computing Machinery and Intelligence." *Mind* 59 (1950): 433–460. Reprinted in Anderson (1964), pp. 3–30.

VON HELMHOLTZ, HERMAN LUDWIG. "The Conservation of Force" (1847); "The Application of the Law of the Conservation of Force to Organic Nature" (1861), in *Selected Writings of Hermann von Helmholtz,* edited with an introduction by Russell Kahl, pp. 3–55, 109–121. Middletown: Wesleyan University Press, 1971.

WATSON, J. B. *Behaviorism.* London: Kegan Paul, Trench and Trubner, 1925.

WEBB, JUDSON. *Mechanism, Mentalism, and Metamathematics: An Essay on Finitism.* Dordrecht, Netherlands: D. Reidel, 1980.

WEIZENBAUM, JOSEPH. *Computer Power and Human Reason: From Judgment to Calculation.* San Francisco: W. H. Freeman, 1976.

WINOGRAD, TERRY. "Understanding Natural Language." *Cognitive Psychology* 1 (1972): 1–19.

WITTGENSTEIN, LUDWIG. *Philosophical Investigations,* 3rd ed., edited and translated by G. E. M. Anscombe. New York: Macmillan, 1968.

INDEX